RACINE AND THE *ART POÉTIQUE* OF BOILEAU

THE JOHNS HOPKINS STUDIES IN ROMANCE LITERATURES
AND LANGUAGES

EXTRA VOLUME XII

RACINE AND THE *ART POÉTIQUE* OF BOILEAU

PQ
1905
H34
1976

BY

SISTER MARIE PHILIP HALEY

OCTAGON BOOKS

A DIVISION OF FARRAR, STRAUS AND GIROUX

New York   1976

Reprinted 1976
by special arrangement with The Johns Hopkins Press

OCTAGON BOOKS
A DIVISION OF FARRAR, STRAUS & GIROUX, INC.
19 Union Square West
New York, N.Y. 10003

Library of Congress Cataloging in Publication Data

Haley, Marie Philip, Sister, 1899-
    Racine and the Art poétique of Boileau.

        Reprint of the ed. published by Johns Hopkins Press, Baltimore,
        which was issued as Extra v. 12 of the Johns Hopkins studies in
        Romance literatures and languages.
        Originally presented as the author's thesis, University of Minne-
        sota, 1931.
        Bibliography: p.
        1. Racine, Jean Baptiste, 1639-1699—Criticism and interpreta-
        tion. 2. Boileau-Despréaux, Nicolas, 1636-1711. L'art poéti-
        que. I. Title. II. Series: The Johns Hopkins studies in
        Romance literatures and languages. Extra volume; 12.
PQ1905.H34   1976   842'.4   76-21264
ISBN 0-374-93379-0

Printed in USA by
Thomson-Shore, Inc.
Dexter, Michigan

To My Father

PHILIP JOSEPH HALEY

AND

To the Memory of My Mother

DEAN CONDON HALEY

PREFACE

A word may be said as to the origin of this volume. When I began my research, I desired to investigate the dramatic practice of Racine in the light of the tenets and counsels which Boileau set forth in *Chant III* of his *Art Poétique*. In view of the intimacy of these friends, whose lives and works were closely linked and who by themselves epitomize that final era of French classicism known as the period of " taste," I expected to find concurrence between the literary doctrine of the one and the theory and artistic workmanship of the other. A certain affinity does exist. But regarding it two quite contrary opinions prevail. Some scholars, lending a ready ear to all the claims made by Boileau in his old age, are inclined to accept the tradition that he " formed " Racine. Others with a keener sense of chronology hold that the precepts formulated by Boileau toward the end of the classic age are a summary of French tragedy at its height, hence a sort of compendium of Racine's technique. Both opinions, it seemed, stood in need of revision. Those who maintain the former view are going against the teachings of experience; literary lawgivers, for all their pretensions, have seldom if ever been known to create and direct a literature, much less to " form " a poet like Racine. On the other hand, those who believe that Boileau merely reduced Racine's practice to laws and counsels are not reckoning seriously enough either with the bookishness that characterizes many of his remarks or with the prestige that surrounded the plays of Corneille even as late as the seventies.

I was aware from the outset that a consideration of Boileau's precepts in their relation to Racine's dramatic creed would involve, in addition to the æsthetic study, a thorough investigation of the friendship of the two poets up until 1674, the year that saw the completion of the *Art Poétique*. This historical approach to my subject proved so rich in controversial matter that it soon became evident that a complete treatment of my original problem would require the publication of more than one volume. I have, accordingly, limited my subject for the pur-

7

poses of the present study, choosing to deal here only with the relationships between the two poets before and during the composition of the *Art Poétique* and with a comparison between Racine's theoretical writings and the pronouncements of Boileau. Although complete in itself, this volume thus forms the basis for another work, now under way, in which the dramatist's technique is being studied in each successive tragedy. We must defer until the conclusion of that work the answer to the question: To what extent may Boileau's precepts be considered a summary of Racine's practice?

Knowledge of Racine is gained primarily from his letters, his marginal annotations on copies of the ancients, and his prefaces. Valincour's *Éloge* delivered before the French Academy, where he succeeded Racine, and his letter to d'Olivet are the testimony of a friend who knew Racine intimately the last eighteen years of the poet's life. They are, naturally enough, extremely laudatory in all that touches Racine's literary reputation. Jean-Baptiste Racine gathered information with a view to writing an authoritative life of his father. He made some of this material available to his younger brother who actually accomplished the task. Louis Racine's *Mémoires sur la Vie de Jean Racine* and the critical studies of his father's plays have not been totally disregarded, the author's pietistic and filial leanings notwithstanding. Almost all the documents bearing upon the life or works of Racine are included in Mesnard's edition of the poet's works published in the *Grands Écrivains* series. Among studies by contemporary scholars, those of Jules Lemaître and Professor Karl Vossler are highly valuable. M. Georges Le Bidois has emphasized some important aspects of the action in Racinian tragedy.

In weighing the evidence regarding Boileau's growing fame and the influence he exerted on his contemporaries, I have endeavored to guard against exaggerations in the direction both of praise and of blame. I have considered carefully the contemporary testimony of Brossette. Although there can be no doubt concerning the integrity or the sincere admiration of this Boswell for his master, Brossette's *Éclaircissements* tend to be shortsighted and simplistic. Le Verrier's *Commentaire avec les corrections autographes de Despréaux* is valuable, but like Brossette's reflections and L. Racine's *Mémoires*, savors of Auteuil traditions. Monchesnay has recorded in the *Bolœana* precious testimony as regards Boileau's literary taste. Much of the biographical material found in the *Satires* and *Épîtres* must be taken *cum grano salis* on account of the poet's tendency in his later years to over-estimate the influence he had exerted in the decade of the sixties. His *Préfaces* are written in a more humble tone. I have taken into account the frankly hostile testimony of Cotin and Chapelain and the more moderate castigations of Boursault, especially in those matters where the flicks of Mme de Sévigné give weight to their recriminations. Among the editions of Boileau that of Berriat-Saint-Prix is the most useful. In matters concerning the history of Boileau's publications, I have followed Berriat-Saint-Prix and M. Émile Magne, I have made abundant use of Revillout's important study, " *la Légende de Boileau*," which opens an approach to the two poets. This scholar pointed out a new Boileau, who was not the innovator " forming " the second generation of French classicists, but rather the codifier of existing literary forms that had already earned the approval of an élite. His careful scrutiny of dates did much to dispel the legend that had grown up concerning the legislator of Parnassus, who, in his later years as the sole survivor of his literary generation, was not averse to the flattery that made much of the precocity and vigor of his talents and of the direction he claimed to have given Molière, La Fontaine, and Racine. M. Jean Demeure's interesting article demolished the legend of the " Quatre Amis."

My subject being, in the main, an æsthetic one, I have aimed at keeping to the fore the Aristotelian and pseudo-Aristotelian doctrine that was the intellectual heritage of the generation of poets who reached maturity in the early sixties. Heinsius, Chapelain, La Mesnardière, Vossius, d'Aubignac, and Corneille have been cited frequently in the text. Saint-Évremond's dissertations represent a taste that is slightly more urbane. Rapin's *Réflexions,* which appeared in the same year as the *Art Poétique,* are of special importance. M. René Bray's book, *la Formation de la Doctrine Classique en France,* clarifies practically all of the fundamental ideas. Although I have tried to confine my study to seventeenth-century French interpretations of Aristotle, it has been necessary occasionally to have recourse to the work of contemporary Aristotelian scholars. In citing Aristotle I have used the translation of S. H. Butcher, and for the interpretation of verisimilitude and *hamartía,* I have accepted the authority of the same scholar. In the more controversial matters of katharsis, peripeteia, and imitation, I have also taken account of the more recent studies by Professor McKeon, Rostagni, and Gudeman.

Additional acknowledgments have been made in the notes, and a complete bibliography is appended.

In citing works I have preserved the spelling and accentuation of the original.

The preparation of this book has had the discerning and kindly guidance of Professor Colbert Searles of the University of Minnesota, who has given it, over a period of years, the benefit of his authoritative knowledge of seventeenth-century French literature. It is a pleasure to express here my grateful appreciation of his helpfulness at every stage of the work. I owe much to Professor William A. Nitze, of the University of Chicago, under whose inspiration this study was begun. He read the book in manuscript form and aided me with valuable suggestions and active help. I am under special obligation to the eminent French scholar, Professor Daniel Mornet, of the Sorbonne, for his careful reading of the work and for his illuminating criticism. I thank Dean McKeon of the University of Chicago, and Professor Ogle of the University of Minnesota, who were good enough to criticize certain chapters. For suggestions in regard to the form I am indebted to my colleagues, Sister Helen Margaret and Sister Antonine of the College of St. Catherine, and to Professor Irville C. Lecompte of the University of Minnesota. Above all, I owe sincere thanks to my community, the Congregation of the Sisters of St. Joseph of Carondelet, for the support and encouragement received during the composition of this book. While acknowledging my indebtedness for the help so generously given me, I wish to say that I alone am responsible for any errors that may remain in the work.

S. M. P.

The College of St. Catherine
St. Paul, Minnesota
September 8, 1937

CONTENTS

ABBREVIATIONS

Berriat-Saint-Prix: *Œuvres Complètes de Boileau.*

Bib. Nat.: Bibliothèque Nationale.

Bray: *La Formation de la Doctrine Classique en France.*

Ed.: edition.

Éd.: *édité* or *édition.*

Lachèvre: *Les Satires de Boileau commentées par lui-même. Reproduction du commentaire inédit de Pierre Le Verrier avec les corrections autographes de Despréaux.*

Laverdet: *Correspondance entre Boileau Despréaux et Brossette publiée sur les manuscrits originaux.*

Magne: *Bibliographie Générale des Œuvres de Boileau-Despréaux.*

Mesnard: *Œuvres de Jean Racine.*

MF: Mercure de France.

MP: Modern Philology.

n.: footnote.

Revillout: "la Légende de Boileau."

RHLF: Revue d'Histoire littéraire de la France.

RLR: Revue des Langues Romanes.

We have enclosed in brackets the dates ascribed by Mesnard to undated letters of Racine.

THE RELATIONS BETWEEN BOILEAU AND RACINE

The Fame of the Two Poets before 1674

A study of the mutual influence of Boileau and Racine upon each other must first of all take into consideration the question of dates and the prestige that each one gained year by year. Boileau would have us believe that his beginnings were timid. He wrote for his own pleasure and, if we can trust his account, read his satires somewhat reluctantly to a few friends.[1] One day in 1662, the abbé Furetière, not finding Gilles Boileau at home, paid a visit to Despréaux, who was living in the same house.[2] Until then the poet had shown his *Satire I* to only a few friends. He read it on this day to the newly elected academician. Although it was far from being in its definitive form,[3] Furetière acknowledged that it excelled anything he himself had written. Brossette, who records this incident, adds:

Il encouragea ce jeune poète à continuer, et lui demanda même une copie de la nouvelle satire, qui devint bientôt publique par les autres copies qu'on en fit.[4]

A letter of Chapelain dated March 13, 1665, contains an important indication in regard to Boileau. The former complains that Boileau " s'est acharné contre deux académiciens qui ne connoissoient ni sa personne ni son nom." [5] The academicians were, of course, Chapelain and Cotin. Now Boileau made his

---

[1]   " A peine, quelque fois, *je me force à les lire,*
        Pour plaire à quelque ami que charme la satire . . .
        Enfin c'est mon plaisir, je veux me satisfaire."
                            (*VIIe Satire*, vss. 85-86 and 89.)
   [2] Their father's house presided over at that time by the eldest brother, Jerome.
   [3] " Cette satire était alors dans un état bien différent de celui auquel l'auteur le mit avant de la faire imprimer, car de 212 vers qu'elle contenait, il n'en a conservé qu'environ 60. Tout le reste a été ou supprimé ou changé." (Brossette's remarks on *Satire I.*)
   [4] His remarks on *Satire I.*
   [5] Cited by Revillout, *RLR*, XXXVII, 88, n. 4.

first attacks upon Chapelain in 1663.[6] Chapelain was that very
year engaged in compiling the list of the first authors to receive
a pension from the young king and was, therefore, in a position
to know the poets who had won a reputation in respectable
circles. He insists, nevertheless, that he knew neither Boileau's
" personne " nor his " nom." Even Boileau himself admitted in
1663 that

> Personne ne connoît ni mon nom ni ma veine.[7]

He also complains of the difficulty of finding a " Mécénas ":

> Et, fait comme je suis, au siècle d'aujourd'hui,
> Qui voudra s'abaisser à me servir d'appui ? [8]

A most curious passage in Le Verrier's *Commentaires,* sub-
scribed to by Boileau himself, tells us that in these early years
the satirist chose his victims more or less at random.[9] He
attacked both poets whom he knew and poets whom he did not
know and those of either category who had written or spoken ill
of him. Often it was simply a matter of finding a name that
would fit into a niche in his verse, and he would consult the
collections of poetry published by de Sercy. The addition made
by Boileau to Le Verrier's explanation of the motivation of the
satirist's attacks reveals the modest pretensions of the poet in
those years. Boileau adds, by way of attenuating the impression
produced by Le Verrier's explanation:

> et il sacrifioit à la Satire ceux (names found in de Sercy's collections
> of poems) qui avoient le malheur de lui plaire car il ne croioit pas leur
> faire grand tort par ses vers qu'il n'avoient pas dessein de donner au
> Public et qu'il ne pensoit pas que les Hommes dûssent regarder.[10]

Despréaux, then, in the early sixties, seemed quite satisfied with
the audience he found in the cabarets which he frequented.

---

[6] Interpolation concerning pensions, *Satire I,* vs. 81 *et sqq.* and the
reference to the forced verses of *la Pucelle, Satire VII,* vs. 30.

[7] *VII⁰ Satire,* vs. 82.

[8] *Satire I,* vss. 87-88. An interpolation of 1663.

[9] Cf. also the *Discours au Roi* (1665), vss. 76-80:

> " Des sottises du temps je compose mon fiel ;
> Je vais de toutes parts où me guide ma veine,
> Sans tenir en marchant une route certaine ;
> Et, sans gêner ma plume en ce libre métier,
> Je la laisse au hasard courir sur le papier."

[10] Lachèvre, p. 56.

The first works of Boileau to appear in print were his *Stances sur l'Escole des Femmes* and his *Sonnet sur la Mort d'une parente.* They were included, without name of author, in a collection of verse entitled *les Délices de la poésie galante des plus célèbres Autheurs du temps.*[11] It came off the press on September 25, 1663. The following year the second part of this collection appeared with the *Satire à M. Molière* on pages 125 to 128. Berriat-Saint-Prix thinks that the poem was printed without the authorization of Despréaux. In one copy that he found, the pages containing the *Satire* were cut out, and other pages of trivial verse were substituted for them. Berriat-Saint-Prix suggests that the poet, fearing the recriminations of Ménage, Quinault, and Scudéry, might have insisted on this change.[12] *Satire II* was reprinted three times, the *Sonnet* was reprinted twice, the *Stances sur l'Escole des Femmes* were printed once more, *Satire IV* and the *Discours au Roy* were published, and the former was reprinted once, before the unauthorized edition of the *Satires* appeared early in 1666. Besides these anonymous publications, Boileau's verses circulated in manuscript form.

We come now to *la Dissertation sur "Joconde,"* written according to M. Bray [14] while La Fontaine's *conte* was still circulating in manuscript form.[15] It is a fine piece of criticism some twenty pages in length. Boileau apparently considers himself a professional critic, if indeed we may say that there were such in the seventeenth century. For he takes a fling at those "demi-critiques" who by virtue of their "common sense," perverted though it be, claim the right to pass judgment on everything. The *Dissertation,* although a masterpiece of criticism carrying in germ most of the ideas, aversions, and literary principles enunciated later on by the critic, remained unpublished until 1669, when it figured in the Dutch edition of La Fontaine's *Contes.*[16]

---

[11] Item 1 in the list of surreptitious publications. (Magne, I, 55.)

[12] I, cxxx. M. Magne was unable to verify this statement as that copy belonging to the *Bib. Nat.* has since disappeared. (I, 55.)

[13] Items 1, and 3-6, in Magne, I, 55-56.

[14] "La Dissertation sur 'Joconde.' Est-elle de Boileau?" *RHLF,* XXXVIII, 346.

[15] The *privilège* to publish La Fontaine's work was granted to Barbin on Jan. 14, 1664. The *achevé d'imprimer* is Dec. 10, 1664.

[16] *Contes et Nouvelles en vers de M. La Fontaine. Nouvelle édition revue et augmentée de plusieurs Contes du même auteur et d'une dissertation sur la Joconde.* Leyde: Jean Sambix le jeune.

It was ascribed by the publisher to "un des plus beaux esprits de ce temps." How can we account for the fact that in 1664 or 1665 Boileau evidently found no publisher who would accept the work, all the furor [17] caused by the two versions of Ariosto notwithstanding? If the work circulated, it was only within a restricted circle of friends. La Fontaine seems not to have noticed it. No contemporary author mentions the *Dissertation* until long after its publication, when Brienne makes some erroneous conjectures as to its authorship. M. Bray, after studying the question from every angle, concludes that Boileau, unbidden and unnoticed, took upon himself the task of defending the *Joconde,* not in the capacity of an established critic nor because of his interest in La Fontaine, but merely to attract attention to himself by thus linking his name with that of an already famous poet.[18] He probably played no rôle in the wager and merely defended the *conte* as he had previously championed *l'École des Femmes,* incurring in either case no risk. His *Dissertation* seems to have taken on importance only with the literary ascendancy of the author. When it was published in 1669 there were indeed weighty considerations that would prevent the future moralist and legislator of Parnassus from claiming the authorship of the work. When he does so in later years, it is not without expressing regret at having thus used his talent in defense of so licentious a tale.[19]

Brossette tells us that in 1664 Boileau was invited, together with Molière and the singer Lambert, to the house of Du Broussin, where the two poets read their verses.[20] This does not imply that they were mingling on an equal footing with the distinguished guests present, but that they were entertainers on that occasion.

A letter of Pomponne [21] dated February 4, 1665, presents further evidence that Boileau had, at that time, made his entrance into a society somewhat different from that of his companions of

[17] Cf. *le Journal des Savants,* Jan. 26, 1665, cited by M. Bray, *RHLF,* XXXVIII, 338-339.

[18] *Op. cit., RHLF,* XXXVIII, 517.

[19] Cf. *infra,* p. 158, n. 132.   [20] Commentary on *Satire II.*

[21] The letter is printed in Monmerqué's *Mémoires de Coulanges* (Paris: J. J. Blaise, 1820), pp. 382-384. Revillout was, however, unable to find the original. (*RLR,* XXXVII, 89, n. 1.)

cabaret fame. He was present and read his *Satires* at the Hôtel
de Nevers on the day that Racine delighted the distinguished
group with three and one-half acts of the *Alexandre*.[22] La
Rochefoucauld, Mme de la Fayette, Mme and Mlle de Sévigné
were the guests of Mme Du Plessis-Guénégaud on that occasion.
Since the writer says that " Boileau " was present, there is a
possibility that he meant Gilles Boileau,[23] who also wrote satires,
as Nicolas Boileau was generally known to his contemporaries as
" Despréaux." But even if the latter were present at the Hôtel de
Nevers, it is clear that he was there merely to furnish en-
tertainment.

Louis Racine, explaining the dedication of *Satire V*, completed
in 1665, affirms that Despréaux then knew only two men at the
court. He had dedicated his new poem to Dangeau. Boileau's
enemies said the satirist was ridiculing the latter by dedicating
to him a *Satire* on the nobility.[24] Both Le Verrier and Louis
Racine take pains to correct this calumny, claiming that the poet
first thought of addressing the verses to La Rochefoucauld but,
upon finding the difficulty of putting that name in verse,[25] he
changed his mind and dedicated the work to Dangeau,

le seul homme de la cour, avec M. de la Rochefoucauld, qu'il connût
alors.[26]

---

[22] Mesnard (I, 497) is inclined to make much of the simultaneous
appearance of the two poets at the Hôtel de Nevers early in the year
1665. He concludes that they were " déjà très-étroitement liés." Now
nothing in M. de Pomponne's letter suggests that this was the case.
Cf. *infra*, pp. 51-52.

[23] An academician since 1659. In the years 1665 and 1666, he received
a gratification of 1200 *livres* from the king. This was more than the
sum granted to Racine or even to Molière. Cf. *infra*, p. 28, n. 69.

[24] " Quand elle (the *Satire*) parut, on trouva fort extraordinaire que
l'autheur l'eust adressée à M. Dangeau quoiqu'ils fussent amis, mais
M. Dangeau estoit jeune. Il avoit l'honneur de jouer avec le Roy et
avec Mlle de La Valière au Palais Brion, à la verité *on ne le regardoit
point comme un homme d'une qualité très distinguée*, quoiqu'il soit
d'ancienne noblesse et allié des Du Plessis-Mornay." (Lachèvre, p. 47.)

[25] Revillout thinks there must have been a better reason. Perhaps
La Rochefoucauld refused to accept the dedication of this diatribe
against the nobility. Or perhaps he did not like Despréaux's talent.
Moreover, Dangeau was at the time in the king's favor and it would
have been to Boileau's advantage to dedicate the work to him, rather
than to La Rochefoucauld. (*RLR*, XXXVII, 449.)

[26] *Mémoires*, Mesnard, I, 232.

2

In 1666 before the authorized edition of the *Satires* appeared, an enemy of Boileau composed a *Discours au Cynique Despréaux.* It remained inedited until M. Magne published it in his *Bibliographie Générale,* ascribing the authorship to Chapelain. M. Demeure, however, holds that " jamais aucun texte n'a permis de l'attribuer avec quelque apparence de certitude à Chapelain." [27] Internal evidence in *Satire IX,* which is a direct answer to the *Discours* [28] as well as to Cotin's *Satire des Satires,* would indicate that Boileau attributed both pamphlets to Cotin.[29] We should like to know whether Chapelain or Cotin was responsible for the *Discours.* If the author was the official distributor of pensions, the "homme d'honneur" whose faith, probity, candor, civility, and sincerity even Despréaux admits, we should attach greater value to the accusations brought against the satirist. Furthermore, since the *Discours* and *la Satire des Satires* agree on many precise points, we should like to know whether we have in them the testimony of one or of two persons. Although testimony

[27] *RHLF,* XLI, 215.

[28] Cf. *Discours,* " *Quelle mousche vous a picqué* pour vous faire si souvent et si rudement jetter sur Quinaut dont neanmoins notre théâtre se pare et le Louvre est charmé? " (Cited by Magne, II, 142.) Then Boileau tells his " esprit " what people are saying about him:

> " Gardez-vous, dira l'un, de cet esprit critique;
> *On ne sait bien souvent quelle mousche le pique."*
> (*Satire IX,* vss. 119-120.)

Boileau is evidently citing the *Discours* in this instance. Boileau made no correction on Le Verrier's remark (he made none on the entire commentary of this *Satire,* which probably indicates that he had not read it carefully) that the underlined expression is an apt imitation of the " fœnum habet in cornu " of Horace (*Satire IV,* Book I). Le Verrier's comment (p. 95) is, indeed, in this instance wide of the mark.

[29] Le Verrier's note (p. 103) to vs. 305 ascribes to Cotin " quelques ouvrages où il l'(Boileau) accusoit de lèze Majesté divine et humaine." Cotin's name appears as the butt of ridicule no less than nine times in the *Satire.* Chapelain receives more extended treatment, but, mingled with condemnation of his poetry and irritation at his unduly large pension, there is lavish praise of the man (vss. 209-216). In commenting on the poem, Le Verrier mentions Chapelain's " 8.000 l. (an error) de pension " and *la Pucelle,* but there is no question of a " libelle diffamatoire " 's being ascribed to him. This indicates that Boileau attributed both the *Satire des Satires* and the *Discours* to Cotin. It is true that the two pamphlets bring the same charges against Boileau. The tone of the *Discours,* written in prose, is, however, far more trenchant.

in the form of a pamphlet by one of Boileau's victims needs to be discounted, the *Discours* must be cited as having more than a grain of truth. The author does not mince words in describing the kind of fame already earned by Boileau:

On parle de vous comme d'un fameux Pilier de Cabaret, d'un fameux Joueur de farces, d'un fameux bateur de Pavé, d'un fameux assassin d'honneur. . . . Vous prenez ridiculement le tiltre (of moral censor) en même temps que vous faites ouverte profession de Parasîte, de farceur, d'Impie, de Blasphémateur dans les lieux où l'on s'enyvre et dans les maisons de desbauche . . . Comment vous estes-vous pu promettre un bon succez d'une si folle entreprise (that of criticising works to which the public has given its approval) quand vous ne seriez pas un petit compagnon fraischement sorti de dessous la férule; un Enfant naguères sevré sur le mont des neuf Sœurs, sans doctrine, sans expérience et sans commerce qu'avec des filoux de lettres qui ne sçavent pas seulement en quoy consiste la nature de la Poésie et qui la reduisent toute à la seule versification: quand dis-je, vous ne seriez pas un Inconnu, un Champignon sorti de terre en une nuit, auriez-vous la présomption de pouvoir tenir seul contre les sentimens de la Cour et de la Ville? . . . Laissez la tasche de leur réforme (that of the poets) à qui elle appartient, et, sans mettre vostre faucille en la moisson d'autruy, ne songez qu'à vous réformer vous mesme, qu'à redresser ce qu'il y a de tortu dans vostre Esprit et dans vos mœurs.[30]

Even Louis Racine, who can hardly be suspected of desiring to stress the less glorious side of Boileau's career, makes mention of this phase of the poet's life. His talent for mimicry, say the *Mémoires,* made the satirist much sought after in society. Although Louis Racine intimates that it is at the court that this talent was especially appreciated, we know that such a gift stood him at least in equally good stead at the taverns. Louis Racine testifies:

Quoique ce talent qui le faisoit rechercher dans les parties de plaisir lui procurât des connoissances agréables pour un jeune homme, il m'a avoué qu'enfin *il en eut honte,* et qu'ayant *fait réflexion que c'étoit faire un personnage de baladin,* il y renonça, et n'alla plus aux repas où on l'invitoit, que pour réciter ses ouvrages, qui le rendirent bientôt très-fameux.[31]

The " baladin " of Louis Racine's apparently expurgated account

[30] Cited by Magne, II, 139-143. There are two manuscript copies: MS 892 of the *Bib. Nat.,* and MS collection Godefroy, *Portefeuille* 217, *Bib. de l'Institut.*

[31] Mesnard, I, 233.

is telling evidence. It confirms the truth lurking in the more venomous diatribe of the *Discours.*

The author of the *Discours au Cynique Despréaux* reveals, furthermore, the names of three of Boileau's victims that prove him to be a monster of ingratitude without " la moindre teinture d'honneur et d'humanité." They are Maucroix, Chapelain, and Gilles Boileau. Chapelain, as a sort of patron, and Gilles, as a brother, were entitled to Boileau's respect. As for Maucroix, what had he done to incur an attack?

> Maucroix sur tous, qui doit être de vos amis puisqu'*il est de ceux qui vous gouvernent* et qui vaut mieux seul que tous tant qu'ils sont.[32]

Now Boileau had included a certain " Mauroy "[33] among the " froids rimeurs " excoriated in the early texts of *Satire VII.* The pamphleteer may or may not have erred in assuming that Boileau was aiming his satirical arrow at Maucroix.[34] The indication that we gather for our purposes is that Boileau was regarded as a disciple[35] of Maucroix and that there were others engaged in directing Despréaux's talents at this time. Intimations of this kind tend to take the wind out of such epistolary sails as:

> Le temps . . . . . . où ma Muse en sa force
> Du Parnasse français formant les nourrissons . . .[36]

Cotin, writing his *Satire des Satires* in 1666[37] after the authorized publication of the *Satires,* brings against Despréaux the same

[32] Magne, II, 142.

[33] For a detailed discussion of the identity of "Mauroy," cf. M. Demeure's article entitled "Mauroy" in *RHLF,* XLI (janvier-mars and avril-juin, 1934). M. Demeure maintains that "Mauroy" was a disguise intended to suggest Maucroix. He refutes M. René Bray's conclusion that "Mauroy" designates a certain Testu de Mauroy. Cf. M. Bray's article, "Boileau et Maucroix en 1666," *RHLF,* XXXVIII (1931), 101 *et seq.*

[34] *Satire VII,* vs. 45 in early editions.

[35] Maucroix's directing Boileau must be taken with due reservations. It is evidently the intention of the pamphleteer to show how ignominious was the conduct of the latter in turning his satire against those to whom he was indebted. It is possible, then, that he exaggerated Despréaux's obligation to La Fontaine's friend.

[36] *Épître à mes Vers* (1695), vss. 14-15.

[37] *Satires du sieur Despréaux Boileau, avec la Satyre de ses Satyres.* Paris: Louis Billaine, 1666.

charges as the author of the *Discours*.   Although of a very
peaceable nature, Cotin is driven to writing satire by the presumption of " le cadet Boileau,"

> Lui qu'on ne voit jamais dans le sacré vallon, . . .
> Lui qu'on ne connoît qu'à cause de son frère, . . .
> Ce malheureux sans nom, sans mérite et sans grâce,
> Se place en conquérant au sommet du Parnasse.

Furthermore, he is irreligious, even blasphemous, and yet " il se
pique d'une belle morale." He is a wanton parasite and a gri-
macing " bateleur." [38]
There are also in the *Satire des Satires* two suggestions that
Despréaux, without deserting the taverns, is finding his way into
higher social circles.   Cotin says that the Marais approves of the
morality preached in the *Satires,* and he ironically bids both
Boileau's tavern audience and his more aristocratic clientèle to
follow it :

> Lieux d'honneur, cabarets dont il est amphibie,
> Réglez sur ce pied-là le cours de votre vie ;
> Et Priape et Bacchus, dont vous faites vos dieux,
> S'ils venaient vous prêcher ne prêcheraient pas mieux.

We see that Despréaux's " amphibious " character adapts him to
frequent either the aristocratic Marais or riotous taverns.   Moreover, this new " Aretino " takes the liberty of castigating *Parlement* because he has protectors at the Louvre.   These are important indications.

Boursault and Mme de Sévigné, giving more equitable judgments a few years later, will confirm many of the assertions of
the *Discours au Cynique Despréaux* and of *la Satire des Satires*.

[38]   " Despréaux, sans argent, ' Crotté jusqu'à l'échine,
> S'en va chercher son pain de cuisine en cuisine.'
> Son Turlupin l'assiste, et, jouant de son nez,
> Chez le sot campagnard, gagne de bons dîners.
> Despréaux, à ce jeu, répond par sa grimace,
> Et fait, en bateleur, cent tours de passe-passe ;
> Puis, ensuite, enivrés et du bruit et du vin,
> L'un sur l'autre tombant renversent le festin."
> (Appendix of Brunetière's *Boileau, Œuvres Poétiques,* p. 307.)
Pierre Perrin, in *la Bastonnade, satyre contre Boisleau* (cited in
Magne, II, 199-203) makes similar charges: Puymorin, after his dis-
gusting drinking stunts, makes an organ out of his nose and sings inde-
cent songs, finally reading in energetic tones the verses of Despréaux.

If in 1668 Boileau's fame is still attributed to the sensation
caused by " les gens qu'il maltraite," [39] if his youth and inex-
perience are still held against him,[40] if Mme de Sévigné in 1671
is leading her son a " vie enragée " on account of the company
he is keeping with " Ninon et une comédienne, Despréaux sur le
tout," [41] we have greater reason to believe that, at the time when
the first *Satires* appeared, there was ground for censuring the
audacity and libertinage of the young poet who was enjoying
what might be called a *succès de scandale.*[42]

It was probably at this time that Despréaux became acquainted
with the premier président de Lamoignon. According to the
Préface of the collective edition of his works given in 1683, he
began to frequent the magistrate " dans les temps que mes
satires faisaient le plus de bruit." Boileau tells us forthright
what was the immediate advantage of this connection :

L'accès obligeant qu'il me donna dans son illustre maison fit avantageusement mon apologie contre ceux *qui voulaient m'accuser alors de
libertinage et de mauvaises mœurs.*[43]

---

[39] Émilie, in Boursault's play, *la Satire des Satires*, defends in moderate terms the cause of Boileau. She acknowledges his talent but
regrets that the poet uses it to engage in a warfare of personalities :
> On court à ses Écrits, mais chacun les achete,
> Moins pour voir ce qu'il fait que les gens qu'il maltraite.
>   (*Théâtre de Boursault*, II, 32.)

[40] Boursault's play ends with this final judgment of Émilie :
> Non qu'enfin Despréaux n'ait beaucoup de génie ;
> Quand il aura plus d'âge, & les yeux mieux ouverts,
> Pour venger ceux qu'il choque, il relira ses vers :
> Devenu raisonnable, & ravi qu'on le croye,
> Il fera son chagrin de ce qui fait sa joye ;
> Et sentira dans l'âme un déplaisir secret,
> D'avoir pû si bien faire, et d'avoir si mal fait.
>   (*Théâtre de Boursault*, II, 68.)

[41] Letter to her daughter, March 18, 1671. (*Lettres*, Grands Écrivains
de la France edition, II, 118.)

[42] Furetière is said to have remarked apropos of *Satire VII* (1663) :
" Voilà qui est bon, mais cela fera du bruit." (Brossette's remarks on
Satire VII, vs. 88.)

[43] In 1701 Boileau detached the part of the general *Préface* that contained these remarks. He published it as an *Avis au Lecteur* in front
of *le Lutrin*. (Berriat-Saint-Prix, II, 283.) Henceforth unless otherwise indicated, references to Boileau's works will be to the edition of
Berriat-Saint-Prix.

It was only a "monstrueuse" pirated edition [44] of his works
that forced Boileau to give the authorized edition of the *Discours
au Roi* and the first seven *Satires* in 1666.[45] The editor, who
would naturally not be prone to underrate unduly the poems he
was publishing, represents Boileau as a modest man afraid to give
his work to the public lest he be accused of increasing the number
of "méchants livres qu'il blâme en tant de rencontres"[46] and
of meriting thereby a place in his own *Satires*. It is more than
likely, however, that "modesty" was not the sole cause of
Boileau's reluctance to publish his satires. A storm of indignation had been called forth by the "monstrueuse" edition, and it
was perhaps fear of *coups,* quite as much as humility, that made
Despréaux hesitate to publish the satires originally destined
to regale a few convivial patrons of the Croix de Lorraine or the
Croix blanche. In any case, the authentic version appeared with
attenuations and changes of names. The publisher strains a
point to placate, in advance, those who might take offense at the
satirist's mention of their works. It matters very little whether
it was modesty or fear of brutal treatment, or both, that accounts
for Boileau's unwillingness to have his satires appear in print.
The fact remains that in 1666 he was a wary poet feeling his
way somewhat timorously.

Le Verrier stresses Despréaux's unpretentiousness in those
days, and states precisely who were his companions in the taverns :

L'autheur (Boileau) ne songeoit point à obtenir aucune pension du Roy,
ny même à publier ses ouvrages. Il se contentoit de les lire à quelques-
uns de ses amis particuliers, à Molière, à Chappelle, à Racine, au Duc
de Vivonne, au Duc de Lédiguière, au Comte de Fiesque, au Duc de La
Rochefoucault, à M^r le Prince. Tout cela se passoit d'ordinaire au
cabaret. Mr de Ranché alors capitaine aux Gardes et à présent Gouverneur de Quesnoy estoit souvent des parties les plus particulières.[47]

---

[44] *Recueil contenant plusieurs discours libres et moraux en vers et un
Jugement en prose sur les sciences où un honneste homme peut s'occuper.*
It is item 7 in Magne (I, 56).

[45] This edition is 11 in Magne (I, 65). The *privilège* given Barbin
on March 6, 1666, was not registered until Aug. 6. The book appeared,
then, sometime after that date. There is no *achevé d'imprimer.*

[46] *Le Libraire au Lecteur.* Cf. also *Mémoires,* Mesnard, I, 237 :
"Jamais poète n'eut tant de répugnance à donner ses ouvrages au
public."

[47] Lachèvre, p. 85. Boileau made no corrections on Le Verrier's remarks

Boileau continued,[48] in two more *Satires* and in *le Discours sur la Satire,* his attacks on academicians and lesser literary lights and his defense of what he considered to be the prerogatives of a satiric poet. M. Magne lists twenty-six complete or separate editions of his works between the original edition of the *Satires* in 1666 and the end of 1668.[49] A brief study of these editions attests the growing fame of Boileau during those years. The twenty-six editions of the *Satires,* complete to date or separate editions, are distributed over the years as follows: two in 1666 (in addition to the original and the pre-original editions); three in 1667; and twenty-one (of which sixteen are separate editions of *Satire VIII* or *Satire IX*) in 1668. The year 1669 saw three complete editions of the *Satires* (a reprint and two new editions), a separate edition of *Satire IX,* and two editions of *la Disserta-*

on *Satire IX.* Indeed, he seems not to have pursued his careful emendation of Le Verrier beyond the commentary on *Satire VIII.*

[48] This is the place to evaluate a claim made by Boileau in a conversation with Mathieu Marais on Dec. 12, 1703. He said that it was he who prevailed upon Denys Thierry to publish the first edition of La Fontaine's fables (*privilège,* June 6, 1667, *achevé d'imprimer,* Mar. 31, 1668). The publisher had been unwilling to undertake the work. " Je l'en pressai, dit Boileau, et ce fut à ma considération qu'il lui donna quelque argent. Il y a gagné des sommes infinies " (cited by Sainte-Beuve, *Causeries du Lundi,* VI, 501, n. 1). This would indicate that as early as 1667 Boileau had considerable influence with publishers. Several considerations, however, lead us to doubt the truth of Boileau's statement. La Fontaine had already such powerful protectors as the duchesse de Bouillon and the duchesse douairière d'Orléans. His talent was highly esteemed. The *Contes* had been edited or reprinted nine times between December, 1664, and the end of 1667. *Joconde* had provoked a quarrel that left La Fontaine definitely the victor. Chapelain in a letter of Feb. 12, 1666, had praised the *Contes* and urged him to continue writing in that *genre.* (*Lettres,* II, 439.) Moreover, the *Préface* to the first collection of *Fables* speaks of the favor the public had already accorded to some of his fables (probably circulating in manuscript form). The association of two publishers — Barbin ceded half the rights to Denys Thierry—would indicate that they anticipated an unusual success for the volume. In any event Boileau's intercession seems quite unnecessary and improbable. His claim seems to be an instance of the tendency he had in his later years to magnify and antedate the service rendered his friends. His defense of La Fontaine in *la Dissertation sur " Joconde "* in 1664 would of course serve as a convenient point of departure for such an illusion.

[49] I, 69-78 and 97-106.

tion sur la "Joconde" published anonymously in a volume of *Contes et Nouvelles en Vers de M^r de La Fontaine.*[50]

Boursault's judgment might be invoked at this point. His *Satire des Satires* gives a contemporary's appraisal of Boileau's fame toward the end of 1668. The fact that Despréaux was made the protagonist and that the play was announced by the Théâtre du Marais [51] indicates that the satirist was already well known. Although an adversary of Boileau, Boursault acknowledges the "délicatesse" of his pen and the approbation he has received from "tant de personnes capables de juger des belles choses." He refrains from condemning what is good in the *Satires.* Boileau's works, however, have made a "grand fracas," and the satirist's glory derives mainly from "beaucoup de mauvais bruit." On the other hand, Boursault admits that Despréaux could "s'attirer des applaudissements sans restrictions" if he used his talent in more impersonal satire.[52] Boursault, taking a part in *la Satire des Satires,* thinks he is fair to the poet when he says :

> Il ne faut pas avoir l'esprit fort délicat,
> Pour nommer l'un fripon, appeler l'autre fat.
> Qu'a-t'il fait jusqu'ici, qu'exciter des murmures?
> Insulter des Auteurs, et rimer des injures? [53]

On the other hand, Boileau had in that year a clever champion in the person of Marie-Catherine Des Jardins, dame de Villedieu, one of the most famous blue-stockings of the second half of the century. Barbin published a collection of her letters, of which one addressed to her lover, M. de Gourville, contained a vigorous defense of Despréaux.

Robinet's *Lettre en vers* of February 2, 1669,[54] indicates that he holds the profession and the person of the satirist in low regard. Without naming Despréaux, he nevertheless includes him in this sweeping invective :

[50] *Ibid.,* I, 188, and Berriat-Saint-Prix, I, cxxxix, item 24.

[51] The *Parlement* on October 22, 1668, at the instigation of Boileau, forbade the performance of *la Satire des Satires.* It was printed in 1669.

[52] *Avis au Lecteur.* (*Théâtre de Boursault,* II, iii.)

[53] *Ibid.,* II, 42.

[54] In announcing the publication of *les Nouvelles galantes et comiques* of Jean Donneau de Visé he takes the opportunity to commend that author's scorn for satirists.

> Maudits Frelons des Républiques,
> Lesquels s'érigent en Censeurs
> Et des Ouvrages et des Mœurs,
> Quoi que le Vice et l'Ignorance
> Fassent toute leur compétence.

He claims that theirs is a false glitter that dazzles only for a time. In May [55] he tells that upon reading Boursault's *Satire des Satires* he laughed in his sleeve, " en ayant une joye extrême."

In 1669, the editor of the Dutch edition [56] of *la Dissertation sur " Joconde "* refers to the author as " un des plus beaux esprits de ce temps." [57] Had Despréaux earned that title? It is not likely that the poet's reputation in 1669 warranted that praise. M. Bray [58] ascribes it at least in part to the avidity of an editor bent on selling his wares.

About this time Boileau confided his project of an *Art Poétique* to Patru, who considered the plan presumptuous in view of the difficulty of expressing in French verse " des matières aussi sèches que le sont de simples préceptes." He fell in with Boileau's idea only after the work was under way, " voyant la noble audace avec laquelle notre Auteur entroit en matière." [59]

A marginal note in Boileau's handwriting, found among his corrections in Le Verrier's *Commentaire sur les Satires*, seems to be additional proof that in polite circles Boileau did not enjoy any pre-eminence as a poet or critic before 1669 or 1670. Boileau's correction consists in altering a part of Le Verrier's comments on those verses of the *Discours au Roi* [60] denouncing poetasters who were singing the king's praises for their personal gain. The verses were written on the occasion of the distribution of pensions in 1664, when Boileau was indignant at Chapelain's choice of authors who were to benefit from the king's bounty. Le Verrier avers, however, that it was not Boileau's own interest which prompted him to speak, for he was still an obscure poet with no thought of receiving a pension from the king:

[55] *Lettre à Madame*, May 25, 1669, cited by Magne, II, 225.

[56] The original edition.

[57] Magne, I, 188.

[58] " La Dissertation sur *Joconde*," *RHLF*, XXXVIII, 353-354.

[59] Brossette's *Remarques*, *Œuvres de Boileau* (Saint-Marc's new ed., II, 216).

[60] Vss. 15 *et sqq*.

Dans ce temps là, il n'estoit pas connu, je ne sçay s'il se connoissoit bien luy-même. A proprement parler, il ne fut bien connu dans le monde *qu'après avoir passé douze années à étudier dans son cabinet tout ce que l'antiquité nous a laissé de meilleur et à composer de génie d'après de si excellens originaux.*[61]

Boileau deleted the italicized words and substituted " qu'à cinq ou six années de là." [62] His fame " dans le monde " began, then, according to his own testimony as late as 1669 or 1670. Although this commentary and Boileau's corrections were written in 1701, some thirty years [63] after the period in question, they may in this instance be taken as trustworthy, for when Le Verrier and Boileau err, it is by way of stressing the critic's precocious talent and the preponderant influence he exerted upon his friends.

His prestige during the next years was increased by the reading of his verses before distinguished gatherings. His *Dialogue des Héros de Roman,* circulating *sub rosa,* continued to cause much merriment.[64] We find in the correspondence of Mme de Sévigné indications that Boileau was being gradually accepted by society. The publication of *Bajazet* early in 1672 led her to compare the merits of Racine and Corneille. To give weight to her preference for the latter she invoked, in the same breath, Despréaux and " le bon goût." [65] She reported in the fall of the next year a visit that the poet paid to Condé and a witticism of his that was being bandied about the capital apparently much to his credit. Gourville had taken him to Tournay, where Mon-

---

[61] Lachèvre, p. 8.

[62] Why did Boileau make the change? Perhaps in order to make the statement more definite. " Five or six years " after 1664 dates his fame as beginning in 1669 or 1670. Le Verrier's interesting but diffuse remark doubtless had the same import but was less clear. He probably figured twelve years of study and imitation that began in 1657, the year in which Boileau's father died and when Despréaux turned to letters as a career.

[63] Le Verrier's *Préface.* (Lachèvre, p. 2.)

[64] According to Boileau's own version, it was out of deference to Mlle de Scudéry that he refrained from publishing it, or even from writing it down during her lifetime. Cf. his letter to Brossette on March 27, 1704 (Laverdet, p. 177) and also the *Discours sur le Dialogue,* which Boileau composed in 1710. The first edition of *les Héros de Roman* was in 1713. M. Demeure (*MF,* CCV, 50, n. 9) suspects that it was fear of maltreatment that prevented Boileau from publishing the *Dialogue.*

[65] *Lettres,* II, 536. The letter is dated March 16, 1672.

sieur le Prince was in command of a wretched army. After
sending him to see the army, Condé asked Despréaux what he
thought of it. " Monseigneur, elle sera fort bonne quand elle
sera majeure," was his reply. Mme de Sévigné explains that the
eldest man in the Prince's army was under eighteen years of
age.[66] In a letter to her daughter dated December 15, 1673,[67]
Mme de Sévigné told of a dinner at Gourville's house, where
Despréaux read his *Poétique* before M. le Duc, M. de la Rochefoucauld, Mme de Thianges, Mme de la Fayette, Mme de Coulanges, l'abbé Testu, M. de Marcillac, and M. de Guilleragues.
She hailed it as a " chef-d'œuvre."

It was probably about this time that Boileau was presented at
court. The occasion was the reading of a part of *le Lutrin* including the revised ending of *Chant II.* On the same day Boileau
recited the last forty verses of his *Épître I.* This was a new
ending in praise of the king.[68] Louis XIV was delighted and
gave the poet a pension of 2000 *livres* [69] and the *privilège* to

---

[66] *Ibid.,* III, 262. The letter was written to Mme de Grignan on Nov.
2, 1673.

[67] *Ibid.,* III, 315-316.

[68] Delaporte (*L'Art Poétique de Boileau commenté par Boileau et
par ses contemporains,* I, 30, n. 1) thinks the presentation took place
in 1669 immediately after the *Épître* was written. Lanson, however
(*Boileau,* p. 24) points out among other things that *le Lutrin* was not
begun and the new ending of the *Épître* was not written before 1672.
The presentation, then, could not have been before this date. The
Bolœana, p. 14, states that at the time of Chancellor Séguier's death in
1672, Boileau had not yet appeared at court. This confirms Lanson's
terminus a quo. Revillout (*RLR,* XXXVIII, 127), basing his argument
on the dates of the pension and the *privilège* as well as on indications
of M. de Vivonne's (it was he who presented Despréaux) absences from
Paris, places the presentation at court as late as the end of 1673 or
January, 1674. He discounts the anecdote related in the *Mémoires*
(Mesnard, I, 232-233) which would put Boileau's presentation at court
before the death of Molière on February 17, 1673. According to Louis
Racine, the king one day asked Despréaux to imitate Molière "qui étoit
présent." He then asked Molière if he recognized himself. "Nous ne
pouvons juger de notre ressemblance," replied Molière, "mais la mienne
est parfaite, s'il m'a aussi bien imité qu'il a imité les autres." Revillout
is of the opinion that Louis Racine is confusing two different occasions
on which Boileau imitated the gestures and manners of Molière, one
when Molière was present, the other subsequently, for the king's benefit.

[69] Cf. Guiffrey, *Comptes des Bâtiments du roi,* I, column 780, where the
pension paid on Feb. 7, 1674, is listed under the heading " Bibliothèque

print all his works.[70]   The latter document, signed on March 28, 1674, contains the king's express commendation of Boileau's works. He accorded the *privilège*

afin de le traiter favorablement et de donner au public par la lecture de ses ouvrages la même satisfaction qu'il en a reçue.[71]

An anecdote of Le Verrier, referring no doubt to this period of Despréaux's life, throws an interesting light on Boileau's ingress to society. The duc de Montausier, on account of his friendship for Chapelain, resented Boileau's repeated attacks on the author of *la Pucelle*. He was further infuriated [72] when Boileau, with malice aforethought, incorporated into *Satire IX* [73] the desire often expressed by Montausier, that the entire " brood " of satirists would go head first to rime in the bottom of the river. Montausier, however, was obliged to acknowledge that no one had written finer verse than Despréaux, and while he blustered that the poet should be sent to the galleys for his satires, he admitted that it should be with a crown of laurels on his head.[74]   Despite the rancor that he felt for the satirist, he begged Puymorin [75] several times to bring his brother to dine

et Accadémie des Sciences." The gratification of 1200 *livres* given in 1665 and again in 1666 " au sieur Boileau, pour luy donner moyen de continuer son application aux belles lettres " (*ibid.*, I, columns 113 and 163) was, of course, Gilles Boileau's.

[70] For these details see Brossette's remarks on *le Lutrin, Chant II*, vs. 121, and on the last verses of *Épître I*.

[71] Clément, *Lettres, Instructions et Mémoires de Colbert*, V, 361, n. 2.

[72] Montausier spoke of nothing so much as of his desire to punish the insolent rimer. His vengeance did not go farther than saying often and publicly that he rose each morning with the intention of beating the satirist. His anger, however, was allayed each day by his morning prayer. (*Réponse à l'avertissement qui a été ajouté à la nouvelle édition des Œuvres de M. Despréaux*, envoyée de Paris à M. Le Clerc, et insérée dans sa *Bibliothèque Choisie*, XXXVI, 64: pub. in *Œuvres de Boileau*, Amsterdam, 1735, III, 357, 358. This work is summarized by Revillout, *RLR*, XXXVII, 455-456.) Montausier, touched by the deference shown him in *Épître VII*, vs. 100, finally relented (Brossette's remarks on this verse).

[73] Vss. 134-136.

[74] Bussy-Rabutin in Oct., 1673, reports this conversation between Montausier and Vineuil, the king's secretary. Cf. Revillout, *RLR*, XXXVIII, 79.

[75] After Gilles Boileau's death in 1669, Puymorin was given the

at his house. Le Verrier tells us what were Despréaux's objections:

Mais l'autheur (Despréaux) qui naturellement est distrait, qui est extrêmement vif et qui accompagne ses discours d'une action véhémente,
craignoit de se trouver à la table de ce duc, car avec un très grand
fond de bonté, il ne pardonnoit point la moindre faute. Un jour il
(Montausier) trouva dans la Chambre du Roy l'autheur (Despréaux)
à qui il dit: voulez-vous que toute la Cour croye que nous sommes mal
ensemble? Si vous ne le voulez pas, venez donc disner avec moy. Il y
alla. Le Duc luy enseigna comment il falloit se tenir sur son siège,
de quelle manière il falloit d'abord mettre la nape sur ses genoux, puis
la serviette par dessus, enfin tout ce qu'il falloit pour observer les règles
d'une politesse et d'une adresse fort outrées. L'autheur sortit de ce repas
sans avoir fait de faute, et il s'admire encore aujourd'huy là-dessus.[76]

This document showing that Boileau, even after his presentation
at court, had serious misgivings in regard to his mastery of
rather elemental rules of social usage, is valuable evidence when
we are considering Boileau's prestige and, in particular, his rise
in society. It would be an error, we believe, to assume from
evidence like the letters of Mme de Sévigné cited above that
Despréaux was mingling, on anything like an equal footing, with
such persons as Mme de Thianges and Mme de la Fayette.[77]

In the *Préfaces* to the several editions of his works given in
1674 and 1675, Boileau refrains from an apology which might
only serve to lay him open to new attacks. His poetry, moreover, calls for neither praise nor justification:

Je ne crois point mes ouvrages assez bons pour mériter des éloges ni
assez criminels pour avoir besoin d'apologie.[78]

The poet has a natural aversion to long apologies in favor of
"bagatelles aussi bagatelles que sont mes ouvrages." [79]   The

former's charge as "contrôleur de l'argenterie" at the court. Here he
became acquainted with Montausier.

[76] Lachèvre, p. 98.

[77] Nor do we find justification for Revillout's conclusions that from
this time on, with Molière dead, Corneille "éteint," La Fontaine of no
consequence, and Racine already passing for "l'élève et le protégé de
son ami le satirique, c'est Boileau qui règne." (*RLR*, XXXVIII, 223.)

[78] Préface of the 4to edition of 1674 and the small 12mo of 1675.

[79] *Préface* of the large 12mo editions of 1674 and 1675. The comte de
Brienne alludes to the humility Boileau assumed in his prefaces (*Mémoires*, I, 47).

semblance of modesty, however, in no way disguises the self-assurance that the author feels at this time. He could easily answer the accusations published against him. He has nothing to fear from further attacks and relies upon the number of readers with good judgment to set right the "petits esprits" who might be misled by objections made to his works. Boileau speaks, indeed, as one having authority.

In 1674 the bookseller Barbin, in dedicating to Boileau les *Nouvelles Œuvres de M. Sarazin,* feels that he is placing the work under a powerful protector, for

Qui oseroit l'attaquer si vous le défendez? et qui entreprendra de le détruire si vous daignez le soutenir? Vostre discernement est devenu la règle des Ouvrages du Siècle.

Louis Racine likewise testifies to the prestige Despréaux enjoyed from this time on:

Il avoit acquis une grande autorité sur le Parnasse, depuis qu'en 1674 il avoit donné son *Art Poétique* et ses quatre *Épîtres.*[80]

Boursault's account of Boileau's intercession in favor of Corneille, whose pension had just been suspended, is added evidence of the critic's fame only recently established. The incident must have taken place in 1674.[81]

M. Despréaux, ayant appris à Fontainebleau, qu'on venoit de retrancher la pension que le Roy donnoit au grand Corneille, courut avec précipitation chez Mme de Montespan, et luy dit que le roi, tout équitable qu'il étoit, ne pouvoit sans quelque apparence d'injustice, donner Pension à un homme comme luy, *qui ne commençoit qu'à monter sur le Parnasse,* et l'ôter à un autre qui depuis si long-tems étoit arrivé au sommet.[82]

The security which he nevertheless feels is well expressed in the *Épître à Guilleragues.* Enjoying the king's gratifications, he no longer fears the effete results of envy or cabals:

C'en est trop: mon bonheur a passé mes souhaits;
Qu'à son gré désormais la fortune me joue,
On me verra dormir au branle de sa roue.[83]

---

[80] *Mémoires,* Mesnard, I, 260-261.

[81] Corneille's pension was discontinued in 1674, and it was resumed in 1682 (Guiffrey, *op. cit.,* I, column 714—II, column 238). The king promised Boileau a pension when the poet was presented at court late in 1673 or in January, 1674. Cf. *supra,* p. 28, n. 69.

[82] *Lettres Nouvelles,* p. 390.   [83] *Épître V* (1674), vss. 132-134.

Mme de Thianges' new year's present [84] to her nephew, the duc du Maine, attests Boileau's popularity in court circles in 1675. The gift was a miniature "chambre du sublime" guarded by Despréaux, who, by means of a pitchfork, kept at a distance seven or eight mediocre poets who were seeking admittance. In the alcove were wax figures of the duc du Maine, de la Rochefoucauld, the prince de Marcillac, the Bishop of Condom, Mme de Thianges, and Mme de la Fayette. "Au dehors du balustre" were Despréaux, Racine, and, a short distance away, La Fontaine. Revillout remarks very aptly that, in this arrangement of the images, despite the honor paid to the poets, "les distances sociales sont observées." [85]

It must be remembered that Boileau's authority, however great at court or among the intellectual élite, was, nevertheless, far from being absolute. In his *Deffense du Poëme Héroïque avec quelques remarques sur les Œuvres Satyriques du Sieur D * * *,*[86] Desmarets de Saint-Sorlin even denied him the title of poet, maintaining that a satirist could not be considered a poet until he had given proof of his talent in another *genre.* He also pointed out faults of taste and criticized certain errors in grammar and prosody that Boileau corrected in subsequent editions. Boileau was not a member of the French Academy until 1684, when he was received only at the express command of the king. There his enemies were firmly in the saddle. Deltour,[87] basing his study on contemporary testimony, concludes that Racine and Boileau were always in the literary minority, and that, at least during their productive years, they were often worsted in their rivalry with Chapelain and his coterie. An incident reported by Monchesnay testifies to the little credit that Boileau enjoyed among the academicians even at a later date. One day an opinion which he held received only two dissenting votes. He expressed surprise at his success. "Je m'attendais

----

[84] January, 1675. Cf. Bussy-Rabutin's letter of Jan. 12, 1675 (*Correspondance avec sa famille et ses amis,* ed. by Lalanne, II, 415-416). The anecdote as reported in the *Ménagiana* is cited by Lanson in his *Boileau,* p. 23.

[85] *RLR,* XXXVIII, 229.

[86] 1674 and a reprint, 1675.

[87] *Les Ennemis de Racine au XVIIe Siècle,* pp. 96 et sqq.

bien, disoit-il, à être condamné; car, outre que j'avais raison, c'étoit moi." [88]

Boileau's authority was hotly contested during the early phase of the quarrel of the Ancients and Moderns. The Moderns thought that his authority was not sufficiently established " pour décider sur le bon et sur le mauvais." [89] On the other hand, certain erudite partisans of the ancients thought that Boileau was presumptuous in constituting himself the defender of their cause. Did he possess the necessary qualifications? Huet is reported to have said to Boileau, who was warming up to the attack:

Monsieur Despréaux, il me semble que cela nous regarde plus que vous. [90]

Until a critical edition of Boileau's works is made, it will be difficult to determine with certainty the influence he exerted upon his friends and enemies. The most recent investigations, however, all point to a Boileau who is less of a legislator, less sure of himself, and quite subject to fluctuations of taste and opinion. M. Mornet hints that studies on the variations from edition to edition will reveal a truer Boileau " tout remué de mouvements divers." [91]

We have seen that the fame of Boileau was not established before 1669 or 1670 and that, to all appearances, it was not full-fledged until the publication of the *Art Poétique,* a part of *le Lutrin,* and his translation of Longinus in 1674.

[88] *Bolœana,* pp. 60-61. Monchesnay testifies: " M. Despréaux n'alloit guères à l'Académie; mais quand il s'y trouvoit, s'il venoit à ouvrir quelque avis, il y perdoit toujours sa cause à la pluralité des voix." Louis Racine in his *Mémoires* (Mesnard, I, 293) reports the same or a similar incident. He maintains, however, that Boileau was for a long time " assez exact aux assemblées, dans lesquelles il avoit souvent des contradictions à essuyer."

[89] Pierre Perrault's *Avertissement* to *La Secchia Rapita, Poème héroï-comique du Tassoni,* Nouvellement traduit d'Italien en Français (Paris, 1678), cited by Magne, II, 186.

[90] Cited by Lanson, *Méthodes de l'Histoire Littéraire,* p. 21.

[91] His review of Albert Cahen's critical edition of the *Satires, RHLF* (1932), XXXIX, 465. He thinks it curious that we have no critical edition of Boileau. " Est-ce par une sorte de justice immanente qui laissait Boileau, à cet égard, en arrière de La Fontaine, Racine ou Molière pour suggérer qu'il n'était que leur compagnon, peut-être timide, et non pas leur maître? " Cf. also his *Racine,* p. 66.

3

What of Racine's reputation and self-assurance during these years? He had acquired, as early as 1663, a singularly rich æsthetic and literary background, and he had published some verse. We shall have occasion later [92] to speak of his knowledge of Sophocles and Euripides that dates from his sojourn at Port-Royal. Although the marginal comments made in his copies of the Greek tragedies may belong to a later period of Racine's life, we know that, even in these early years, he was a painstaking student who read thoughtfully, annotating his texts as he went. He wrote extensive comments in the *Parallel Lives* and *Moralia* of Plutarch in 1655 and 1656. The marginalia, written in polished Latin in copies of Quintilian and Tacitus and authentically dated 1656, attest the thoroughness of his preparation for a career of letters. His careful reading of Homer, Ariosto, Virgil, Pindar, Petrarch, Plato, and Aristotle during his stay at Uzès is reflected in his correspondence. Studying Saint Thomas Aquinas did not appear to dampen his interest in the theater, as he constantly makes inquiries concerning what is going on in Paris. The imagination, sensibility, powers of observation, and the potential passion evidenced by his early letters,[93] are a positive asset to the future dramatist.

Before meeting Boileau, Racine had written, besides some verse unpublished during the poet's lifetime,[94] *la Nymphe de la Seine, l'Ode sur la convalescence du Roi,* and *la Renommée aux Muses.* The first two poems were published,[95] one in 1660, the other in 1663. The third may have been the poem that Le Vasseur submitted to Boileau's criticism, and consequently the occasion of the first meeting of the two poets. It was probably published late in the year 1663.[96] *La Nymphe de la Seine* in its revised form pleased Chapelain, and, according to Louis Racine [97] and Brossette,[98] earned for the poet a gratification of 100 *louis* from the king. Early in the year 1663, he received a further gratification of 800 *livres.*[99] In a letter of July 23, 1663, Racine

[92] Cf. *infra*, pp. 115 *et sqq.*   [93] Mesnard, VI, 394-510.

[94] *Le Paysage ou promenade de Port-Royal des Champs* and *les Stances à Parthenice.*

[95] Mesnard, IV, 50 and 65.   [97] *Mémoires,* Mesnard, I, 224-225.

[96] *Ibid.,* IV, 71-72.   [98] Mesnard, I, 58, n. 3.

[99] La Place, *Pièces intéressantes et peu connues pour servir à l'histoire et à la littérature,* cited by Mesnard, I, 58.

tells his sister that a pension has been promised him. He figures, accordingly, in the *Comptes des Bâtiments du roi*[100] for 1664, receiving 600 *livres*. *La Renommé aux Muses* won for him the protection of the Comte de Saint-Aignan, to whom he later dedicated his first tragedy. In November, 1663, he was present at the king's *lever*. In writing of this and similar preoccupations, he styled himself " à demi-courtisan," but expressed little enthusiasm for the " métier." [101]

Besides the lyric poetry already mentioned Racine seems to have written a play called *Amasie,* which the comedians of the troupe du Marais at first received enthusiastically. The unfavorable verdict they gave after reconsidering the piece was a keen disappointment to Racine.[102] The plan of a second play based on Ovid's love affairs was completed in June, 1661.[103]

It is quite evident after weighing the assets of Boileau and those of Racine in 1663, that the advantage is indubitably on the side of the latter. By the end of 1670 Racine had given one comedy and five tragedies including *Britannicus,* which in 1676 [104] he still considered the most solid and the most praiseworthy tragedy he had written. Four *Préfaces* had been printed before the end of 1670, and the *Préface* of *Bérénice* was soon to be published. Racine then gave *Bajazet*. It was the following year, in the midst of the triumph of *Mithridate,* that he was received into the French Academy.[105] His *Préfaces* became less polemical in tone, indicating that he no longer felt obliged to fight his way inch by inch.[106] *Bérénice* is the last play to have a *Dédicace*. The dedicatory letters of earlier plays are gradually suppressed in re-editions after 1672. Racine evidently no longer felt the need of sustaining his tragedies by means of powerful protectors. *Iphigénie* was performed at Versailles on August 18,

[100] Guiffrey, *op. cit.,* I, column 56. Guiffrey begins with Colbert's accounts for 1664.
[101] Letter to Le Vasseur, Mesnard, VI, 516.
[102] Letter to Le Vasseur, Sept. 5 [1660]. (Mesnard, VI, 387-388.)
[103] *Ibid.,* VI, 417.
[104] *La Seconde Préface* in the first collective edition of his works.
[105] January 12, 1673.
[106] The *Préfaces* of *Alexandre* and of *Andromaque* were attenuated in the re-editions of those plays in 1672 and 1673, respectively. Cf. Michaut, *la Bérénice de Racine,* p. 44.

1674, some five weeks after the *Art Poétique* came off the press.[107] All Racine's secular plays, therefore, with the exception of *Phèdre,* antedate the publication of the *Art Poétique.* Seven, and the most enlightening, of his prefaces had appeared previous to 1674. No one could, in the light of these facts, claim that the tenets of tragedy as they were actually enunciated in *Chant III* affected Racine's conception of that *genre.*

On the other hand, we shall see that intimate relations between the two poets were probably established about 1671.[108] It would not, therefore, be unreasonable to suppose that, during the composition of the *Art Poétique,* the two poets often discussed the æsthetic principles involved in tragedy.

The Friendship of Boileau and Racine

We shall at this point in our study examine Louis Racine's assertion that the two poets " ont dans tous les temps partagé entre eux les faveurs des Muses et de la cour." [1] It is manifestly the time element in his statement that needs to be investigated.

If there existed any doubt regarding the intimacy of their friendship, it would be dispelled by the warmly affectionate correspondence which they carried on between 1687 and the year of Racine's death.[2] They were closely associated after October, 1677, in their work as historiographers of the king. At court Racine winced at the blunders that escaped the lips of his friend, who was by nature far less of a courtier than he.[3] If we may trust Monchesnay, it was " pour la gloire de son ami," [4] that Boileau took upon himself the proof-reading and emenda-

---

[107] July 10, 1674.

[108] Cf. *infra*, pp. 38-44.

[1] *Mémoires*, Mesnard, I, 213. Cf. *ibid.*, I, 229.

[2] Mesnard, VI, *passim*, 557-624, and *ibid.*, VII, 3-193.

[3] Cf. especially Despréaux's blustering denunciation, in the presence of Mme de Maintenon, of Scarron and the burlesque style.

[4] *Bolœana*, p. 107. " M. Racine, quelques années avant de mourir, avait une sorte d'indifférence pour ses Ouvrages. Il ne voulut jamais corriger les épreuves d'une nouvelle édition, ni changer des endroits qui méritoient d'être réformés. M. Despréaux prit ce soin pour la gloire de son ami." Louis Racine says the same thing in his *Mémoires.* (Mesnard, I, 301.)

tions in the late editions of Racine's plays.[5] Despréaux's name
figures among those of the relatives and friends on the marriage
certificate of Marie-Catherine Racine.[6] Louis Racine relates
that his father, knowing that he was about to die, asked Jean-
Baptiste to write to M. de Cavoye soliciting the payments of his
pension. The letter was read to Racine, who ordered it to be
rewritten:

> Pourquoi . . . ne demandez-vous pas aussi le payement de la pension
> de Boileau? Il ne faut point nous séparer. Recommencez votre lettre;
> et faites connoître à Boileau que j'ai été son ami jusqu'à la mort.[7]

The poet's tender farewell to Despréaux is also related in the
Mémoires. Racine regarded it a blessing to die before his friend.[8]
The first time that Boileau appeared at Versailles after his
friend's death, he received in public the condolences of the king.[9]
Intimate relations between the poet's family and Despréaux continued until the latter's death in 1711. When Louis Racine
was studying philosophy at the Collège de Beauvais, he wrote
some verse.[10] Mme Racine was alarmed upon discovering this
tendency in her son as she " avoit souvent entendu parler du
danger de la passion des vers." She took the piece to Boileau,
and, reminding him of what he owed to the memory of his friend,
besought him to remonstrate with the young man.[11]

Now, although indisputable testimony leaves no room for
doubt [12] concerning the intimacy of their friendship in later

[5] The most important editions, besides the first collective edition of
1676, are those of 1687 and 1697.

[6] *Pièce Justificative n⁰ XXVI*, Mesnard, I, 190. The document is
dated Jan. 7, 1699.

[7] *Mémoires*, Mesnard, I, 350. The incident is also reported first-hand
by Jean-Baptiste in an *Avant-Propos* destined for Louis Racine's edition
of his father's letters. It is cited by Mesnard, VI, 557.

[8] Mesnard, I, 351.

[9] *Bolœana*, pp. 20-21; also Vuillard's letter to M. de Préfontaine, May
6 [1699] (Mesnard, VII, 329) ; and Jean-Baptiste Racine's letter to his
brother, November 6 [1742] (*ibid.*, VII, 337).

[10] The poem was about a dog which had been dissected in an anatomy
class at the college.

[11] *Mémoires*, Mesnard, I, 356-357.

[12] Cf. a very interesting article, " Boileau contre Racine," in the *Revue
de Paris*, VI (nov.-déc., 1902), 861-870. Jean Lemoine gives the history
of a lawsuit between Boileau and Racine in the years 1684-1685. The

years, one is not justified in assuming that the same close relationship existed between the two poets from the time of their first meeting, which probably took place in the winter of 1663-1664. In an effort to establish the date at which their relations became intimate, it will be necessary to examine and evaluate the several accounts of their first meeting and the documents that bear upon the years immediately following it.

There are seven versions of the beginning of the relations between Boileau and Racine. Five state that a piece of verse was the occasion of bringing the two poets together. The time of the meeting is more or less explicitly given in each instance.

We have, in the first place, Brossette's edited account.[13] In the edition of Boileau's works which he gave in 1716, he makes the following comment apropos of the epigram *In Marullum*:

> Le célèbre La Fontaine la montra à M. Racine qui ne connaissait pas encore M. Despréaux. Elle fut cause de leur connaissance. M. Racine le pria de lui donner ses avis sur la tragédie des *Frères Ennemis*, à laquelle il travaillait alors.

The time of their first meeting would be between Racine's return from Uzès and June 20, 1664, when *la Thébaïde* was performed. Racine's correspondence shows that he is completing the tragedy early in the winter of 1663-1664.

Fragments of Brossette's notes under date of October 8, 1702, present a slightly different version in which *la Thébaïde* is

former, according to the documents cited, was taking action to recover 3000 *livres* which he claimed to have loaned Racine on Jan. 13, 1683. As Racine did nothing to meet the obligation, a house, rue de la Grande Fripperie, bought by him in 1681 was attached and put up for sale to the highest bidder. All due publicity was given the legal proceedings. Those holding mortgages on the property were informed by the prescribed written and verbal notices. Court proceedings were stopped, however, on July 5, 1685, as, on the previous night, Racine had paid the plaintiff the sum he owed him. Lemoine interprets the litigation between the two friends as an added proof of their intimacy. The house in question was encumbered with mortgages when Racine acquired it. As mortgages were not recorded at that time, Racine was continually harassed by the appearance of unknown mortgagees. To rid himself of this nuisance, he resorted to a lawsuit which would force all those who held a mortgage on the property to declare themselves at that time or forego their claim. Boileau aided him in the scheme.

[13] *Œuvres de Boileau-Despréaux*, etc. (1716), I, 488, cited by M. Demeure, *MF*, CCV, 35-36.

adduced as the piece of poetry that first brought the two poets together. The meeting took place, according to both of Brossette's accounts, during the composition of *la Thébaïde*.

Racine y travailla. Il apprit en ce tems-là que M. Despréaux, qui étoit fort jeune aussi bien que luy, et qu'il ne connoissoit pas, passoit pour un critique judicieux, quoiqu'il n'eût encore fait aucun ouvrage, jugeoit fort bien des ouvrages d'esprit. Il luy fit présenter sa pièce par un abbé nommé Levasseur. M. Despréaux fit ses corrections et Racine les approuva. Il eut une forte envie de faire connoissance avec M. Despréaux, et la Fontaine que Racine connoissoit le mena chez M. Despréaux.[14]

Dubos, in 1719, said that Racine had just given *Alexandre* when " il se lia d'amitié avec l'auteur de l'Art Poétique." The author of the *Réflexions Critiques sur la Poésie et la Peinture* gives us to understand that Boileau, then and there, judged that Racine had sufficient talent to learn to write verse " avec peine." [15] Dubos, then, would place the beginning of their relations shortly after December 4, 1665, but his account contains too many improbabilities for us to give credence to the details reported therein. All that we can conclude from it is that Dubos, who was none too well informed, believed that the two poets became acquainted early in Racine's literary career.

Louis Racine gives more details. He tells us in the *Mémoires* that the abbé Le Vasseur had taken the *Ode de la Renommée* to Boileau, whom he knew. The satirist's written remarks seemed " très-judicieuses " to the young poet, who desired henceforth to make the acquaintance of Despréaux. Their mutual friend brought this about, and thus were formed " les premiers nœuds de cette union si constante et si étroite "[16] that it was impossible to write the life of one without also writing that of the other.[17]

The fifth account is a note written by Louis Racine for an edition of his father's letters. It is an explanation of the end of

[14] Laverdet, *Appendice*, p. 519.

[15] Cf. *infra*, p. 45, n. 41, where the passage is cited.

[16] It would be easy for Racine's son, who was only six years old at the time of his father's death, to jump to the conclusion that Boileau and Racine were always bound by the same close ties of friendship that he had witnessed during his father's last years. We have seen that he insists elsewhere on the constancy of their relations. Cf. *supra*, p. 36.

[17] Mesnard, I, 229.

the last letter we have of Racine to Le Vasseur.[18]   The version
of the meeting of Boileau and Racine is the same as that of the
Mémoires.   The time of the meeting, according to him, would be
late fall or the early winter of 1663-1664, as Racine's letter [19]
to Le Vasseur in November shows that *la Renommée* was completed at that time and that the Comte de Saint-Aignan had
found it " très belle."   The first edition of the *Ode* is undated.
Mesnard thinks it was printed late in the year 1663.[20]

Jean-Baptiste Racine prepared a note on the same part of his
father's last letter to Le Vasseur.   He calls attention to the
passage where his father expressed gratitude to the unnamed
person who, at Le Vasseur's request, had made some rather
extensive criticisms on one of Racine's poems:

Voici un passage bien considérable, puisqu'il est, pour ainsi dire,
l'époque de l'étroite amitié [21] qui a été entre M. Despréaux et mon père,
et qui n'a fini qu'à leur mort.   C'est de lui (Boileau) qu'il est ici
parlé.   Mon père ne le connoissoit pas encore, et l'abbé le Vasseur, leur
ami commun, lui communiqua quelques critiques que M. Despréaux
avoit faites sur son ode de la Seine.[22]

The account of J.-B. Racine differs from Louis Racine's only
in the name of the poem that Despréaux had criticized.   Inasmuch as Racine's letter is of December, 1663, and as the criticisms had been received recently, it is not probable that Le
Vasseur, or Racine either, should be concerned with getting
detailed remarks on *la Nymphe de la Seine,* which had been
published three years before.   Louis Racine's version is more
likely, as in a preceding letter to Le Vasseur there is mention
of *l'Ode à la Renommée.*   It is possible that Louis Racine, too,
erred in recording the name of the poem that Boileau criticized.
It may have been verses of *la Thébaïde,* which Racine was finish-

[18] *Ibid.*, VI, 520, n. 7.   The letter dated by Mesnard, December, 1663,
is cited *infra,* p. 47.

[19] Mesnard, VI, 515.

[20] *Op. cit.*, IV, 71-72.

[21] Very loosely stated.   He must mean the formation of their close
friendship.   It could not be " l'époque de l'étroite amitié," as Racine,
at the end of the letter, expresses a vague hope of meeting the author
of the remarks sometime in the future: " Je ne sais si (*sic*) il ne me
sera point permis quelque jour de le connoître."

[22] Mesnard, VI, 520, n. 7.

ing at this time. From the rest of Racine's letter one could easily infer that it was *la Thébaïde,* as that tragedy was uppermost in his mind when he wrote the letter in question.

Before considering the last document bearing upon the first meeting of the two poets, it would be well to see what conclusions may reasonably be drawn from the evidence that has been cited thus far. The common inference is that Boileau and Racine met, very probably, in the winter of 1663-1664, and that their first relation was a literary one. We agree with M. Demeure that what Boileau, at Auteuil, told Brossette, Jean-Baptiste, and Louis Racine in regard to this part of his life has only a " valeur relative." [23] However, we do not believe, with M. Demeure, that these accounts, even coming as they do from a common source, deserve to be discarded entirely.

What probability is there that Racine and Boileau should become acquainted at this time? Paris was not so large a city that two young men of practically the same age, with literary aspirations, should remain long without knowing each other. Both poets were making a stir in 1663. Despréaux's first verse appeared in print in September of that year. In various taverns he was already known through his early satires. Racine had returned from Uzès and was resuming the associations so much dreaded by Port-Royal. He had published three poems by the end of 1663, and was receiving a gratification from the king. The Hôtel de Bourgogne was negotiating for *la Thébaïde.*[24]

Moreover, since Molière was a friend to both of them, it is not likely that Racine and Boileau should long remain utter strangers to each other. Boileau drew near " cet illustre poète comique "[25] about the time of the *École des Femmes.* Similar character and talent " les portèrent bientost à se voir souvent et l'estime mutuelle qu'ils avoient l'un pour l'autre alla toujours en augmentant." [26] The next year he composed his " *Stances à*

[23] *MF*, CCV, 38.

[24] Mesnard, VI, 520. Letter to the abbé Le Vasseur [décembre, 1663]. " On promet depuis hier *la Thébaïde* à l'Hôtel: mais ils ne la promettent qu'après trois autres pièces." It was finally given its first performance by Molière's troupe.

[25] Le Verrier's *Commentaire* on *Satire II*, an insert in Boileau's handwriting (Lachèvre, p. 25).

[26] *Loc. cit.*

M. de Molière sur sa Comédie de ' l'École des Femmes' que
plusieurs gens frondaient." Now Racine wrote in November
of that same year that he had been at the king's *lever* where he
had seen Molière, who received on that day special marks of
royal favor. Racine told the abbé Le Vasseur:

J'en ai été bien aise pour lui: il a été bien aise aussi que j'y fusse
présent.[27]

A little later he wrote that he had not yet seen *l'Impromptu*
"ni son auteur depuis huit jours: j'irai tantôt." [28] In 1664
Boileau wrote *Satire II*, dedicated to Molière, that

> Rare et fameux esprit, dont la fertile veine
> Ignore en écrivant le travail et la peine.[29]

According to both Monchesnay and Brossette, *Satire IV*, written at this time, was inspired by a conversation with Le Vayer
and Molière. Brossette[30] reports that during the same year
Despréaux and the comic poet were present on one occasion at
the home of Du Broussin, where they both read their verse.
This is the year that Molière's troupe played *la Thébaïde* on
June 20. In 1665, while *Tartuffe* was suspended, Boileau made
bold, in his *Discours au Roi*, to denounce those who " tout blancs
au dehors, sont tout noirs au dedans " [31] and who on this account
fear " *Tartuffe* et Molière." [32] The latter played Racine's *Alexandre* on December 4. Now it is not possible that these two
poets, both on intimate terms with Molière during the years
1663 to 1665, should persist in not knowing each other. There
is strong probability in favor of the assertions of Brossette and
of both Louis and Jean-Baptiste Racine that Boileau and Racine
became acquainted in the winter of 1663-1664.

M. Demeure made *tabula rasa* of the testimony we have just
considered in order to bring forth, as definitive, a real document

---

[27] Mesnard, VI, 515.   [28] *Ibid.*, VI, 517.

[29] *Satire II*, vss. 1-2. Le Verrier (Lachèvre, p. 25), commenting on
this satire, wrote: " L'Autheur donne icy à son ami une facilité de
tourner un vers et de rimer, que son ami n'avoit pas, mais il est question de le louer et de luy faire plaisir." Le Verrier's notes on this
satire were very carefully corrected by Boileau. There were no changes
made, however, in the sentence cited here.

[30] Remarks on *Satire II*.

[31] *Discours au Roi*, vs. 84.   [32] *Ibid.*, vs. 102.

sworn to by Boileau himself during the lifetime of Racine.[33]
On February 16, 1696, when Racine was a candidate for the
charge of " conseiller secrétaire du roi," three persons were
summoned to give testimony concerning his " vie, mœurs et
religion," and his fidelity and affection in the service of the
king. Before giving evidence, each of the three witnesses took
an oath to tell the truth, protested that he was not a relative
of Racine, and told how long he had known the candidate.
François Dupuy said he had known Racine " depuis vingt ans
ou environ." Charles de Cartigny said he knew Racine " depuis
très longtemps." Divry and Cousin, who were charged with
the investigation, recorded Boileau's testimony as follows:

Maître Nicolas Boileau, sieur Despréaux, avocat en Parlement . . .
après serment par lui fait de dire vérité, a dit n'être parent ni allié
audit sieur Racine; qu'il le connoît depuis vingt-cinq ans pour être
homme de probité et de grand mérite; qu'il est de très-bonne famille de
la Ferté-Milon.

Now there is, to be sure, nothing vague about Boileau's testimony. If, at the beginning of 1696, he said he had known
Racine for twenty-five years, he means us to infer that they
became acquainted in 1671. This date, as M. Demeure points
out, coincides with that of the " soupers délicieux, c'est-à-dire
des diableries " of which Mme de Sévigné wrote on April 1,
1671,[34] when she was deploring her son's associations with
Ninon, " une petite comédienne, les Despréaux et les Racine
avec elle." That the two poets are at that time on intimate
terms is beyond doubt. We do not agree, however, with M.
Demeure, who disposes summarily of all evidence of contacts
between the two poets before this date, and concludes that
Racine did not know Boileau at all before 1671. We shall, in
the course of this study, consider carefully all such evidence.
Meanwhile, let us suppose that in making the affidavit referred
to, Boileau asserted that for twenty-five years he had known
Racine intimately enough to be able to vouch for his probity
and merit. This, moreover, seems to be the meaning of the
text. M. Demeure[35] does not cite the part of the deposition
which might compromise the decisiveness of his proof, namely

---

[33] *Pièce Justificative nº XXXIV.*   (Mesnard, I, 194-198.)
[34] *Lettres,* II, 137.   [35] *MF,* CCV, 39.

that " il le connoît depuis vingt-cinq ans pour être homme de
probité et de grand mérite." This affidavit concerning the
duration of their intimate friendship does not preclude the
possibility of some acquaintance before 1671.

Now it is certain that legend has done much to distort the
history of the relations of the poets between the winter of 1663-
1664 and the year 1671. There is need for much caution in
examining the evidence that we have touching the contacts the
two poets may have had during these years.

The tradition that the four friends—La Fontaine, Boileau,
Racine, and Molière (or Chapelle)—met in taverns, where they
gaily imbibed wine and literature, has colored all studies that
bear upon the years following 1663. Mesnard [36] and Revillout [37]
accepted what M. Demeure [38] later proved to be only a legend.
This last scholar traced the belief in the quatuor to the *Préface*
of *Psyché*,[39] and by a study of the dates when the various friend-
ships involved became intimate, he pointed out the error in the
inferences that had been made from La Fontaine's *Préface*. He
showed the gradual strengthening of the legend until it gathered considerable force in the nineteenth century. He went
farther and succeeded in identifying three members of the four-
some who used to meet in the combined interests of jollity and
letters. They were La Fontaine, Maucroix, and Pellisson. The
fourth member is unknown. Although La Fontaine, Boileau,
Molière, and Racine did not form the group in question, it is
certain that they were acquainted. Racine's association with
Molière, however, was of short duration.[40]

Now, what evidence exists of actual contacts between the
satirist and Racine during the early years of their acquaintance? There is, first of all, Boileau's boast of having taught
Racine the art of writing verse. The legend seems to have had

[36] I, 62-67.

[37] *RLR*, XXXV, 553.

[38] " L'introuvable Société des ' Quatre Amis,' " *RHLF*, XXXVI (1929).

[39] January, 1669.

[40] (*Mémoires*, Mesnard, I, 236.) The performance of *Alexandre* at
the Hôtel de Bourgogne and the withdrawal of la Du Parc in 1667
caused between them " un refroidissement qui dura toujours quoiqu'ils
se rendissent mutuellement justice sur leurs ouvrages." Cf. *infra*, pp.
52-55.

its origin at Auteuil. Dubos [41] and Louis Racine [42] repeat Brossette's account of Boileau's teaching Racine to " faire des vers difficilement." [43] It is very significant that they use almost the same wording.

Racine's earliest letters to the abbé Le Vasseur prove, however, that, even three years before he knew Boileau, Racine was far from being a facile poet contented with what he wrote. He sent his friend a sonnet [44] which he had revised, " un nouveau sonnet," he calls it, " car je l'ai tellement changé hier au soir, que vous le méconnoîtrez." He had modified it in accordance with the rules of the sonnet that the *abbé* had prescribed:

La force de vos raisons étant ajoutée à celle de ma conscience a achevé de me convaincre. Je me suis rangé à la raison, et y ai aussi rangé mon sonnet. . . . Ma conscience ne me reproche plus rien, et j'en prends un assez bon augure.[45]

Another example of the painstaking manner of his early writing is found in a letter of September 13 [1660]. His ode, *la Nymphe de la Seine,* had been submitted to Chapelain for criticism. He claims to have followed very closely the latter's suggestions. Chapelain had, in particular, disapproved of tritons

[41] " Ce dernier (Racine) venoit de donner sa Tragédie d'Alexandre, lorsqu'il se lia d'amitié avec l'auteur de l'*Art Poëtique.* Racine lui dit, en parlant de son travail, qu'il trouvoit une facilité surprenante à faire ses vers. Je veux vous apprendre à faire des vers avec peine, répondit Despréaux, et vous avez assez de talent pour le sçavoir bientôt. Racine disoit que Despréaux lui avoit tenu parole " (*Réflexions Critiques sur la Poésie et la Peinture,* II, 105-106). This passage is cited by Parfaict, *Histoire du Théâtre Français,* X, 213, n. *a.* The error in the date of the beginning of their friendship, the subtle insinuation that Boileau was at that time the author of the *Art Poétique,* and the condescension attributed to the latter make the account doubtful.

[42] " Il est vrai qu'elle (tragedy of *Alexandre*) avoit plusieurs défauts, et que le jeune auteur s'y livroit encore à sa *prodigieuse facilité de rimer.* Boileau sut la modérer par ses conseils, *et s'est toujours vanté de lui avoir appris à rimer difficilement.*" (*Mémoires,* Mesnard, I, 236-237.) Cf. also *ibid.,* I, 271.

[43] " M. Racine avoit une *facilité prodigieuse* à faire des vers, mais c'étoit le moien de n'y jetter pas beaucoup de force. M. Despréaux m'a dit qu'il *avoit appris à M. Racine à faire des vers difficilement.*" Brossette's *Mémoires,* Oct. 8, 1702. (Laverdet, p. 520.)

[44] Probably a sonnet addressed to Cardinal Mazarin celebrating the peace of the Pyrenees.

[45] Letter dated by Mesnard 1659 or 1660. (VI, 384.)

that Racine lodged in the river. This alteration that involved
the reworking of an entire stanza cost the poet much labor and
annoyance. Racine had no sooner made the corrections indicated by the critic than he conceived some doubt " si ces changements n'étoient point eux-mêmes à changer." [46] In the absence
of the *abbé* he almost had recourse, after the manner of Mal-
herbe, to an old servant, but knowing her to be a Jansenist and
therefore capable of exposing him, Racine was obliged to be the
sole judge of the " bonté " of his verses.

Two more examples taken from Racine's early correspondence
will suffice to prove that he was a conscientious dramatist before
he came under Boileau's influence. In 1661 Racine was beginning a play depicting Ovid's love-affairs. In preparation for
this task he had read and marked " tous les ouvrages " of Ovid.
He had worked and reworked the plan and had finally brought
it to perfection. Far from begrudging the time spent on this
initial step, he would willingly have devoted another fortnight
to it. He had, moreover, followed all the suggestions made by
Mlle Beauchâteau, an actress at the Hôtel de Bourgogne.[47]
These are all indications of the poet's serious purpose. Two
years later, when he was finishing *la Thébaïde,* Racine wrote
again to the abbé Le Vasseur. He had little news to tell, for
he had been doing nothing " except retouching continually the
fifth act " of his play. He spoke of the changes that he had
made rather reluctantly in the *stances,* in accordance with the
suggestions of " ceux qui me les (stances) avoient demandées." [48]

Although he was in the main fairly docile and felt the need
of having his own opinions corroborated, Racine in his early
twenties shows a certain flare of independence. M. Vitart, in
spite of the poet's disapproval, had shown *la Nymphe de la
Seine* to Charles Perrault. The latter had made some good
suggestions that Racine was not sorry to have followed. There
were one or two others, however, that Racine discarded forthright, protesting that he would not follow those counsels even
if they were to come from Apollo himself.[49]

[46] *Ibid.,* VI, 391.
[47] Letter to Le Vasseur [juin 1661], Mesnard, VI, 416-417.
[48] Letter dated [décembre 1663], Mesnard, VI, 519.
[49] *Ibid.,* VI, 393. Perrault condemned a certain comparison to Venus
on the ground that the goddess had been a prostitute.

A letter written by Racine toward the end of 1663 shows the same independence. Le Vasseur, who was at Crône, had submitted some of Racine's verse to a friend. He then wrote the poet a letter which included the corrections made by the third person, who was probably Boileau.[50] Racine, in answering the *abbé's* letter, wrote:

Je viens de parcourir votre belle et grande lettre, où j'ai trouvé assez de difficultés qui m'ont arrêté, et *d'autres sur lesquelles il seroit aisé de vous regagner.* Je suis pourtant fort obligé à l'auteur des remarques, et je l'estime infiniment. Je ne sais si il (*sic*) ne me sera point permis quelque jour de le connoître.[51]

What, then, of Despréaux's repeated boast that he had taught Racine to write easy verse " difficilement "? Now we have seen that Racine, before his meeting with Despréaux, was a painstaking poet who, in his desire to succeed, sought criticism and accepted it with considerable docility. There were times, however, when he was willing to hold out against the suggestions offered him. Moreover, since the two poets were not on intimate terms until about 1671, and since after that date [52] Racine scarcely stood in need of Boileau's lessons, there is little likelihood that he was responsible for teaching Racine to write verse. The truth of the matter seems to be that, if anyone was responsible for teaching Racine to write verse, it was Subligny, not Boileau. The stylistic changes in *Andromaque* indicate that

[50] Cf. *ibid.*, VI, 520, n. 7. Mesnard thinks it was Despréaux because Boileau's father owned a house at Crône. It is possible that it still belonged to the family in 1663 and that Boileau was spending some time there.

[51] Letter dated by Mesnard, December, 1663. (VI, 520-521.)

[52] Louis Racine said that it was upon noting the perfection of the verses of *Britannicus* that Boileau said for the first time what he repeated afterward: " C'est moi qui ai appris à M. Racine à faire des vers difficilement " (*Mémoires*, Mesnard, I, 249). From *Britannicus* (1669) on, even his enemies praised Racine's verse. Boursault is forced to admit that " il est constant que dans le *Britannicus* il y a d'aussi beaux vers qu'on en puisse faire et cela ne me surprend pas; car il est impossible que M. Racine en fasse de méchants " (*Artémise et Poliante*, cited by Mesnard, II, 226). The only criticism on record of Racine's prosody from this time on is Boileau's judgment on the verses of *Bajazet*, which, if Monchesnay can be relied upon, he found " trop négligés " (*Bolœana*, p. 107).

Racine corrected a number of expressions which Subligny, in his *Folle Querelle,* had condemned in the name of "pureté de langue." [53] Robinet [54] says explicitly that the greater clarity of style in *Britannicus* is due to Subligny's criticisms. In any event, the facts do not bear out Boileau's assertion transmitted to us by Brossette, Dubos, and Louis Racine. It has, moreover, all the hall marks of the legends spun at Auteuil.

Boileau, in a letter of December 10, 1701, to Brossette, acknowledges having had " quelque part," together with Racine and Furetière, in the composition of the original *Chapelain Décoiffé.* [55] He adds by way of attenuating the blame that attaches to the authorship of so trivial a parody:

Mais nous n'y avons jamais travaillé qu'à table, le verre à la main. Il n'a pas esté proprement faict *currente calamo* mais *currente lagenâ,* et nous n'en avons jamais escrit un seul mot.

Moreover, according to Despréaux, the copy sent him by Brossette bears scarcely any resemblance to the early form of the piece. He recognizes as his own only two couplets of that version. [56] Now, it is possible that Boileau was not entirely sincere in disclaiming to that extent his responsibility in the composition of the *Chapelain Décoiffé.* [57] Why, however, should he

---

[53] *Préface* of *la Folle Querelle ou la Critique d'Andromaque,* cited by Lanson, *le Théâtre choisi de Racine.* The play was performed on May 18, 1668, by Molière's troupe. It was printed by Thomas Jolly, coming off the press on Aug. 22, 1668. The detailed criticisms of style that the author could not work into the third act of the play were set forth in the *Préface* along with more general criticisms pertaining to the " conduite de théâtre." They were very numerous. Cf. Lanson's edition, where they are indicated in the footnotes.

[54] *Lettre en vers,* 21 décembre, 1669.

[55] The question of the authorship of the *Chapelain Décoiffé* is a difficult one. Van Roosbroeck (*Boileau, Racine, Furetière,* etc., *Chapelain Décoiffé, a Battle of Parodies,* p. 42) renounces, in the present state of our knowledge, solving it with any degree of definiteness. He tabulates (p. 43) the contemporary ascriptions of the parody.

[56]   " Mille et mille papiers dont ta table est couverte,
                    Semblent porter escrit le destin de ma perte ";
and
                " En cet affront la Serre est le Tondeur,
                    Et le tondu père de *la Pucelle.*"   *Loc. cit.*

[57] Cf. his letter to Brossette (March 27, 1704), which contains a frank disavowal of the published version of the *Dialogue des Héros de Roman*

say that Racine had a hand in it, if this collaboration had no
foundation in fact? It would seem unlikely that only two and
one-half years after Racine's death, Despréaux should make to
him an entirely gratuitous ascription of a poem that could bring
only discredit upon his friend. Tallemant des Réaux[58] is the
only other contemporary who attributes the work in part to
Racine. It must be admitted, however, that Boileau's written
testimony, substantiated by Tallemant des Réaux, is weighty
evidence. It indicates a contact between the two poets in 1664.[59]
It does not, of course, argue any degree of intimacy in their
relations, but merely a casual collaboration made *currente lagena*
on a work that must be attributed in the main to Furetière or
Chapelle.[60]

The next function of Boileau, according to the devotees of
Auteuil, was to turn Racine toward a cult of " la nature."
According to Louis Racine, Boileau brought the young poet
back to the natural after he had wandered astray in an early
sonnet and in some verses of *la Thébaïde*.[61] The facts, however,
do not confirm this assertion. In his next play, *Alexandre,*
Racine leans very hard on the *romanesque* and is, indeed, farther away from nature, as it was understood in the seventeenth

and the assertion that M. le Marquis de Sévigné was the " principal
author " of the written dialogue. M. Cahen (*Satires*, p. xi), however,
after comparing it with the definitive version, believes that the work as
it was published in the *Œuvres de M. de Saint-Evremond* was substantially the same as the primitive oral text of Boileau.

[58] MSS of La Rochelle, MS 672, fol. 246. Van Roosbroeck (*op. cit.,*
p. 42) thus summarizes it: the parody was, according to Tallement
des Réaux, composed by Chapelle and enlivened by Racine and Furetière.

[59] *Chapelain Décoiffé* was published in Paris by Nicolas Tibaud in
1665.

[60] Boileau says that Furetière " avoit le plus de part à cette pièce,"
and he ascribes to him the lines:

. . . . " O Perruque, ma mie!
N'as-tu donc tant vécu que pour cette infamie! "

Tallemant des Réaux says that Chapelle composed the greater part of
the parody.

[61] " Les principes du bon goût, qu'il avoit pris dans la lecture des
anciens et dans les leçons de Port-Royal, ne l'empêchoient pas, dans le
feu de sa première jeunesse, de s'écarter de la nature, dont il s'écarte
encore dans plusieurs vers de *la Thébaïde*. Boileau sut l'y ramener."
(*Mémoires*, Mesnard, I, 226.)

4

century, than he was in the earlier tragedy. It must be remembered that Louis Racine got from Boileau much of his information regarding his father's literary career, as the poet had
rarely spoken to his children of that period of his life.[62] It is
quite probable that, in this instance, as well as in his account
of Boileau's teaching Racine to rime, Louis Racine's version
reflects the tendency to self-aggrandizement that Boileau showed
during the last years of his life.

Brossette is responsible for the anecdote that would make
Racine indebted to Boileau for the subject of his second tragedy.
He says:

M. Despréaux invita M. Racine à suivre une autre route que Corneille,
qui n'avoit mis sur le théâtre que des héros romains.   Prenez, lui dit
Despréaux, les héros de la Grèce.   Il lui indiqua Alexandre le Grand,
qui fut le sujet de sa seconde tragédie.[63]

Mesnard, making no comment, cites the anecdote for what it is
worth.   It contains too many discrepancies for us to attach any
importance to it.   In the first place, it was not true that Corneille had portrayed only Roman characters.   He had already
written *Médée*,[64] *Œdipe*,[65] and *la Toison d'Or*.[66]   Whatever may
be said of the other two plays, Boileau could not, in 1664, have
overlooked the *Œdipe*, which had much success both at Paris
and at Versailles during the entire reign of Louis XIV.[67]   Racine, moreover, did not wait to be told by Boileau what course
he should follow.   He had already treated a Greek subject in
la Thébaïde and, if Louis Racine's account is true, he had, even
earlier, attempted to write a tragedy on the subject of Theagenes
and Charicleia.[68]   The counsel to follow " une autre route que
Corneille " smacks of the parallels [69] that were made after

[62] *Ibid.*, I, 229.

[63] *Mémoires*, Oct. 8, 1702. (Laverdet, p. 520).

[64] 1635.   [65] 1659.   [66] 1660.

[67] Cf. Despois, *le Théâtre en France sous Louis XIV*, pp. 377-380.

[68] *Mémoires*, Mesnard, I, 228.

[69] Subligny, in the *Préface* of *la Folle Querelle*, says of Racine: " S'il
n'avoit pas fait toutes les fautes qui y sont contre le bon sens, *je
l'aurois déjà égalé sans marchander à notre grand Corneille.*"   The
Préfaces of *Britannicus* and *Bérénice* show that Racine is already conscious of a differentiation between his tragedy and Corneille's.   Cf. also
la Critique de Bérénice by the abbé de Villars: " L'auteur a trouvé à
propos, *pour s'éloigner du genre d'écrire de Corneille,* etc." (cited by

Racine had given at least one masterpiece. It would be improbable that Boileau—if indeed he counselled Racine at this juncture—should advise the young dramatist, about to write his second tragedy, to depart from the *procédés* that had brought success to the great Corneille. Boileau was at this time, and continued to be all during his life, an ardent admirer of Corneille's theater.[70]

What conclusions in regard to the intimacy of the two poets may be drawn from M. de Pomponne's account[71] that "Boileau" was present at the Hôtel de Nevers early in 1665, when Racine read three and one-half acts of the *Alexandre?* In the

Mornet, *Racine*, pp. 372-373). Mme de Sévigné (*Lettres*, II, 535-536), after seeing *Bajazet*, still casts her lot with the older dramatist. According to Louis Racine, " l'Académie avoit envie de faire le parallèle de Corneille et de mon père." Boileau in an epigram suggested another outlet for the activity of this body:

> Je consens que chez vous, messieurs, on examine
> Qui du pompeux Corneille ou du tendre Racine
> Mérita dans Paris plus d'applaudissements.
> Mais cherchez donc en même temps
> (La question n'est pas moins belle)
> Qui du fade Boyer ou du sec La Chapelle
> Mérita plus de sifflements.

(Letter of L. Racine to Brossette, June, 1740, *la Correspondance de J.-B. Rousseau et de Brossette*, II, 241). The principal contemporary studies revealing the differences in their art are: La Bruyère's *Caractères* (1688); VII⁰ *Réflexion sur Longin* (1694); Fontenelle's *Parallèle* (1693); and Longepierre's *Parallèle* (1686). Granet's *Recueil de Dissertations sur plusieurs Tragédies de Corneille et de Racine*, I, 47 et *sqq.* contains Longepierre's *Parallèle*.

[70] Even if Despréaux did urge him to follow another path from that of his illustrious predecessor, the author of *Alexandre* is still, although to a less degree than in his first tragedy, the disciple of Corneille in his first manner. The subject, like the clemency of Augustus or the generosity of Caesar, calls forth admiration rather than the Aristotelian pity and fear. "Les grands intérêts" loom large despite the gallantry that Racine introduced. Cf. Act II, sc. 2 and Act V, sc. 3, which, according to Mesnard (I, 516) "ont la forme et souvent l'accent des grandes scènes de Corneille." Saint-Évremond (*Dissertation sur l'Alexandre*), notwithstanding his objections to the play, saw in Racine the successor of Corneille and hoped that the older dramatist would adopt the poet " pour former, avec la tendresse d'un père, son vrai successeur." (*Œuvres*, I, 197.)

[71] Cf. *supra*, pp. 16-17.

first place, it must be recalled that "Boileau" indicated to contemporaries, not Nicolas but Gilles Boileau, and that the former was generally known as "Despréaux." Did M. de Pomponne mean to tell us that Gilles Boileau was there and read his satires? It is surely possible, as he was well known in literary circles before his younger brother finished his studies. He had been an academician since 1659.[72] Supposing that the author of the letter meant Despréaux, which is also possible, what can be inferred in regard to their friendship? Mesnard concludes that they were "déjà très-étroitement liés." [73] Revillout is of the same opinion.[74] Now nothing in the letter itself suggests that this was the case, and, as M. Demeure fittingly remarks, "le texte ne dit pas que les deux poètes ont exécuté un duo ni qu'ils avaient été invités ensemble parce qu'amis l'un de l'autre." [75] We have in M. de Pomponne's letter, even if the reference is to Despréaux, the record of nothing more than another casual meeting of the two poets.

It would be well to consider, at this point in our study, what was the probable effect on Boileau of the estrangement between Molière and Racine apropos of the *Alexandre*.[76] Brossette tells us that when the poet had completed his *Alexandre le grand* he wanted to have the piece performed by Molière's troupe. L'abbé de Bernay, however, with whom Racine was then living, showed much obstinacy in trying to persuade him to give his second tragedy to the Hôtel de Bourgogne. It was a pleasantry of Boileau, inspired, no doubt, by a desire to do Molière a good turn, that put an end to the altercation. Brossette testifies:

Comme ils étoient en grande contestation là-dessus, M. Despréaux intervint, et décida par une plaisanterie, disant qu'il n'y avoit plus de bons acteurs à l'Hôtel de Bourgogne: qu'à la vérité il y avoit encore le plus habile moucheur de chandelles qui fût au monde, et que cela pouvoit bien contribuer au succès d'une pièce. Cette plaisanterie seule fit revenir l'abbé de Bernay qui étoit d'ailleurs très-obstiné; et la pièce fut donnée à la troupe de Molière.[77]

---

[72] His writings sold like bread, according to Tallemant des Réaux. (*Historiettes*, V, 235-240, referred to by Revillout, *RLR*, XXXIV, 457.)
[73] I, 497.
[74] *RLR*, XXXVII, 92.   [75] *MF*, CCV, 44, n. (7).
[76] M. Demeure takes up the question. (*MF*, CCV, 52.)
[77] Commentary on *Satire* III vs. 185, cited by Mesnard, I, 504.

The play was given its first performance at the Palais-Royal on December 4, 1665. Now La Grange, on December 18, recorded the surprise of Molière's troupe upon finding that the piece was also being given at a rival theater.[78] " Comme la chose s'était faite de complot avec M. Racine qui en usait si mal que d'avoir donné et fait apprendre la pièce aux autres comédiens," the actors had no scruples in withholding the author's share of the proceeds for that day.[79] Whatever the reason for Racine's action,[80] it caused a breach in the friendship of Molière and Racine that was never entirely repaired.

There seems to have been open hostility between the two poets for some three years. Racine's taking la Du Parc [81] at Easter, 1667, to create the rôle of *Andromaque* at the Hôtel de Bourgogne was not destined to assuage Molière's resentment. The latter must have watched with the keen eye of a producer the tremendous success that Racine's tragedy was having at a rival theater. At any rate, on May 18, 1668, he mounted Subligny's parody of *Andromaque*. It had more than twenty-eight performances before the end of the year,[82] and contemporaries, according to Grimarest even Racine himself,[83] attributed to Molière the authorship of *la Folle Querelle*. This is evidence that toward the middle of 1668 Racine and Molière were still considered enemies. That this animosity continued for at least some months is indicated by a statement of Valincour concerning Molière's judgment on *les Plaideurs* and by Racine's *Préface*

---

[78] It had been performed nine times at the Palais-Royal.

[79] *Registre*, p. 79.

[80] The *Mémoires* (Mesnard, I, 236) and the *Bolœana* (p. 104) attribute it to the poor acting of tragedy at the Palais-Royal. Perhaps Molière's illness at that time had something to do with it. According to Robinet (*Lettre*, Dec. 20), Molière did not play a rôle. His theater was shortly afterward closed for two months on account of Molière's poor health. Or did Racine, without any cause, merely jump at a chance to supplant his rival, Boyer, at the first theater of Paris?

[81] " Ce qui mortifia Molière," say the *Mémoires*. (Mesnard, I, 236.)

[82] An interruption in La Grange's *Registre* between May 13 and May 25 makes it impossible to tell exactly how many performances there were.

[83] Racine not only ascribed it to Molière, according to Grimarest, but " il estimoit cet ouvrage comme un des meilleurs de l'auteur." (*Vie de Molière* cited by Mesnard, I, 68.)

to that play. The comedy, given in November of that year, did
not at first have much success. Molière, however, was present
at the second performance, and Valincour reports his saying,
contrary to the verdict of the public: " Ceux qui se moquoient
de cette pièce méritoient qu'on se moquât d'eux." [84] Valincour
adds, by way of enhancing Molière's impartiality, that the latter
was not at that time on friendly terms with the author of the
play. The *Préface* of *les Plaideurs* would indicate that Racine
was less generous than Molière. If the purpose of comedy is to
provoke laughter, Racine judges that his play has attained its
end. He then flings, presumably at Molière, this disparaging
appreciation of comedy:

*Ce n'est pas que j'attends un grand honneur d'avoir assez longtemps
réjoui le monde.* Mais je me sais quelque gré de l'avoir fait sans qu'il
m'en ait coûté une seule de ces *sales équivoques* et de ces *malhonnêtes
plaisanteries* qui coûtent maintenant si peu à la plupart de nos écrivains, et qui font retomber le théâtre dans la turpitude d'où quelques
auteurs plus modestes l'avoient tiré.

Mesnard [85] seems certain that Racine is not impugning Molière
in the last sentence of the *Préface*. He admits that perhaps
Racine went too far in saying that he did not expect much honor
to come to him from having amused people for a rather long
time with his comedy. The remark is, indeed, a cutting one
and no doubt touched Molière. As for the " sales équivoques "
and " ces malhonnêtes plaisanteries," how could Molière help
hearing in them reverberations of the quarrel of the *École des
Femmes*? During this period when *le Tartuffe* was suspended,
Molière was not a stranger to these, nor even to more serious
accusations.[86] The *Préface* confirms Valincour's assertion that
there was enmity between the two poets.

[84] Valincour's letter to the abbé d'Olivet for the article on Racine.
(*Histoire de l'Académie française*, II, 332.)

[85] *Op. cit.*, II, 136, n. 1.

[86] Monchesnay (*Bolæana*, p. 50) claims that Boileau preferred Terence
to Molière because the latter " dérogeoit souvent à son génie noble par
des *plaisanteries grossières* qu'il hazardoit en faveur de la multitude,
au lieu qu'il ne faut avoir en vûe que les honnêtes gens." Cf. *Art
Poétique, Chant III*, vss. 394-405. Arnauld in 1677 took Boileau to task
for his unqualified praise of Molière in his *Épître à Racine*, telling him
that " un homme comme lui devoit prendre garde aux gens qu'il louoit,
et de quelle manière il louoit, que Molière avec tout son esprit, avoit

Besides performing *la Folle Querelle*, Molière was in the eyes of Racine guilty of another offense that must have damped any hope of reconciling them. In 1667 he lured Corneille away from the Hôtel de Bourgogne, *Attila*, *Tite et Bérénice*, and *Psyché* being played by the troupe of the Palais-Royal. Now Racine's bitterness toward Corneille had been growing since the latter's unfavorable judgment of the *Alexandre* in 1665. Surely Racine could not brook Molière's patronage of the rival about whom he was to make such scathing insinuations in the *Préfaces* to *Britannicus* and *Bérénice*.

We have seen that there was, for a long time, open hostility between Molière and Racine. According to *les Mémoires*,[87] the "refroidissement . . . dura toujours, quoi qu'ils se rendissent mutuellement justice sur leurs ouvrages." [88] Now what was the rôle of Boileau during the quarrel of Molière and Racine? Again we cite *les Mémoires*: "Boileau resta uni à Molière, qui venoit le voir souvent et faisoit grand cas de ses avis." [89] The *Satire des Satires* is further evidence that Boileau and Molière were considered friends in 1666. Cotin climaxes all his invectives against the satirist with an ironical couplet that discloses at the same time his contempt of Molière:

> A ses vers (Boileau's) la Béjar applaudit,
> Il règne sur Parnasse, et Molière l'a dit.

Knowing Boileau's intimacy with Molière,[90] we should expect his sympathy in the affair of the *Alexandre* to be with him. Moreover, friendship apart, with the wrong, at least in the beginning, patently on Racine's side, it is likely that Despréaux's sense of justice would be outraged by the desertion of the young playwright, whose early efforts Molière himself had encouraged. If it is true that in the beginning Boileau urged Racine to give his play to the Palais-Royal, he would undoubtedly be piqued by the subsequent change in billing, made apparently without his knowledge. The *Bolœana* reports an incident that shows

bien des hauts et des bas, et que ses Comédies étoient une École de Mauvaises Mœurs." (*Bolœana*, p. 37.)

[87] Mesnard, I, 236.

[88] Saint-Marc, on the other hand, maintains, in his *Vie de Chapelle*, that "leurs amis communs les réconcilièrent dans la suite: mais ils n'eurent plus de liaison particulière." (Cited by Mesnard, I, 68.)

[89] *Ibid.*, I, 270.   [90] Cf. *supra*, pp. 41-42.

the position of Boileau between Racine and Molière toward the
end of 1668: his loyalty to the author of *l'Avare* is unmistak-
able. Monchesnay says:

Molière donna son *Avare* où M. Despréaux fut des plus assidus. Je
vous vis dernièrement, lui dit Racine, à la Pièce de Molière, et vous
riiez tout seul sur le Théâtre. Je vous estime trop, lui répondit son
ami, pour croire que vous n'y ayiez pas ri, du moins intérieurement.[91]

In the open enmity that existed between Racine and Molière
from December, 1665, until at least the end of 1668, it is quite
certain that Boileau sided with the latter. The rupture must
have been a serious obstacle in the way of Racine's and Boileau's
becoming intimate friends during these years.

During the very year [92] in which Racine was completing his
Alexandre, Boileau composed *le Dialogue des Héros de Roman*,
which he recited everywhere. It contained the following reference to Alexander, a hero well known both through history and
through La Calprenède's *Cassandre*: [93]

J'ai bien de la peine, dis-je, à m'imaginer que les Cyrus et les Alexandre
soient devenus tout à coup, comme on me le veut faire entendre, des
Thyrsis et des Céladon.[94]

Now although Boileau's flair for actualities is well known, it
scarcely seems possible that he should have Racine's hero in
mind, for until the play was performed on December 4, 1665,
the reference would have been lost on most persons.[95] It was
not long, however, before a rapprochement to Racine's hero was
made, and copies of the *Dialogue* made from memory without

[91] *Bolœana*, p. 105.
[92] Three and one-half acts of *Alexandre* were read at the Hôtel de
Nevers early in the year 1665. (Letter of Pomponne to Arnauld
d'Andilly reported by Mesnard, I, 497.) "Boileau" was present and
read some of his *Satires*. *Alexandre* was performed on December 4,
1665. Boileau's dating of the *Dialogue* is somewhat inexact: "Le
lieutenant criminel et sa femme furent assassinés à Paris la mesme
année que je fis ce dialogue, c'est à sçavoir en 1664" (Laverdet, p.
333, n. 1). Tardieu, however, was assassinated on Aug. 24, 1665.
[93] Professor Lancaster called this to my attention.
[94] Words of Pluto. (*Œuvres*, III, 40-41.)
[95] If Boileau composed the *Dialogue* in 1664, he could not have had
Racine's play in mind.

the author's consent soon included a piquant scene ridiculing that character.[96]

Satire III, completed soon after the performance of *Alexandre*, makes it even more difficult to determine what Boileau really thought of the love element in *Alexandre*. The two ridiculous " campagnards, grands lecteurs de romans," [97] stupid by nature and tipsy at the close of the banquet, open a discussion of letters. They judge authors " en maîtres du Parnasse." One of them proclaims in doctoral tones:

> Je ne sais pas pourquoi l'on vante l'*Alexandre,*
> Ce n'est qu'un glorieux qui ne dit rien de tendre,
> Les héros chez Quinault parlent bien autrement,
> Et jusqu'à " Je vous hais," tout s'y dit tendrement.[98]

This condemnation of *Alexandre* that Boileau places in the mouth of the country bumpkin is, of course, intended to reveal the latter's stupidity and therefore indicates that the satirist approved of the play taken as a whole.[99] It is not, however, so simple a matter to decide precisely what Boileau thought of the *tendresse* in the play. Does he mean to infer that there is just enough of this element, or that there is an over-dose of it? His intention throughout seems to be to render the " campagnard " as ridiculous as possible. His caricature is made with large brush strokes, and the grossest exaggeration would be in keeping with the general tone of the satire. Now, if this loutish fellow failed to discern any *tendresse* at all, even where an excess of it was present, Boileau's aim in drawing the bumptious " campagnard " would be more fully achieved. It does not seem credible that the author of *le Dialogue des Héros de Roman* would fail to detect what was the principal defect in Racine's play. Boileau did not like gallantry, and considered his admi-

[96] The interpolation is given in Mesnard, I, 517-19. M. Demeure (*MF*, CCV, 54) suggests that Boileau might even have composed this part of the *Dialogue* and that he disavowed it years later when he was writing the work down at the behest of Brossette.

[97] Vs. 43.

[98] Vss. 185-188.

[99] M. Demeure sees in these lines only open hostility toward the dramatist (*MF*, CCV, 54). He seems here to be unduly influenced by the thesis he is brilliantly defending, namely, that Racine was not acquainted with Boileau until 1671 and that the latter, as a partisan of Corneille, was inimical toward Racinian tragedy until the year 1672.

ration for the novels of La Calprenède and Mlle de Scudéry one
of the follies of his early youth.[100]   Neither is it possible that
an acquaintance of less than two years' standing should blind
him to Racine's faults.[101]   If he failed to notice the excess of
tendresse in *Alexandre*, is it because his critical acumen was
not fully developed in 1665?   It is, of course, true that up
until that time his satires had been moral rather than literary
in scope.   When he flayed an author, he did so without giving
reasons for his condemnation.[102]   He had in nowise constituted
a body of doctrine.   On the other hand, he had composed *la
Dissertation sur "Joconde"* and *les Héros de Roman*, in both
of which he had shown himself extremely sensitive to aberra-
tions in the line of gallantry.   It would seem reasonable to suppose that Boileau did perceive the defect in Racine's tragedy.
He may either have been endeavoring by a complimentary reference to curry favor with Racine, or have condoned the flaw, in
virtue of the real merits of the play, contenting himself with
the slight innuendo in *Satire III*.   It is quite probable that he
was not sure enough of his judgment of works that were just
appearing to make in public any too definite pronouncement on
the *tendresse* in the tragedy.   We must bear in mind that the
arbiters of good taste had passed sentence upon the *Alexandre*
as early as February fourth of that year, when Pomponne and
his circle judged that it was " assurément d'une fort grande
beauté." [103]   There was no gainsaying their judgment.   It seems
likely that Boileau's reticence in this instance shows him to be
the " campagnon peut-être timide," [104] and not the master of
Racine.

[100] *Discours sur le Dialogue suivant* (1710).   (III, 35.)

[101] Cf. La Harpe: " L'amitié sans doute aveuglait Despréaux."
(*Lycée*, IIᵉ partie, livre Iᵉʳ, chap. III.)

[102] Cf. *supra*, p. 14.

[103] Letter to Arnauld d'Andilly describing Racine's reading of three
and one-half acts of *Alexandre* before La Rochefoucauld, Mme de la
Fayette, Mme and Mlle de Sévigné, cited in Mesnard, I, 497. Cf. *Épître
VII*, vs. 96, where Pomponne and La Rochefoucauld are cited among
those who " se laissent pénétrer " by beautiful passages. Cf. also *la
Première Préface* of *Alexandre*: " Les premières personnes de la terre et
les Alexandres de notre siècle " have declared themselves in favor of the
play.

[104] Mornet, reviewing M. Albert Cahen's edition of the *Satires*, *RHLF*,
XXXIX (1932), 465.

The document that concerns the relations between the two poets during the next years is a letter of Père Tournemine in the form of a *Défense du Grand Corneille*. It was printed at the beginning of the *Œuvres Diverses de P. Corneille* which were published in Paris in 1738.[105] In discussing Boileau's epigrams on *Agésilas*[106] and *Attila*,[107] Tournemine says that they were inspired by the satirist's desire to immolate to his idol, Racine, the latest works of the older dramatist. Louis Racine protests against this accusation, shying especially at the word "*idole*":

Ce n'étoit pas certainement lui immoler de grandes victimes; et Boileau ne pensa jamais à élever son idole (pour répéter le terme du P. Tournemine) au-dessus de Corneille; il savoit rendre justice à l'un et à l'autre; il les admiroit tous deux, sans décider sur la préférence.[108]

It is permissible to discount Père Tournemine's letter by virtue of its date. Writing, presumably in 1738, of an epigram composed early in Boileau's career, he likely antedated the close relations that he had known to exist between Boileau and Racine. We have seen that it is quite impossible that Racine was Boileau's "idol" in 1667.

Jean-Baptiste Racine's notes, which were evidently utilized in the composition of the *Mémoires*,[109] indicate what would at first sight seem to be solid evidence that in that year Boileau intervened in the quarrel between Racine and Port-Royal. In the first *Visionnaire*,[110] Nicole had aimed at Desmarets the well-known invective against "un faiseur de romans et un poète de théâtre," each of whom he considered an "empoisonneur public non des corps, mais des âmes des fidèles."[111] Racine, accord-

[105] Published by Granet at the house of Gissey and Bordelet.

[106] 1666.

[107] 1667. For the epigrams cf. *Œuvres*, II, 454. For a discussion of their import, cf. H. C. Lancaster, *A History of French Dramatic Literature*, Part III, 594-595.

[108] *Mémoires*, Mesnard, I, 259. Cf. *VIIe Réflexion sur Longin*. Posterity alone can be the judge of works of literature.

[109] Mesnard, I, 238-244.

[110] It was dated Dec. 31, 1665. The last eight *Imaginaires* were directed against Desmarets de Saint-Sorlin and bore the subtitle of *Visionnaires*.

[111] Cited by Mesnard, IV, 260.

ing to the notes of his son, assuming that Nicole's denunciation
was meant for him in particular, straightway

prit la plume; et sans rien dire à personne, il fit et répandit dans le
public une lettre sans nom d'auteur, où il turlupinoit ces Messieurs de
la manière la plus sanglante et la plus amère.[112]

Two anonymous responses [113] in behalf of Port-Royal appeared, one on March 22, the other on April 1, 1666. Racine
intended to reply with a second *Lettre* written on May 10, and
addressed to the *Deux Apologistes de l'auteur des Hérésies
Imaginaires*. This letter, for reasons that we shall consider
later, was not made public. Nicole in the following year [114]
included in the collective edition of *les Imaginaires* the two
anonymous responses made to Racine's first letter against Port-
Royal. Racine, although not named in Nicole's *Avertissement*,
was referred to as a young poet who had taken upon himself
" l'intérêt commun de tout le théâtre " and who in his letter [115]
" contoit des histoires faites à plaisir." Everything that Racine
had said was, according to the *Avertissement*, false and contrary to common sense. The *solitaire*, moreover, prefaced the
responses, later ascribed to Du Bois and to Barbier d'Aucour,

[112] A note of J.-B. Racine that was available to the editors of 1807.
It is cited by Mesnard, IV, 261.

[113] Cf. Mesnard, IV, 296-328, for the text of the two responses.

[114] The first letter of Racine is undated in the original edition. A
reprint bears the date of January, 1666. We know that it was written
sometime between Dec. 31, 1665, when the first *Visionnaire* appeared,
and March 22, 1666, the date of Du Bois' response to Racine. Now in
Racine's *Préface pour une édition des deux lettres*, etc., written " eight
days " after the appearance of the 1667 edition of *les Imaginaires*, the
author says that the public saw the first of his two letters " il y a un
an " (*Préface*, Mesnard, IV, 277). That assertion gives an approximate
date for the composition of the *Préface*. A letter from Port-Royal to
Nicolas Vitart (Mesnard, IV, 270) is evidence that Racine was still
considering publishing the polemical documents as late as May 8, 1667.
One would infer, moreover, from two passages in this letter that the
edition of Nicole's *Imaginaires* had appeared only recently. The writer
of the letter had just received a copy from the author. He tells Vitart
that he would be glad to do something to quiet the affair, but that
suppressing the edition was out of the question, as " c'est une impression
dont on n'est pas maître, et dont l'imprimeur a déjà envoyé une partie
de côtés et d'autres." (*Ibid.*, IV, 271.)

[115] The first letter, which was the only one that Nicole knew.

with words of praise that infuriated the poet. The latter, within eight days [116] of the appearance of the new edition of *les Imaginaires*, had written a virulent *Préface* destined for an edition of the two letters against Port-Royal, one of which, although it had been written for some ten months, was still unpublished. Racine says in regard to the second letter:

Lorsque j'étois prêt à la laisser imprimer, *quelques-uns de mes amis* me firent comprendre qu'il n'y avoit point de plaisir à rire avec des gens délicats qui se plaignent qu'on les *déchire* [117] dès qu'on les nomme; qu'il ne falloit pas trouver étrange que l'auteur des *Imaginaires* eût écrit contre la comédie, et qu'il n'y avoit presque point de régent dans les collèges qui n'exhortât ses écoliers à n'y point aller. *Et d'autres des leurs* me dirent que les lettres qu'on avoit faites contre moi étoient désavouées de tout le Port-Royal; qu'elles étoient même assez inconnues dans le monde, et qu'il n'y avoit rien de plus incommode que de se défendre devant mille gens qui ne savent pas seulement que l'on nous ait attaqués. Enfin ils m'assurèrent que ces Messieurs n'en garderoient pas la moindre animosité contre moi; et ils me promirent de leur part un silence que je n'avois pas songé à leur demander.[118]

Racine adds that, satisfied with the promise made by the emissaries of Port-Royal, he was content to let the matter drop. He changed his mind, however, when there appeared a new edition of *les Imaginaires* containing, besides Du Bois' and d'Aucour's responses to Racine's first letter, an *Avertissement* at which the poet took offense.

The details of the quarrel advanced thus far are those given by Racine himself. Before examining the other contemporary accounts, we wish to call attention to an important variation in the *Préface* which has not, to our knowledge, been considered in previous studies. In the passage of the *Préface* just cited, Racine had first said that when the second letter was ready for publication it was " quelques-uns de leurs amis," that is, friends of Port-Royal, who came to plead with him. The next sentence, still referring to them, began: " Ils me dirent." Racine, in the autograph, crossed out everything from " quelques-uns de leurs amis " to " me " in the following sentence. He then rewrote between the lines what he had struck out, making only

two changes in what he had originally written, namely, a substitution of " mes amis " for " leurs amis," and, in the following sentence, the substitution of " et d'autres des leurs " for
" ils," a change necessitated by the first alteration. The variations show that, in the original draft of the *Préface*, Racine was
entirely preoccupied with what the friends of Port-Royal had
said to him. The ironical turn which Racine in his anger so
naturally gave to their first argument—or was it merely the
record of the impression made upon him by their arguments—
evidently pleased the poet, for after suppressing the passage, he,
upon second thought, restored it. Racine was aware, however,
that an argument so little flattering to the dignity and to the
spirit of detachment of the *messieurs*, might better be put to
the account of his own friends. From both versions of the
Préface it is evident that friends of the *solitaires*, whether or
not directly delegated by Port-Royal, intervened in the quarrel.
In the definitive version only, does he assign a part to his own
friends, and then the arguments that he ascribes to them are a
part of those originally attributed to the representatives of
Port-Royal.

We shall now study, in the light of what Racine himself said,
the accounts of the quarrel as they are given by his sons. The
latter make no distinction between the suppression of the second
letter written on May 10, 1666, and that of the two letters and
the *Préface* intended for a collective edition sometime in 1667.
Indeed, they seem to have disregarded entirely the date of the
second letter and the reasons given by Racine in the *Préface* for
having withheld it from immediate publication. Louis Racine
would lead us to infer that the second letter and the *Préface*
were written at the same time,[119] while in reality they were
composed at an interval of at least ten months, the former as an
answer to the pamphleteers, Du Bois and d'Aucour, and the latter
as a retort to the *Avertissement* of Nicole. According to J.-B.

---

[119] Mon père, moins piqué de ces deux réponses que du soin que
Messieurs de Port-Royal prenoient de les faire imprimer dans leurs
ouvrages avec un pareil avertissement, fit contre eux la seconde lettre,
et mit à la tête une préface qui n'a jamais été imprimée. . . . Content
de cette préface dont je n'ai rapporté qu'une partie, et de sa seconde
lettre, il alla montrer ces *nouvelles productions* à Boileau. . . ."
(*Mémoires*, Mesnard, I, 240-243.)

Racine's notes, which were the source of what Louis Racine said later in the *Mémoires*, it was Despréaux who deterred Racine from publishing these works:

Mon père . . . se préparoit à faire imprimer sa seconde lettre à la suite de l'autre, et il y pensoit si sérieusement que j'ai entre les mains une Préface écrite de sa main, qu'il vouloit mettre en tête de l'édition. Son ami, M. Despréaux, qui n'étoit point pour lors à Paris, arriva heureusement, comme il se disposoit à donner cette édition. Mon père fut aussitôt lui communiquer le tout; l'autre écouta de grand sang-froid, loua extrêmement le tour et l'esprit de l'ouvrage, et finit en lui disant: Cela est fort joliment écrit, mais vous ne songez pas que vous écrivez contre les plus honnêtes gens du monde. Cette parole fit aussitôt rentrer mon père en lui-même . . . il supprima sa seconde lettre et sa préface, et retira le plus qu'il put des exemplaires de la première lettre.[120]

If we were certain that Jean-Baptiste Racine's account was reliable, we should see in it the eagerness of Racine in 1667 to communicate his work to Boileau, and the readiness of the latter to give counsel. It is, however, precisely in this direction that the sons of Racine, nurtured as they were at Auteuil, are prone to err. They exaggerate the duration of the friendship of the two poets and the influence of Boileau upon their father.[121]

After reporting the incident in the *Mémoires*, Louis Racine refutes a statement that Brossette made in his edition of Boileau's works in 1716. The latter said, apropos of Racine's first letter against Port-Royal, included for some reason in *Œuvres de Boileau*, that the *messieurs*, alarmed by Racine's redoubtable talent, took steps to placate their adversary and that they found " le moyen d'apaiser et de regagner le jeune Racine; et même ils le regagnèrent tellement que jusqu'à sa mort il a été un de leurs plus zélés partisans." [122] Louis Racine maintains, on the contrary, that " Port-Royal garda le silence et ne fit aucune démarche pour la réconciliation " and that, " dans la suite," his father alone took the initiative in restoring friendly relations between himself

---

[120] Cited by Mesnard, IV, 266.

[121] One example will serve to illustrate this tendency. Louis Racine (*Andromaque, Œuvres*, V, 345), in pointing out the development of his father's talent between the time of the composition of *Alexandre* and that of *Andromaque*, makes this statement: " *Cette vigueur lui fut inspirée par Boileau devenu son ami, et par ses ennemis.*"

[122] *Œuvres de Boileau* (1716), II, 329, cited by Mesnard, IV, 267.

and Port-Royal.[123]   Louis Racine, in taking exceptions to Brossette on this point,[124] is, of course, ignoring the early phase of the quarrel so explicitly set forth in the *Préface*.   The author of the *Mémoires,* in arraigning Brossette, explains how the latter could not help being ill informed on this point when he wrote his commentary, for, at that time, neither he nor anyone else knew of the existence of the second letter:

Lorsque Brossette fit imprimer la première lettre, il ne connoissoit pas la seconde, *qui n'étoit connue de personne, ni de nous-mêmes.*   Elle fut trouvée, je ne sais par quel hasard, dans les papiers de M. l'abbé Dupin: et ceux qui en furent les maîtres après sa mort [125] la firent imprimer.[126]

Now if, in 1716, they did not know of the existence of the second letter, it follows that they were also ignorant of the *Préface pour une édition des deux lettres à l'auteur des Imaginaires,* one-fifth of which deals with the circumstances attendant upon the writing and suppression of that letter.

Boileau had evidently never related to them the incident, for how could he have done so without mentioning the second letter and the *Préface?*   If the sons of Racine knew nothing of the existence of those documents until after Boileau's death, upon whose authority do they give the detailed account of their father's rushing straightway to Despréaux (who had been out of town) with his second letter and the *Préface?*   Boileau's advice, reported as it is in direct speech by Jean-Baptiste Racine, becomes very doubtful in the light of this added remark of Louis Racine. Racine's sons, confronted with a *Préface* and a second letter against Nicole that had manifestly been withheld from publication by their father, probably sought the easiest explanation of their suppression.   Did they, by a sort of analogy, ascribe to Boileau, who was the mediator in the reconciliation of 1677, the

---

[123] *Mémoires,* Mesnard, I, 243.

[124] The journalists of Trévoux also record in their *Mémoires* (March, 1724) the attempts of Port-Royal to silence Racine.   They err, however, in saying that the second letter was printed and add that " elle devint, bientôt rare, parce que l'auteur la supprima, ayant été regagné par M. N. (Nicole)."   Cited by Mesnard, IV, 265, n. 2.

[125] The abbé Dupin died in 1719.

[126] *Mémoires,* Mesnard, I, 243-244.   It was first printed in 1722 in an edition of Boileau's works published at La Haye.

rôle of a wise and disinterested admonitor in the crisis of 1667?[127] It is possible that such was the case.

There was a similar confusion in the mind of the only other contemporary who recorded Boileau's intervention in 1667 in Racine's controversy with Nicole. J.-B. Rousseau, in a letter to Brossette dated December 4, 1718, took him to task for the same statement that Louis Racine was to censure him for in the *Mémoires*. After denying that Port-Royal had made any overtures to Racine, Rousseau adds that it was Despréaux who appeased the poet by making him ashamed of his ingratitude toward those to whom he owed his education. Rousseau alleges another argument used by Despréaux to dissuade Racine from publishing the second letter. The satirist

lui fit envisager le péril où il s'exposoit en attaquant une compagnie de théologiens qui l'accableroit de volumes, dès qu'elle viendroit à le déterrer, et l'obligeroit de renoncer pour sa défense à une occupation plus convenable à son génie que le genre polémique.[128]

Rousseau then relates Racine's repentance and his reconciliation with Arnauld, as if the latter immediately followed the episode of the second letter.[129] This, of course, makes us suspect that the author was, like Brossette, confusing two crises in Racine's life that were in reality ten years apart. Besides, a flagrant error in the form of a statement that Mère Angélique persistently refused to see the poet, even after the reconciliation, makes us mistrust the entire account.[130]

What may we conclude in regard to the assertion made fumblingly by J.-B. Rousseau, and clearly, but with an apparent discrepancy, by Jean-Baptiste and Louis Racine? Did Boileau prevent Racine from publishing the letter in question and, if so, precisely what part did he play in the controversy? Brossette's silence on a point that would reflect so much credit upon Boileau is, indeed, disconcerting. How could the latter, who " boasted

[127] Louis Racine (*Mémoires*, Mesnard, 237) made just such an error in confusing the circumstances of two different *privilèges* to print Boileau's works. The permissions were both obtained by Barbin, one in 1666, the other in 1672.

[128] Cited by Mesnard, IV, 267.

[129] Rousseau does not mention the *Préface*.

[130] Mère Angélique died in 1661.

all his life of having taught Racine to write verse," [131] have
refrained from telling Brossette of the service he rendered his
friend at this critical time in his career? We must also bear in
mind that this contact between the two poets would have taken
place during the years when there was apparently some slacken-
ing in the friendship between Boileau and Racine due to the
affair of the *Alexandre*.[132]

Admitting for the time being that Boileau did intervene in
the quarrel, let us examine step by step the part ascribed to him
and see what degree of intimacy with Racine can be inferred
therefrom.   J.-B. Racine tells us that his father made the first
letter public " sans rien dire à personne." [133]   He did not, then,
even inform Despréaux, much less consult with him in the
matter.   Even if J.-B. Racine's account is erroneous and if Racine
did show the letter to Despréaux, the latter did not have enough
influence over him to obtain its suppression, although all the
arguments attributed to Boileau the next year apropos of the
second letter might fittingly have been adduced at the very
opening of the quarrel.   In the next place, Racine kept the
second letter among his papers for some ten months before
hostilities were again brought to a head by Nicole's new edition
of the *Imaginaires*.   The fact that Boileau did not see the letter
during this period cannot be explained by any prolonged absence
of the satirist, J.-B. Racine's manuscript note notwithstanding.[134]
Boileau, preoccupied during these years with several editions of
his *Satires*,[135] could not have been away from Paris for very long
at a time.   The fact that Racine kept a letter of such burning
interest without showing it to Boileau is strong evidence that the
satirist did not have his complete confidence in 1666 or during
the first half of 1667.

We must next consider Boileau's affiliations at this time with
Port-Royal.   Louis Racine errs in relating that Boileau acted
in the quarrel simply as an " amateur de la vérité " and that
he had not as yet established any " liaison " with Port-Royal.[136]
Despréaux's friendship with the Comte de Brienne, a militant

---

[131] *Mémoires*, Mesnard, I, 271.
[132] Cf. *supra*, pp. 52-56.
[133] Cf. *supra*, p. 60.   [135] Cf. *supra*, p. 24.
[134] Cf. *supra*, p. 63.   [136] *Mémoires*, Mesnard, I, 242.

Jansenist [137] to whom Port-Royal later entrusted the editing of Pascal's *Pensées,* dates from the early sixties. Boileau, moreover, was acquainted with Arnauld d'Andilly at the beginning of 1665.[138] The latter, according to Brossette,[139] although he admired the work as a whole, found fault with certain verses in *Satire II.* Boileau, in accordance with the suggestions drawn from Arnauld's criticism, revised these lines for the collective edition of 1666. In 1667,[140] the crucial year of Racine's hostilities with Nicole, Despréaux showed his colors by ironically dedicating his *Satire sur l'Homme* [141] to Claude Morel, a doctor of the Sorbonne and an ardent Molinist.[142] This consideration of Boileau's loyalty to Port-Royal should help us in determining the part that he played in the controversy between Racine and the *solitaires.* If there is a grain of truth in the assertion made by the sons of Racine and by J.-B. Rousseau that Boileau dissuaded Racine from continuing the scandalous quarrel, it would seem to be this: the satirist intervened, not as a friend of Racine, but as an advocate of Port-Royal. The hypothesis [143] is an interesting one. Boileau's natural uprightness and his acquaintance with Racine would fit him for the delicate task of mediation. Boileau would then be one of "leurs amis," in the first version, and of "d'autres des leurs" of the definitive form of the *Préface,* whose arguments and promises caused Racine to withhold his second letter from publication. Even the arguments attributed to him by Racine's sons and by J.-B. Rousseau might be those of a more or less official envoy of Port-Royal. We should expect Racine, in giving his version of their arguments, to pass over their indictment of his ingratitude toward those who had been his devoted teachers, and he does not, indeed, mention it. Boileau,

---

[137] He became a Jansenist after his exile from Paris toward the end of 1662 (*Mémoires de Brienne,* II, 227-236). For his relationship with Despréaux cf. Revillout, *RLR,* XXXVII, 106-107.

[138] Cf. *ibid.,* XXXVII, 104.

[139] Remarks on vss. 53 and 57 of *Satire II.*

[140] Berriat-Saint-Prix, I, 185, n. 2.

[141] *Satire VIII,* in which he would prove
Que l'homme, qu'un docteur est au-dessous d'un âne (vs. 272).

[142] The fact that Morel was called "la mâchoire d'âne" on account of the size of his jaw doubtless gave piquancy to the dedication.

[143] It was suggested by Professor Searles.

according to J.-B. Rousseau, also pointed out the harm that Racine would do himself by diverting his talent from an " occupation plus convenable à son génie " into the ungrateful *genre* of polemics. This argument harmonizes fairly well with one reported by Racine; for friends of Port-Royal, according to the *Préface,* reminded Racine that nothing would be, from his standpoint, more " incommode " than to carry on a futile controversy before spectators who did not even know that he had been attacked.

At any rate, Boileau—if indeed he figured among the friends of Port-Royal mentioned in the *Préface*—was certainly not the only mediator in the quarrel. We do not know whether it was his arguments or those of someone else that prevailed. A very interesting letter written by a friend of Port-Royal, perhaps by Lancelot himself,[144] to Nicolas Vitart on May 8, 1667, is evidence that the latter had, previous to this date, been an intermediary in behalf of Racine. He was so biased in favor of his cousin that he had threatened Port-Royal with Racine's pen, " comme de la plume qu'on a plus sujet de redouter." [145]   The author of the letter exhorts Vitart in the firmest, yet most amicable terms, to dissuade Racine from adding fuel to the fire:

Si vous aimez véritablement votre cousin, portez-le plutôt à demeurer dans le silence. C'est une affaire faite, dont apparemment on ne parlera plus, qu'autant qu'il en donnera sujet: qu'il s'en tienne là, s'il veut croire mon conseil.[146]

This letter may have convinced Vitart that his cousin was in the wrong, and it was perhaps his influence that concurred to prevent Racine from printing the second letter and the *Préface* in 1667.

We conclude this part of our study by acknowledging that it is very difficult to assign to Boileau a definite rôle in the quarrel of 1666 and 1667. Contemporary accounts, by confusing the dates, fail to distinguish two phases of the crisis, and there is even a possibility that the circumstances of the definitive reconciliation of 1677 are blended with those of the hostilities of 1667. There is no likelihood whatever that Boileau intervened

---

[144] Cf. Mesnard, IV, 268, n. 2.
[145] *Ibid.*, IV, 271.   [146] *Loc. cit.*

in the early part of the controversy as a friend of Racine. If he played a rôle at this time, he did so as a partisan of Port-Royal. The *Préface* and the letter to Vitart are a proof, moreover, that his rôle was not as preponderant as the sons of Racine and J.-B. Rousseau would have us believe.

Andromaque, performed in November of that year, is not mentioned by Boileau until 1670,[147] when he ends the original version of *Épitre I* with a colorless reference to its being a tragedy.[148] The *Bolœana,*[149] however, attributes to Despréaux two criticisms of the play. He objected, it is said, to the character of Pyrrhus, " qu'il traitoit de héros à la Scudéri." Besides, the " sentiment puéril " expressed by Pyrrhus in the last scene of the second act[150] was unseemly and derogated from the " gravité magnifique " proper to tragedy. Louis Racine in his *Examen de l'Andromaque* confirms this last assertion of Monchesnay and, in telling when Boileau made the criticism, he gives us information that is of capital importance in this study:

Je me souviens que daignant un jour m'entretenir de ces matières, quoique je fusse encore très-jeune, après m'avoir avoué qu'il avoit longtemps, comme un autre, admiré la scène fameuse qui commence par ce vers:

Eh bien, Phœnix, l'amour est-il le maître?

il m'assura qu'il avoit depuis changé de sentiment, ayant reconnu qu'elle ne s'accordoit pas avec la dignité du cothurne . . . Il m'ajouta qu'il se repentoit d'avoir fait cette réflexion trop tard, parce que s'il l'eût faite dans le temps, il eût obligé l'auteur à supprimer ce morceau.[151]

Boileau, therefore, admitted to Louis Racine that " for a long time " he had admired the scene like everyone else and that he did not perceive the fault until it was too late to " oblige " the poet to suppress that part of the play. This seems to be a con-

---

[147] Cf. Magne, I, 129.

[148] Despréaux parries the attack of the supercilious reader who,
> " Prêt à juger de tout, comme un jeune marquis
> Qui, plein d'un grand savoir chez les dames acquis,
> Dédaignant le public que lui seul il attaque,
> Va pleurer au *Tartuffe* et rire à l'*Andromaque.*"
> (Berriat-Saint-Prix, II, 19-20, n. 9.)

[149] P. 59.

[150]
> . . . . " Crois-tu si je l'épouse,
> Qu'Andromaque en son cœur n'en sera pas jalouse? "
> (Vss. 669-670.)

[151] *Œuvres de Louis Racine,* V, 355.

fession that he did not notice this weakness in *Andromaque* until after Racine's death.

Other testimony shows us that, in this instance, Boileau was not ahead of his time. Brossette, in a letter of August 6, 1716, to J.-B. Rousseau, tells us the genesis of Boileau's criticism:

M. Despréaux avait remarqué qu'aux représentations d'*Andromaque* l'on ne manquait jamais de sourire en cet endroit. Or, ce n'est pas l'effet que doit produire la tragédie. L'amour doit y être traité autrement que dans la comédie.[152]

J.-B. Rousseau, in answering this letter, said that he, too, had always condemned the scene, although he found in it much beauty:

Cependant, si c'est une faute, on doit être bien aise que Racine l'ait faite par les beautés dont elle est réparée; mais il ne serait pas sûr de l'imiter en cela.[153]

Dubos, three years later, tells us that in truth the *parterre* laughed almost as loud at this scene as it would at a comedy.[154] Louis Racine's testimony, corroborated by Brossette and Monchesnay and enriched by the observations of J.-B. Rousseau and of Dubos, indicates that Despréaux was, in this instance, not a forerunner of taste, but rather the echo of a criticism that was already widespread.

In 1668 Racine wrote *les Plaideurs*. It was inspired, according to the *Préface,* by a reading of the *Wasps.* The author thought of sharing with the public some of the pleasantries found in Aristophanes and destined them originally for the Italian troupe. The departure of Scaramouche for Italy frustrated this project and " fit naître l'envie à quelques-uns de mes amis de voir sur notre théâtre un échantillon d'Aristophane." Racine, if he was to write a comedy, favored the more regular models of Menander and Terence. His friends, however, said it was not so much a comedy they wanted of him; they were curious to see what effect the witticisms of Aristophanes would have in their language. Racine speaks thus of their part in the work:

[152] *Correspondance de J.-B. Rousseau et de Brossette,* I, 70.
[153] *Ibid.,* I, 76.
[154] *Réflexions Critiques sur la Peinture et la Poésie,* I, 132.

Ainsi, moitié en m'encourageant, moitié en mettant eux-mêmes la main
à l'œuvre, mes amis me firent commencer une pièce qui ne tarda guère
à être achevée.[155]

The poet, then, had discussed his plan from all angles with his
friends. He acknowledges not only their encouragement but
their actual assistance in the composition of the piece.

Brossette, in his edition of Boileau,[156] affirms that the comedy
was written in the Mouton blanc, the cabaret where the *Chapelain Décoiffé* had its origin. He adds that young nobles "les
plus spirituels de la cour" were wont to assemble there together
with "MM. Despréaux, Racine, La Fontaine, Chapelle, Furetière et quelques autres personnes d'élite." [157]   He states precisely what was Boileau's contribution to the piece. It was the
idea of the dispute between the countess and Chicanneau that
had its counterpart in a scene enacted before Despréaux's
brother, a clerk of court. Racine "ne fit guère que la rimer,"
according to Brossette. The *Ménagiana* [158] gives the same account. Louis Racine, in his version, follows Brossette's commentaries:

Boileau lui fournit l'idée de la dispute entre Chicanneau et la Comtesse;
il avoit été témoin de cette scène, qui s'étoit passée chez son frère le
greffier, entre un homme très-connu alors, et une comtesse, que l'actrice
qui joua ce personnage contrefit jusqu'à paroître sur le théâtre avec les
mêmes habillements, comme il est rapporté dans le commentaire sur la
seconde satire de Boileau.[159]

Le Verrier, in his commentary on *Satire IX,* speaks of
Boileau's experience at the Palais. He asserts briefly, and in
passing, that the amusing idiosyncracies which Despréaux observed there found a place later on in his friend's comedy:

C'est là (at the *Palais*) où trouvant des ridicules qui ne se trouvent
point ailleurs dans un si haut degré de perfection, il ramassa ces caractères et ces personnages qui joüent leur rolle avec tant de grâces dans
les Plaideurs de Racine.[160]

---

[155] *Préface* to *les Plaideurs.*
[156] *Œuvres de Boileau* (1716), I, 438, cited by Mesnard, II, 132.
[157] Cf. the list of Boileau's tavern companions in Le Verrier's commentary to *Satire IX* cited *supra*, p. 23.
[158] Mesnard, II, 132.
[159] *Mémoires,* Mesnard, I, 246-247.
[160] Lachèvre, p. 96. Boileau made no corrections on the commentary
on *Satire IX.*

It is safe to conclude from the testimony cited that Boileau suggested the "idea" of at least one scene of *les Plaideurs*. That Racine drew upon Despréaux's knowledge of the procedure and jargon of the courts is also quite possible.[161] On the other hand, every witness who speaks of the composition of the comedy mentions several collaborators. Racine, in his *Préface,* always refers to the assistance given him by his "amis." Boileau apparently had no preponderant part in the composition of the play. His collaboration could have gone no farther than suggesting the scene, the "caractères," and "personnages." This is the impression given by the accounts cited above, and it is confirmed by the homogeneous style in which the play is written. We may see, then, in this collaboration nothing more than another casual contact between Racine and Boileau.

We shall examine, in the next place, the testimony concerning the literary relations existing between the two poets while *Britannicus* was being written. J.-B. Rousseau possessed the manuscript of a scene between Burrhus and Narcisse that was not found in the play. He had at one time attributed it to Jean-Baptiste Racine, but in a letter to Brossette dated December 25, 1718, he says that he believes it to be the work of Louis Racine. Brossette, in his answer to Rousseau, tells him that he, too, has had "for a long time" a copy of the scene in question. It was written, he affirms, by Jean Racine, who had intended it to be the first scene in the third act of his tragedy. Brossette then explains that it was at the behest of Boileau that Racine omitted the scene:

M. Despréaux lui conseilla de la supprimer parce qu'il la trouvait faible en comparaison du reste de la pièce et qu'elle en arrêtait l'action. Il n'approuvait pas que Burrhus se commît ainsi avec Narcisse et il disait que cette scène ne pouvait finir que par des coups de bâton. M. Racine la retrancha donc et se contenta d'en retenir quelques vers qui sont encore dans sa tragédie.[162]

Louis Racine verifies the incident and adds that the scene was

[161] Racine says he has used the language of chicanery sparingly: "Je n'en ai employé que quelques mots barbares que je puis avoir appris dans le cours d'un procès que ni mes juges ni moi n'avons jamais bien entendu." (*Préface.*)

[162] Letter dated at Lyons, March 25, 1719. (*Correspondance de Jean-Baptiste Rousseau et de Brossette,* I, 179.)

suppressed before the tragedy was given to the actors.   His version of Despréaux's objections to the scene, while it harmonizes with Brossette's account, is more elaborate.[163]   It does not appear that Louis Racine is repeating Brossette in this instance.   Indeed, he seems not to be aware of the latter's letter to Rousseau, for he affirms that " cette scène n'est encore connue de personne," although it is plain from Brossette's letter that both he and Rousseau possessed copies of it.[164]   A statement in the *Mémoires* also indicates that Louis Racine probably got his information, not from Brossette, but directly from Despréaux. He tells us that he is publishing for the first time a scene " que Boileau avoit conservée, et qu'il nous a remise." [165]   Was it the copy that Racine submitted to him in 1669?   It is possible, as the only papers that we know that Racine asked to have put into Boileau's hands after his death were those concerning the *Histoire du Roi*.[166]   The very definite evidence concerning the deleted scene apparently comes from Boileau through two intermediaries who seem, in this case, to testify independently of each other.   We may conclude that sometime before *Britannicus* was performed Boileau made a suggestion in regard to the play and that Racine saw fit to follow it.[167]

[163] " ' Vous les (spectateurs) indisposerez, lui dit-il, en leur montrant ces deux hommes ensemble.   Pleins d'admiration pour l'un, et d'horreur pour l'autre, ils souffriront pendant leur entretien.   Convient-il au gouverneur de l'Empereur, à cet homme si respectable par son rang et sa probité, de s'abaisser à parler à un misérable affranchi, le plus scélérat de tous les hommes?   Il le doit trop mépriser pour avoir avec lui quelque éclaircissement.   Et d'ailleurs quel fruit espère-t-il de ses remonstrances?   Est-il assez simple pour croire qu'elles feront naître quelques remords dans le cœur de Narcisse?   Lorsqu'il lui fait connoître l'intérêt qu'il prend à Britannicus, il découvre son secret à un traître, et au lieu de servir Britannicus, il en précipita la perte.' Ces réflexions parurent justes, et la scène fut supprimée." (*Mémoires*, Mesnard, I, 252-253.)

[164] Since both Brossette and Rousseau were dead when the *Mémoires* appeared in 1747, it is just possible that Louis Racine is not counting them.

[165] Mesnard, I, 250.   L. Racine presented the manuscript to the *Bibliothèque du Roi*.

[166] *Note de Jean Racine contenant quelques dispositions testamentaires*, 29 octobre, 1685.   (*Ibid.*, VII, 356.)

[167] M. Demeure (*MF*, CCV, 55), however, suggests that the " peut-être " of a couplet of *Épître VII*, if it is not merely a *cheville*, signifies

Other criticisms of *Britannicus* that Boileau is said to have
made belong to a later period of his life.[168] They concern the
dénouement, which Despréaux is said to have considered
" puéril," and the character of Britannicus who was " trop petit
devant Néron." [169] Louis Racine,[170] upon the authority of his
older brother, twice denied that Boileau made the adverse criticisms reported in the *Bolæana*. A discussion of Boileau's comments on *Britannicus* would be out of place at this point in our
study. Even if it were certain that he made them, they represent the judgment of the critic at a much later date.[171]

Boursault's account of the first performance of *Britannicus*
has often been taken as a proof of the intimacy that was thought
to exist between Boileau and Racine toward the end of 1669. At
the beginning of *Artémise et Poliante*,[172] the author, who
avowedly bears a grudge against Racine,[173] facetiously remarks
that the audience was small, for on that day the execution of
the Marquis de Courboyer drew the theatergoers away from the
Hôtel de Bourgogne. Boursault then describes the behavior of
a certain " Monsieur de * * * *, admirateur de tous les nobles
vers de M. Racine." This gentleman did everything that a true

---

that Boileau, in speaking of the genesis of *Britannicus*, was reduced to
a hypothesis. This is the couplet referred to:

> " Et *peut-être* ta plume, aux censeurs de Pyrrhus,
> Doit les plus nobles traits dont tu peignis Burrhus."
>
> (Vss. 53-54.)

[168] Monchesnay was discussing *Britannicus* with Despréaux " en présence du fils de Monsieur Racine." (*Op. cit.*, p. 106.)

[169] *Bolæana*, p. 106.

[170] *Mémoires*, Mesnard, I, 249; and also in a letter to Brossette dated
at Paris, March 21, 1741. (*Correspondance de J.-B. Rousseau et de
Brossette*, II, 269.)

[171] M. Demeure (*MF*, CCV, 57) uses this evidence to show that, " en
1670 encore, Boileau était un cornélien et par conséquent un ennemi de
Racine." He is not justified in inferring from the *Bolæana* that this
was Boileau's judgment *in 1670*. Nor is the conclusion a logical one.
The fact that Boileau made a well-aimed criticism of *Britannicus* does
not constitute him " un ennemi de Racine."

[172] Paris, chez René Guignard, 1670.

[173] Mesnard (II, 226) cites Boursault: " Quoique rien ne m'engage à
vouloir du bien à M. Racine, et qu'il m'ait désobligé sans lui en avoir
donné aucun sujet, je vais rendre justice à son ouvrage."

friend of an author could do in order to contribute to the success of the work, even applauding before the play began.

Son visage, qui à un besoin passeroit pour un répertoire du caractère des passions, épousoit toutes celles de la pièce l'une après l'autre, et se transformoit comme un caméléon à mesure que les acteurs débitoient leurs rôles . . . Je ne sais rien de plus obligeant que d'avoir à point nommé un fond de joie et un fond de tristesse au très-humble service de M. Racine.[174]

The frères Parfaict were the first to say that this was a portrait of Despréaux. They printed Boursault's abbreviation, Monsieur *De * * * **, and insinuated in a note that the author of *la Satire des Satires* thus designated Despréaux.[175] Now there is nothing in the passage that would indicate that the author meant Boileau rather than another of Racine's admirers, who were already numerous. Furthermore, " Monsieur de * * * * " does not seem to be an apt abbreviation for Monsieur Despréaux.[176] What motive could Boursault have for withholding or disguising the critic's name? Boileau had not had the same delicacy toward him in *Satires VII* [177] and *IX*.[178] This brings us to a serious objection to substituting Despréaux's name for the indeterminate Monsieur de * * * *. Boursault had fared badly in two of Boileau's *Satires*. He retaliated with *la Satire des Satires,* a forthcoming performance of which was announced at the Théâtre du Marais. The *Parlement,* however, at the instigation of Boileau, issued an injunction [179] on October 22, 1668,

[174] *Ibid.,* II, 225-226.

[175] *Histoire du Théâtre Français,* X, 431.

[176] Until 1701 his works were published under the name " Monsieur D." (*Préface,* 1701.) " Des " would seem to be a more natural abbreviation for Despréaux than " de ****," and we know that Boileau did, later on, separate the particle, writing his name "Des Préaux." M. Demeure (*MF*, CCV, 41), suggests that the four asterisks may indicate a four syllable name like " de Guilleragues."

[177] Vs. 45, where he figured in the original version among the " froids rimeurs."

[178] Vs. 289, where Boursault's name filled the niche until it was replaced in 1694 by that of Pradon. The satirist says that, in order to placate his censors, he will change his tune:
" Je le déclare donc : Quinault est un Virgile ;
Boursault comme un soleil en nos ans a paru."
(Vss. 288-289.)

[179] Cited in Magne, II, 126.

forbidding any troupe to perform Boursault's play. Hostilities between the two were kept alive by the subsequent publication of the piece on May 4, 1669. The sale of the printed work was also stopped by the courts. The quarrel must have been still rankling when Boursault wrote his account of the *première* of *Britannicus*. Surely Boursault dealt very gently with his adversary, if he meant to portray him in this passage of *Artémise et Poliante*. It would take more than the word of the frères Parfaict, writing some seventy years later, to authorize the substitution of Despréaux's name in the passage in question.

The following year Racine gave *Bérénice*. Dubos, in finding fault with the subject of that tragedy, makes an assertion that, if it were known to be true, would be very pertinent to our study. The author of the *Réflexions Critiques* was the first to affirm that Racine had undertaken this subject " sur les instances d'une grande Princesse." He asserts also that Boileau disapproved of the subject and that, if he had been at hand, he would have prevented Racine from treating it:

Quand il se chargea de cette tâche, l'ami, dont les conseils lui furent tant de fois utiles, étoit absent. Despréaux a dit plusieurs fois qu'il eût bien empêché son ami de se consommer sur un sujet aussi peu propre à la Tragédie que Bérénice, s'il avoit été à portée de le dissuader de promettre qu'il le traiteroit.[180]

Louis Racine in his *Mémoires,* in precisely the same context, that is, apropos of the unhappy subject proposed by the Duchess of Orleans, repeats almost verbatim Dubos' account of Boileau's absence which prevented him from counselling Racine on that occasion.[181] Now if M. Michaut does not altogether disprove the story of Henriette d'Angleterre's suggesting the subject of *Bérénice,* he at least deals it a mighty blow. Although the fact that she collaborated on *Andromaque* [182] lends some plausibility to Dubos' account, this scholar challenges a statement made for the first time some fifty years after the play was written, and he

---

[180] Dubos, *op. cit.*, I, 122.

[181] " La princesse que j'ai nommée lui avoit fait promettre qu'il le (the subject) traiteroit; et comme courtisan, il s'étoit engagé. ' Si je m'y étois trouvé, disoit Boileau, je l'aurois bien empêché de donner sa parole.' " (*Mémoires*, Mesnard, I, 255.)

[182] Cf. the dedicatory letter addressed to her.

traces the subsequent elaborations of it.[183] He concludes that it
is a legend invented by persons who could not admit that Racine
would stoop to snatching a subject from Corneille in order to
enter into direct competition with the older dramatist, although
we know that such a practice was not without precedent.[184] Now
even with the intervention of Henriette d'Angleterre reduced to
the status of a legend, there remains the possibility that someone else urged Racine to compete with Corneille, and the reported assertion of Boileau might still have some foundation in
fact.   Professor Lancaster argues that the actors of the Hôtel
de Bourgogne, piqued at Corneille for selling his *Attila* to the
troupe of the Palais-Royal, might well have induced Racine to
write a play on the same subject as Corneille.[185]

If Boileau did make " plusieurs fois " the statement that
Dubos ascribes to him, what degree of intimacy with Racine
could be implied therefrom?   Perhaps, as in the case of his
criticism of *Andromaque*,[186] after the play was written, he
chimed in with de Villars' and Saint-Évremond's criticisms in
regard to Racine's choice of subject.   Later on, in his conversations at Auteuil, he might easily have antedated his judgment
to the time when Racine was considering the subject of *Bérénice*.
In any event, we can see in the remark an over-statement of
his influence on the dramatist.   How could he be so sure
that he would have " prevented " Racine from treating the
subject?   We know that his opinion did not prevail in a similar
instance in 1688, when his relations with the dramatist were
far more intimate.   Mme de Caylus [187] tells us that, although
Boileau deprecated Mme de Maintenon's commission, Racine
set to work on a play to be given at Saint-Cyr.   According
to this niece of Mme de Maintenon, Despréaux, whom Racine
went to consult,

---

[183] Cf. Fontenelle's *Vie de Corneille* (1729) ; Louis Racine's *Mémoires*
(1747) and his *Examen de Bérénice* (1752) ; *le Siècle de Louis XIV*
(1751) and Voltaire's commentary on *Bérénice* (1764).

[184] *La Bérénice de Racine*, p. 126.

[185] He thinks it reasonable to suppose that Corneille had begun his
play soon after the publication of *Attila* in 1666.   (*Op. cit.*, Part III,
pp. 574-575.)

[186] Cf. *supra*, pp. 69-70.

[187] Racine wrote the Prologue to give her a rôle in the play.

décida brusquement pour la négative: ce n'étoit pas le compte de
Racine. Enfin, après un peu de réflexion, il trouva sur le sujet d'Esther
tout ce qu'il falloit pour plaire à la cour. Despréaux lui-même en fut
enchanté, et l'exhorta à travailler, avec autant de zèle qu'il en avoit eu
pour l'en détourner.[188]

What can be concluded from what Dubos says regarding the
genesis of *Bérénice*? His testimony, standing alone—there is
every indication that Louis Racine used it as his source—and
unrecorded for almost fifty years, is extremely doubtful. Moreover, the bare facts affirmed, namely, Boileau's *absence* and his
repeated assertion that he would have prevented Racine from
treating the subject if he had been able, are not sufficient evidence to warrant any definite conclusion in regard to their relations at the time that *Bérénice* was begun.

The next testimony that we have is certain and shows us the
two poets early in 1671 on very intimate terms with each other
and with la Champmeslé.[189] Mme de Sévigné wrote thus to her
daughter of certain suppers in which her son had a part. Besides
Ninon de Lenclos,

il y a une petite comédienne et les Despréaux et les Racine avec elle:
ce sont des soupers délicieux, c'est-à-dire des diableries.[190]

Years later, in a letter to Racine,[191] Boileau recalls the rôle that
the former played in these gatherings. Racine seems to have

[188] *Souvenirs de Madame Caylus*, p. 165.

[189] La Champmeslé came to Paris with her husband in 1669. She
played for a short time at the Théâtre du Marais. The frères Parfaict
give an account of her début at the Hôtel de Bourgogne in the rôle of
Hermione in the spring of 1670. Racine had not seen her rehearse her
part and lacked confidence in her. After the performance, however, he
rushed to her dressing-room, and throwing himself on his knees thanked
her for the excellent interpretation of the rôle. (*Histoire du Théâtre
Français*, XIV, 513-514.)

[190] *Lettres*, II, 137. The letter is dated April 1, 1671. On March 18,
she had complained of Charles' being at Saint-Germain " entre Ninon
et une comédienne, Despréaux sur le tout: nous lui faisons une vie
enragée. Dieux, quelle folie! dieux, quelle folie! " (*Ibid.*, II, 118.)

[191] August 28, 1687. Boileau thinks that drinking Pantin wine would
not be a bad penance to impose on Champmeslé " pour tant de bouteilles
de Champagne qu'il a bues chez lui, vous savez aux dépens de qui."
Cf. also Boileau's epigram " De six amants . . . " written, according to
Brossette, at one of these suppers. (*Recueil ms. de la Bib. Nat.*, p. 41,
cited by Mesnard, I, 85.)

furnished the champagne of which Monsieur de Champmeslé partook so heartily that Boileau, even in 1687, still twits his friend about it. The important thing for our purposes, however, is the assurance that Racine and Boileau were henceforth intimate friends whose pleasures and literary preoccupations must be studied together. This date, as M. Demeure points out, coincides with Boileau's testimony, in the affidavit of 1696,[192] that he had known Racine (*intimately,* we should like to understand) for twenty-five years.[193]

We shall consider briefly who were the friends and protectors of the two poets during the years preceding 1671. M. Demeure [194] found in the study of their respective milieux a strong support of his thesis that Boileau was Racine's " enemy " until 1671. While such an investigation is far from being conclusive, it may be taken as an indication of which way the wind was blowing. Chapelain, whose encouraging words of criticism Racine reports as he would " le texte de l'Évangile, sans y rien changer," [195] is flouted in the *Satires.* From 1664 on, Boileau engaged in a series of skirmishes with Colbert,[196] the dispenser of royal pensions. A well-known parody of *Cinna* [197] shows how

[192] Cf. *supra,* pp. 42-44.

[193] Bearing in mind, however, the empressement with which Racine entered into relationships with la Champmeslé after seeing her in the rôle of Hermione at Easter time in 1670—she played the rôle of Bérénice in November of that year—we are inclined to assume that the suppers about which Mme de Sévigné wrote in March and in April of the following year had been going on for at least some months and that personal relations between the two poets were pretty solidly established by the end of 1670.

[194] *MF*, CCV, 52-53.

[195] Letter to Le Vasseur, September 13 [1660]. (Mesnard, VI, 393-394.) A letter of Chapelain (*Lettres*, II, 313) to Colbert dated June 22, 1663, is evidence that Racine kept up relations with Chapelain, who was then advising him in regard to *l'Ode sur la Convalescence du Roi.*

[196] For an account of the intermittent advances that Despréaux made meanwhile to Colbert, consult Revillout, *RLR*, XXXVII, 553 *et sqq.* Boileau's intimacy with Lamoignon would tend to keep the relations between the satirist and Colbert strained. Lamoignon and Colbert had been enemies since the trial of Fouquet. (*Lettres de Guy Patin*, Mar. 20, 1665, III, 518.)

[197] *Boileau ou la Clémence de Colbert* represented the magistrate pardoning Despréaux and his brother for their attacks upon him. Cf. Van

open the hostility was between them. Even as late as April 4, 1672, Chapelain succeeded in obtaining from Colbert the withdrawal of the *privilège* that had been given to print Boileau's works. Racine, on the other hand, in dedicating *Bérénice* to the "contrôleur général des finances," extols his rare qualities, "qui ont attiré l'admiration de toute la France." Perrault, who said "de fort bonnes choses" [198] concerning *la Nymphe de la Seine* and who supported the candidacy of Racine at the French Academy in 1672,[199] felt meanwhile the repeated lashes of Boileau's satire. The duc de Saint-Aignan accepted the dedication of *la Thébaïde* in 1664. He received the same honor from Cotin in 1666, when the latter addressed to him *la Satire des Satires*. The brunt of Boileau's castigation of vice in the hierarchy [200] fell upon M. de Péréfixe, who was the archbishop of Paris in 1666, when *Satire I* appeared in print. The following year the "mauvaise humeur" of Molière, and quite likely that of Despréaux also, fell upon the same dignitary regarded as the leader in the cabal against *le Tartuffe*.[201] Racine, on the other hand, this same year in his *Préface* to the letters against Port-Royal, took sides with the archbishop who was persecuting the abbey.[202] Boileau, much to the surprise of Mesnard,[203] attacked even those who were associated intimately with Racine. In *Satire IV* he arraigns, for his alternate avarice and prodigality, the abbé de Bernay, with whom Racine was living.[204] He also ridicules in

Roosbroeck, *Boileau, Racine, Furetière*, etc. *Chapelain Décoiffé, a Battle of Parodies*, pp. 24 *et sqq.*

[198] Letter to Le Vasseur, September 13 [1660]. (Mesnard, VI, 392-393.)

[199] He was received into the Academy on January 12, 1673.

[200] He bids one flee from the city,
    "Où le vice orgueilleux s'érige en souverain,
    Et va la mître en tête et la crosse à la main."
                                    (*Satire I*, vss. 131-132.)
Le Verrier, whose comments on this *Satire* were very carefully supervised, wrote apropos of these verses: "M. de Péréfix, Archevêque de Paris venoit de faire à Port-roial cette procédure si extraordinaire et si connue de tout le monde." (Lachèvre, p. 22.)

[201] *Mémoires* of Brossette dated Nov. 9, 1702. (Laverdet, p. 565.)

[202] According to a rumor reported, but not vouched for, by J.-B. Racine, the archbishop tried to enlist Racine as a writer against Port-Royal (Mesnard, IV, 261). Cf. also *les Mémoires, ibid.*, I, 240.

[203] I, 27, n. 5.

[204] Cf. Le Verrier's commentary on vss. 66-70. (Lachèvre, 43.)

Satire I [205] and *Épître II* [206] a certain Le Mazier, who was a close relative of Madame Vitart. M. Demeure considers all this pertinent evidence and concludes therefrom that Boileau and Racine were themselves enemies until 1671, when parties of pleasure brought them together.[207] M. Demeure, in ignoring all evidence to the contrary, seems to show some bias. His careful study of their friends does indicate, however, that Boileau and Racine were not personal and intimate friends during the years in question.

In this study which is concerned with the extent to which the *Art Poétique* reflects Racinian tragedy, the question of the influence of one poet upon the other is of supreme importance. We are especially interested in that period of their intimate friendship that synchronizes with their productive years. It is marked by such mileposts as Boileau's *Épigramme* [208] of 1674, where he speaks of the " judicieux avis " which he receives from his friend; the famous *Épître VII,* consoling the poet at the time of the cabal of *Phèdre*; and the critic's generous rôle in Racine's reconciliation with Port-Royal. The latter was married in 1677 " en présence, du côté dudit Racine, de Nicolas Vitart, seigneur de Passy, et de M. Nicolas S^r des Préaux." [209] We recall Despréaux's solicitous regard for his friend's literary reputation when he thought it was jeopardized by Mme de Maintenon's order for a religious piece to be performed at St. Cyr. Boileau's laudatory verses,[210] to be inscribed below his friend's portrait, and his delicate appraisal of Racine and Corneille in the *VIIe Réflexion sur Longin* show him to be a warm-hearted and admiring friend.

The two poets showed great eagerness in communicating to each other their works. Boileau encouraged Racine in 1691, when the latter considered his *Athalie* a stage failure.[211] In June

[205] Vs. 123.   [206] Vs. 36.

[207] M. Demeure thinks it is not without reason that Boileau was reticent concerning his early relations with Racine and that feelings of shame made him loath to tell his young admirers at Auteuil of the companions and places of resort associated with the beginnings of their friendship.

[208] Against Desmarets, *Œuvres*, II, 455-456.

[209] *Registre de la paroisse Saint-Séverin, Pièce Justificative n° XXIII,* Mesnard, I, 188.

[210] *Œuvres*, II, 442-443.   [211] *Mémoires*, Mesnard, I, 325.

6

1693, Boileau, acceding to Racine's curiosity, sent him the rest of his *Ode sur Namur,* although he had not intended to show it to him until it was at the stage where it needed nothing except his friend's corrections. He begged him not to spare it. In doubt about certain innovations, Boileau wrote: " Vous en jugerez, sauf à tout changer si cela vous déplaît." [212]

Louis Racine, in speaking of the services they mutually rendered each other, insists upon the equality of their literary friendship:

Ces deux amis avoient un *égal* empressement à se communiquer leurs ouvrages avant que de les montrer au public, *égale* sévérité de critique l'un pour l'autre, et *égale* docilité. [213]

We have reason to believe, however, that the sons of Racine strain a point in their efforts to establish the poet's submissiveness to Boileau. In preparing their father's correspondence for publication, they deleted a passage [214] that reveals a certain amount of independence in regard to what they considered to be Boileau's earliest criticism of Racine's verse. They were evidently harmonizing the passage with the version of the *Mémoires* which tells us that Racine found Boileau's corrections " très-judicieuses." [215] A remark taken from the *Examen de l'Andromaque* also illustrates how ready Louis Racine is to worship at the feet of Boileau. He records the latter's criticism of the scene between Pyrrhus and Phœnix in the second act of the play and the critic's regret at not having perceived this weakness sooner. If he had noticed it in time, " il eût obligé l'auteur à supprimer ce morceau." Louis Racine then makes this very naïve reflection in regard to the dominion that Boileau was thought to have exercised over the dramatist:

Je remarquai alors le sévère jugement de ce grand critique, et quel avoit été son empire sur son ami, puisqu'il ne doutoit point de la docilité avec laquelle il eût sacrifié une scène si brillante. [216]

Without exaggerating Racine's docility, we may infer that he

---

[212] Letter to Racine, Mesnard, VII, 87.

[213] *Mémoires*, Mesnard, I, 250.

[214] The passage is cited above, p. 47. The italicized passage was suppressed in getting the letter ready for publication. This was pointed out by Demeure. (*MF*, CCV, 37, n. 3.)

[215] Mesnard, I, 229.   [216] *Œuvres de Louis Racine,* V, 355.

made excellent use of the criticisms he received [217] and that, after they become close friends, Boileau was first and foremost among those whose judgment he trusted.

That such was the case, M. de Valincour's [218] testimony leaves no room to doubt. Valincour was one of the most intimate friends of the two poets. He was chosen to take the *fauteuil* in the French Academy that was left vacant at the death of Racine. His praise of the dramatist in his reception discourse embraced quite naturally a eulogy of Boileau:

Avant que d'exposer au Public ce qu'il (Racine) avait composé il aimait à le faire lire à ces amis pour en voir l'effet, recevant leurs sentimens avec docilité. Mais rien ne l'assuroit davantage sur ses doutes, que les lumières de cet excellent Critique avec qui il étoit lié d'une amitié si célèbre, et je dois, pour l'honneur de l'un et de l'autre, rapporter ici ce qu'il m'a souvent dit lui-même, qu'il ne se croyoit pas plus redevable du succès de la plûpart de ses pièces aux préceptes d'Horace et d'Aristote, qu'aux sages et judicieux conseils d'un ami si éclairé.[219]

This joint praise was no more than what Boileau expected. A very interesting letter of Vuillart [220] is proof that Boileau was very touchy about such matters. The director of the Academy, M. de La Chapelle, in his response to M. de Valincour, praised Racine and the new member who succeeded him both as academician and as historiographer. He did not mention Despréaux. This silence appeared to Boileau " très malhonnête et très offensant." Vuillart tells us that the satirist would already have written " quelque chose de vif " against La Chapelle, if he had not been busy moving, " car il n'est pas aussi mort à lui-même sur pareil cas, qu'on a sujet de croire que l'auroit été M. Racine." The whole affair " lui tient fort au cœur," and Vuillart hopes that time and the distraction of a new dwelling, together with the prayers of his incomparable friend Racine, will allay the emotion caused in him by the slight.

We have, on the other hand, indisputable testimony that, at times, Racine's criticisms weighed heavily upon Boileau.[221] In

[217] Cf. *supra*, pp. 45-48.
[218] D'Olivet, writing the *Histoire de l'Académie française*, asked Valincour to contribute the article on Racine.
[219] Cited in Parfaict, *op. cit.*, X, 214-215.
[220] Written to M. de Préfontaine, July 9, 1699. It is cited by Sainte-Beuve, *Nouveaux Lundis*, X, 384-385.
[221] For the " docilité de Boileau pour la critique," cf. *Article XVI* in Berriat-Saint-Prix's *Essai sur Boileau*. (I, cxix-cxx.)

a letter to Brossette, Despréaux flays his future commentator roundly for going to the " excès du raffinement " in pointing out blemishes in his poems.   He recalls, for Brossette's benefit, how Racine, although he did not go to the same lengths, sometimes showed an over-nicety in his observations and how, on such occasions, the satirist would beg off with a witty misquoting of a Latin proverb:

Feu M. Patru, mon illustre ami, était non seulement un critique très habile, mais un très violent hypercritique, et en réputation de si grande rigidité, qu'il me souvient que, lorsque M. Racine me faisait sur des endroits de mes ouvrages quelque observation un peu trop subtile, comme cela lui arrivait quelquefois, au lieu de lui dire le proverbe latin: *Ne sis patruus mihi,* "n'ayez point pour moi la sévérité d'un oncle"; je lui disais: *"Ne sis Patru mihi.* N'ayez point pour moi la sévérité de Patru! " [222]

It would appear from this letter that, of the two poets, Racine was the severer critic.

When Boileau wrote the *Épître à mes Vers* in 1695, he was an old man living at Auteuil [223] and enjoying the adulation of " plus d'un héros, épris des fruits de mon étude." [224]   But looking back wistfully upon the past, he recalled the time when he was " forming " a generation of poets: [225]

[222] Letter to Brossette dated at Auteuil, Aug. 2, 1703.   (*Œuvres*, IV, 382.)

[223] Racine, in a letter to J.-B. Racine dated July 24, 1698, thus describes the empressement with which Boileau's admirers sought his company: " Il (Boileau) est heureux comme un roi dans sa solitude, ou plutôt dans *son hôtellerie d'Auteuil.*   Je l'appelle ainsi parce qu'il n'y a point de jour où il n'y ait quelque nouvel écot, et souvent deux ou trois qui ne se connoissent pas trop les uns les autres.   Il est heureux de s'accommoder ainsi de tout le monde.   Pour moi, j'aurois cent fois vendu la maison." (Mesnard, VII, 263.)

[224] Vs. 113.

[225] In the case of La Fontaine and of Molière, both some fifteen years older than the critic, the formative influence of Boileau is slight indeed. The former was by nature independent, showing this disposition even in regard to the ancients: " Souvent à marcher seul j'ose me hasarder." (*Épître à Mgr l'Évêque de Soissons, Œuvres,* IX, 202.)

As for Molière, he had won a great victory for " le bon sens " with his *Précieuses Ridicules* in 1659, before Despréaux had appeared on the literary horizon.   From La Fontaine's *Lettre à Maucroix,* it is evident that as early as 1661 " the entire court was under the spell of Molière " and that

Le temps n'est plus, mes Vers, où ma Muse en sa force,
Du Parnasse français *formant les nourrissons,*
De si riches couleurs habillait ses leçons.[226]

This striking expression of the influence he claimed to have
exerted in earlier years came in the year of La Fontaine's death;
Molière had been dead twenty-two years; of his intimate friends,
only Racine was still alive. Boileau's commentators and admirers, especially Brossette [227] and Louis Racine, later endorsed
these pretensions that were part and parcel of Auteuil tradition.
They were accepted by posterity.[228] But what Boileau wrote
in his *Préface* of 1701 is more in accord with the facts. Acknowledging the obligation he is under to the public, he says:

Je ne saurois attribuer un si heureux succès qu'au soin que j'ai pris de
me conformer toujours à ses sentiments, et d'attraper, autant qu'il m'a
été possible, son goût en toutes choses.

De la façon que son nom court
Il doit être par delà Rome (*Œuvres*, IX, 349).

Le Verrier insinuates that Molière was already famous when Boileau
made his acquaintance (Lachèvre, p. 25). The same commentator (p.
55) wrote this interesting remark apropos of *Satire VI:* " Cette satire
plaisoit si fort à Molière qu'il souhaita de la faire entendre à sa femme.
L'autheur ne voulut pas satisfaire sur cela l'empressement de son ami,
de peur que la femme de Molière ne crust l'autheur fort inférieur à son
mari." Although Boileau did not approve of the commentary, his marginal note carries no denial of the truth of the statement, and the
passage in question was not deleted: " Tout ce que vous dites de Molière
est trop petit pour estre raconté." This incident, which would have
occurred sometime after Molière's marriage on Shrove Monday, 1662,
does not argue any formative influence on the part of the critic. When
Despréaux espoused Molière's cause in the quarrel of the *École des
Femmes,* it was, then, the case of a young man with nothing to lose
allying himself with the winning side. The *Critique de l'École des
Femmes, l'Impromptu de Versailles,* at least three acts of *le Tartuffe,*
and *Don Juan* were written during the next two years. In 1666, the
year that saw the publication of the first seven *Satires,* Molière gave
his *Misanthrope.*

[226] Vss. 114-116.

[227] Cf. Brossette's *Avertissement* in his edition of the *Œuvres* (Geneva:
1716): " C'est à M. Despréaux *principalement* que la France est redevable de cette justesse et de cette solidité qui se font remarquer dans
les ouvrages de nos bons écrivains."

[228] Cf. Sainte-Beuve, *Portraits Littéraires,* I, 11, where we read that
Boileau, from 1664 on, was associated with Racine, " dont il devient le
guide et le conseiller. Les dîners de la rue du Vieux-Colombier s'ar-

We state, by way of summary, that at the time of their first meeting, which took place probably in 1663, Racine had signal advantages over Boileau as regards serious preparation for a career of letters. The satirist, three years older than Racine, was to all appearances only finding himself in 1663, and his fame was restricted to the clientèle of certain cabarets. His satire in imitation of Juvenal was still largely moral, rather than literary in character. Racine, on the other hand, had written and published some lyric poetry, and was receiving a gratification from the king. He was soon to win prestige with his first tragedies. His ideas about tragedy were already crystallized, and *Andromaque* and *Britannicus,* one of his most perfectly wrought plays, had been performed before Boileau began his *Art Poétique.*

But during the period of their intimate friendship, which dates very probably from the end of 1670 or the beginning of 1671, the two poets exercised a mutual influence upon each other. While Despréaux was formulating his rules of poetry, Racine was engaged in writing *Bérénice, Bajazet, Mithridate, Iphigénie,* and their remarkable *Préfaces.* He had long since exhausted Aristotle; in his polemical works from the *Préface* of *Alexandre* on, after a pointed allusion to the pleasure manifested by the spectators, the principal thrust at his adversaries was usually an appeal to the practice of the ancients and to the Aristotelian rules, which he considered as more or less of a professional

rangent pour chaque semaine, et Boileau y tient le dé de la critique. Il fréquente les meilleures compagnies . . . et partout ses décisions en matière de goût font loi." Sainte-Beuve goes even farther in his *Causeries du Lundi,* 3rd ed., VI, 511-512. He wonders what would have become of the great writers, were it not for Boileau and Louis XIV. " Racine, je le crains, aurait fait plus souvent des *Bérénices*; La Fontaine moins de *Fables* et plus de *Contes*; Molière lui-même aurait donné davantage dans les Scapins et n'aurait peut-être pas atteint aux hauteurs sévères du *Misanthrope.* En un mot, chacun de ces beaux génies aurait abondé dans ses défauts. Boileau, c'est-à-dire le bon sens du poète critique autorisé et doublé de celui d'un grand roi, les contint et les contraignit, par sa présence respectée, à leurs meilleures et à leurs plus belles œuvres." Nisard held the same opinion: " Il faut songer à l'influence qu'un esprit excellent, ferme sans complaisance, supérieur par la raison, peut exercer même sur des hommes qui le surpassent par l'étendue et la fécondité du génie (*Histoire de la Littérature Française,* II, chap. VI, p. 287).

secret.[229]   That Boileau was admitted into this secret there can be no doubt. Segrais, who as a partisan of Corneille [230] shows a certain antipathy towards the poets,[231] affirms that " leur entretien roule sur la poésie; ôtez-les de là, ils ne savent plus rien." [232] He even goes so far as to say that La Rochefoucauld was thinking of them when he wrote the maxim: " on ne plaît pas longtemps quand on n'a qu'une sorte d'esprit." [233]   Although there is little likelihood that he had them in mind, the fact that Segrais made the application indicates that the two poets were generally known to talk shop. In the next section we shall consider Aristotelian doctrine as the common ground of their literary conversations.

[229] Cf. especially the *Préface* of *Bérénice*, where Racine asks the audience to leave to poets the responsibility of clarifying the rules: " Mais toutes ces règles sont d'un long détail, dont je ne leur conseille pas de s'embarrasser. Ils ont des occupations plus importantes. Qu'ils se reposent sur nous de la fatigue d'éclaircir les difficultés de la *Poétique* d'Aristote: qu'ils se réservent le plaisir de pleurer et d'être attendris; et qu'ils me permettent de leur dire ce qu'un musicien disait à Philippe, roi de Macédoine, qui prétendoit qu'une chanson n'étoit pas selon les règles: ' A Dieu ne plaise, Seigneur, que vous soyez jamais si malheureux que de savoir ces choses-là mieux que moi! ' " Racine can even condone de Villars' ignorance in regard to the rules " puisque heureusement pour le public, il ne s'applique pas à ce genre d'écrire." (*Ibid.*)

[230] Cf. the anecdote in regard to his receiving Corneille's confidence during one of the early performances of *Bajazet*: " Je me garderois bien de le dire à d'autres que vous, parce qu'on diroit que j'en parlerois par jalousie: mais prenez-y garde, il n'y a pas un seul personnage dans le *Bajazet* qui ait les sentiments qu'il doit avoir et que l'on a à Constantinople; ils ont tous, sous un habit turc, le sentiment qu'on a au milieu de la France." (*Segraisiana*, cited by Mesnard, II, 452.)

[231] Gilbert, in the Grands Écrivains ed. of the *Maximes*, points out in this connection one gratuitous gibe at Boileau in Segrais' memoirs. After citing this *pensée* of Mme de la Fayette, " Celui qui se met au-dessus des autres, quelque esprit qu'il ait, se met au-dessous de son esprit," Segrais adds on his own authority: " Despréaux est de ces gens-là." (*Segraisiana*, cited in les *Œuvres de La Rochefoucauld*, I, 186.)

[232] *Segraisiana*, cited by Mesnard, I, 309. Louis Racine protests against the injustice of the remark, especially apropos of his father. Saint-Simon testifies to the courtly manner of Racine: " Personne n'avoit plus de fonds d'esprit, ni plus agréablement tourné; rien du poète dans son commerce et tout de l'honnête homme, de l'homme modeste " (*Mémoires*, Grands Écrivains series, VI, 170-171). Dangeau in his *Journal* (April 20, 1699) substantiates Saint-Simon's testimony.

[233] *Les Maximes*, I, 186. This maxim (CDXIII) appeared for the first time in 1678, in the fifth ed. of *les Maximes*.

THEIR KNOWLEDGE OF THE ANCIENTS

Boileau's Contacts with the Stagirite's Doctrine

M. Bray's remarkable book, *la Formation de la Doctrine Classique en France*, presents systematic and conclusive evidence that up and down the seventeenth century Aristotle was the principal preoccupation not only of French poets and theorists, but of novelists and literary pamphleteers as well. Although there is no theoretical treatise, no critical dissertation however short, almost no preface which does not cite Aristotle,[1] though usually at second hand, one must not conclude that his doctrine was always accepted without reservations. The dissenters, in comparison with the solid and imposing group of Peripatetics were few, however, and their protests feeble. During the five years that Boileau was working on the *Art Poétique*, Aristotelian studies were being pursued with greater intensity than at any time in the seventeenth century.[2] The doctrinaires of the seventies no longer leaned hard on the Italian Renascence critics [3] as d'Aubignac and the earlier French theorists had done. Besides proposing to follow Aristotle more closely than their predecessors, they aimed to add examples and comparisons "pour établir encore davantage les règles qu'il donne."[4] Conscious that their

---

[1] Bray, p. 50.

[2] Le sieur de Norville gave the first French translation of the *Poetics* in 1671. Rapin, after bringing out his work on *Éloquence* had under way the *Réflexions sur la Poétique d'Aristote* (1674). Le Bossu's *Traité du Poème Épique* (*privilège*, 1674) was "by common consent one of the best poetics in the French language" (cf. Boileau, *IIIe Réflexion Critique*, III, 168). Cassandre's French translation of the *Rhetoric* was heralded by Boileau in 1674 (*Préface* to the *Traité du Sublime* in the original collective 8vo edition of his works). Père Vavasseur's *Remarques sur les Nouvelles Réflexions*, a rejoinder to Rapin, appeared in 1675. Bernard Lamy published that same year *la Rhétorique ou l'Art de Parler* and three years later, his *Nouvelles Réflexions sur l'Art Poétique*.

[3] Rapin brands Scaliger a "pure grammarian" (*La Comparaison d'Homère et de Virgile, Œuvres*, I, 99) and admits that Castelvetro complicated rather than explained Aristotle (*Préface* to *Réflexions sur la Poétique, Œuvres*, II, 107).

[4] *Ibid.* (*Œuvres*, II, 108).

mission was an apostleship of taste, they harked back to the works of the ancients as the unfailing pattern of " bon sens " and " nature." [5]

This tendency to go straight to Aristotle does not of course imply that earlier French treatises and practices [6] had no influence on the period in question. For it is impossible not to see a striking continuity in the development of both dramatic theory and technique in France. Boileau's tenets, for example, are by no means the denial of d'Aubignac's theories. Neither is one justified in looking at la Pratique [7] as a complacent summary of Corneille's practice. Even before 1660, when Corneille in his Discours insulted [8] d'Aubignac, thereby inspiring the latter to make corresponding changes [9] for the second edition of his work and later to take up arms against Sophonisbe, Sertorius, and Œdipe,[10] it is clear that the abbé is not satisfied with the existing conditions of the drama. He hints at many new things [11] that are already in the air. Recent studies tend to show that Racine's dramatic system was not a new thing, but rather the natural outgrowth of the Cornelian theater under the psychological, intellectual, and social conditions that prevailed in the late sixties and in the seventies.[12] Among those conditions must be reckoned the renewal of Aristotelian doctrines by sincere attempts to get at the meaning of the original Greek text and to enrich the interpretation of the precepts by a penetrating analysis of the works of the ancients. Racine emphasizes this point when he tells why the abbé de Villars could not be expected to pass any

[5] *Dessein de Cet Ouvrage* prefixed to the collective edition (*ibid.*, I, 2 recto—5 verso).

[6] E. g., the linking of scenes.

[7] Probably begun as early as 1640, although not completed until a few years before 1657, the date of publication. (Cf. H. C. Lancaster, *French Dramatic Literature in the Seventeenth Century*, Part III, Vol. I, 9.)

[8] Cf. *ibid.*, Part III, Vol. I, 13.

[9] The changes remained unpublished in the 17th century. They are indicated by M. Martino in his edition.

[10] These dissertations are discussed by Professor Lancaster, *op. cit.*, Part III, Vol. II, chap. XIII.

[11] E. g., a kind of tragic action that is simple and dependent upon passion (*La Pratique*, pp. 85-86).

[12] Mornet, *Racine, Introduction.* Cf. also Lanson, *Corneille*, pp. 189-190.

sensible judgment on a tragedy: he had apparently never read
Sophocles and " il n'a même jamais rien lu de la *Poétique,* que
dans quelques préfaces de tragédies." [13] After considering the
evidence bearing on Boileau's contacts with the Stagirite's
doctrine, we shall study Racine's rôle in the general movement
culminating in the numerous treatises and comparisons mentioned above.

Gilles Boileau, the academician, may have more or less un-
intentionally [14] directed his younger brother into the field of
critical erudition. He was a translator of no mean repute, having
turned into French Arrian's *Manual of Epictetus* and the *Pinax*
of Cebes. When he died in 1669, he left a partial translation of
Aristotle's *Poetics.* According to d'Olivet, the work was more
than two-thirds completed. Forty years later, Despréaux, eager
to see the translation finished, turned it over to M. de Tourreil.[15]
Now Gilles Boileau's library, doubtless rich in works of the
ancients, was available to Despréaux as for some years both
brothers continued to live in their father's house.[16] Despréaux,
upon devoting himself to letters after his father's death in 1657,
probably found in Gilles' library much to occupy him during the
following years, which, according to Le Verrier, were spent in
studying " dans son cabinet tout ce que l'antiquité nous a laissé
de meilleur." [17]

The brilliant but unbalanced Louis-Henri de Loménie, comte
de Brienne, may have put Boileau in touch with Heinsius' dissertation on Aristotle. Brienne, who until 1663 was Secretary of
State charged with foreign affairs, frequented most assiduously
the savants and literati of his day. Besides being a connoisseur
of art and Roman antiquities, he had what even Boileau deemed

---

[13] *Préface* to *Bérénice.*

[14] Gilles Boileau seems to have been too self-centered to take an
active interest in orienting his younger brother. An academician since
1659, he soon began to take umbrage at Despréaux's growing fame.
The high point of their quarrel seems to have been between the years
1666 and 1668. Cf. Despréaux's *Épigramme sur Gilles Boileau* (*Œuvres,*
II, 453), in which the author says he finds in Gilles an excellent author
and a pleasing poet but not a brother.

[15] D'Olivet, *Histoire de l'Académie française,* II, 107.

[16] They were still living there in 1662. Cf. *supra,* p. 13.

[17] Cf. *supra,* p. 27.

an excessive devotion to poetry. Among his learned corre-
spondents he counted Daniel Heinsius. Although until 1663 the
relations between Brienne and Despréaux were intermittent,[18]
they were close friends from about that time on until Brienne
was obliged to leave France in 1671. When Despréaux had *Satire
VIII* under way, he consulted de Loménie together with La
Fontaine and Racine, if Brossette's account can be trusted.[19]
A letter of Boileau to Brienne written at the time when *le Lutrin*
was being composed is evidence that the satirist eventually
wearied of the " longue audience de vers " with which he had to
pay for Brienne's pleasing conversations; [20] but association for
almost ten years with one who had been the correspondent of the
learned Dutch commentator of Aristotle must have left its mark
on the young poet.[21]

Boileau's conversation with Brossette reported in the latter's
Mémoires indicates that he knew La Mesnardière's *Poétique*.
Boileau, in explaining to Brossette why he had attacked [22] the
" lecteur de la chambre du roi," said that it was because he had
written a very cold tragedy that did not receive even a second
performance. His *Poétique*, however, " toute médiocre qu'elle
étoit " was read as it was considered something new. Boileau
admitted to Brossette that La Mesnardière's treatise proposed
some rather good rules which the author had taken from Aristotle, Horace, and Scaliger.[23] This judgment of the work implies
that the critic had read *la Poétique*.

[18] In a letter of April 9, 1702, Boileau tells Brossette how in his
" early youth " he came to write an epigram against Brienne. Jacques
Boileau, frequently visited by the count, induced Despréaux to write
some Latin verses in praise of " ce fou qualifié " (Brienne). The latter
did so, as de Loménie, on account of his birth and position, was a person to conjure with. Jacques showed the poetry to Brienne, who judged
it unfavorably. It was to avenge his failure that Despréaux wrote the
epigram against the count. It is not likely that the latter ever saw it.
(Laverdet, p. 106.)

[19] His remarks on vs. 129 of *Satire VIII*.   [20] *Œuvres*, IV, 4.

[21] Cf. *Bibliographie Universelle*, XXIV, 650, for the life of Brienne.
Revillout, *RLR*, XXXVII, 106-107, discusses the relations between
Brienne and Boileau apropos of the latter's affiliations with Port-Royal.
Cf. *supra*, pp. 66-67.

[22] *Art Poétique, Chant IV*, vs. 35.

[23] Brossette's *Mémoires* under date of Oct. 21, 1702. (Laverdet, p.
531.)

Despréaux was also familiar with d'Aubignac's *Pratique du Théâtre*, and we shall see that certain lines of the *Art Poétique* appear to be the versification of the *abbé*'s ideas.[24] Boileau, in his third *Réflexion Critique* praises both the man and his works:

J'ai connu M. l'abbé d'Aubignac. Il etait homme de beaucoup de mérite, et fort habile en matière de poétique, bien qu'il sût médiocrement le grec.[25]

Some verses [26] written by the satirist in 1664 to be placed at the beginning of d'Aubignac's novel, *Macarise*, are an additional proof that there existed between them a definite literary, if not personal, relationship. On April 9, 1702, Boileau told Brossette how he happened to write these verses in praise of the stoic philosophy. The author of *Macarise* enjoyed " alors beaucoup de réputation," and Despréaux was apparently flattered by the invitation to write an epigraph for his allegorical novel. Some forty years later he is ashamed to have thus supported a work which " ne fit de chés Sercy, qu'un saut chés l'Épicier ":

Je fis l'Épigramme pour estre mise au-devant de ce Livre, avec quantité d'autres ouvrages que l'Auteur avoit, à l'ancienne mode, *exigés de ses amis* pour le faire valoir; mais heureusement je lui portai l'Épigramme trop tard, et elle ne fut point mise, Dieu en soit loué.[27]

Corneille's *Examens* and *Discours* appearing in 1660 must have been a challenge to the incipient poet trying to cope with Aristotelian doctrine. An exhaustive study of Boileau's attitude toward Corneille during the four or five years following the publication of the *Examens* and *Discours* would lead us, for the purposes of this dissertation, too far afield. Revillout has thus far made the most complete investigation of their relations during those years. One feels, however, that many points remain to be clarified. Revillout adduces strong evidence that Despréaux was drawn into the difficulties that Molière was having with Corneille at this time. In the *Avertissement* to *les Fâcheux* Molière had poked fun at the recently published *Examens* of the older dramatist:

Le temps viendra de faire imprimer mes remarques sur les pièces que j'aurai faites et je ne désespère pas de faire voir un jour, en grand Auteur, que je puis citer Aristote.

---

[24] Cf. *infra*, pp. 220-221.   [26] *Ibid.*, II, 447.
[25] *Œuvres*, III, 162.   [27] Laverdet, p. 107.

Corneille was thought to be involved in the cabal against both the *École des Maris* and the *École des Femmes*. In the latter play Molière had made bold to parody a couplet of *Sertorius*,[28] Corneille's most recent piece. Contemporaries saw in Boileau's *Stances à M. de Molière sur sa Comédie de l'École des Femmes* a neat thrust at Corneille, whom they identified with the "jaloux esprits"[29] and the "envieux"[30] who were caviling at Molière's success. D'Aubignac, inveighing against Corneille, makes precisely this charge:

Il y a longtemps qu'Aristophane l'a dit, il se ronge de chagrin quand un seul poète occupe Paris depuis plusieurs mois . . . et les vers que M. des Préaux a faits sur la dernière pièce de Molière nous en ont assez appris.[31]

It was in the next year that Despréaux, as a "friend" of d'Aubignac, was asked to write an epigraph for the latter's novel. It is possible that their making common cause against the older dramatist had brought them together. Molière, meanwhile, continued to taunt Corneille in the *Critique*.[32]

Some verses in *Satire IV* show us that Boileau, in the manner of Molière, dealt somewhat jauntily with Aristotle in these years. The pedant is the first of the "fous" whom Despréaux fleers:

[28] . . . . "C'est assez
Je suis maître, je parle, allez, obéissez."
(*École des Femmes*, Act II, sc. 6). Cf. *Sertorius*, Act V, sc. 6.
[29] Vs. 1.
[30] Laisse gronder tes envieux:
Ils ont beau crier en tous lieux
. . . .
Si tu savais un peu moins plaire,
Tu ne leur déplairais pas tant. (Vss. 19-20 and 23-24.)

[31] *IVe Dissertation* cited by Revillout, *RLR*, XXXIV, 467. Cf. also the testimony of a friend of Corneille: "Il (Corneille) en avoit de la jalousie, ne pouvant s'empêcher de le témoigner." (*Segraisiana*, Prault's ed., p. 212, cited by Revillout, XXXIV, 466, n. 2.)
[32] Dorante maintains that comedy is a more difficult *genre* than tragedy, that heroes of tragedy "sont des portraits à plaisir, où l'on ne cherche point de ressemblance; et vous n'avez qu'à suivre les traits d'une imagination qui se donne l'essor, et qui souvent laisse le vrai pour attraper le merveilleux. Mais lorsque vous peignez les hommes il faut peindre d'après nature." (*La Critique de l'École des Femmes*, scene 6.)

> Un pédant, enivré de sa vaine science,
> Tout hérissé de grec, tout bouffi d'arrogance
>
> .   .   .   .
>
> Croit qu'un livre fait tout, et que sans Aristote
> La raison ne voit goutte, et le bon sens radote.[33]

This passage, written according to a tradition [34] after a conversation with Le Vayer and Molière, harks back to just such a gibe in the *Critique de l'École des Femmes* of the preceding year. Lysidas, the pedant of the skit, contends that those who possess Aristotle and Horace see at once that the rules are violated in Molière's play. Dorante, the sensible person in the *Critique*, speaks of the rules in a rather casual fashion:

Vous êtes de plaisantes gens avec vos règles, dont vous embarrassez les ignorants et nous étourdissez tous les jours. Il semble, à vous ouïr parler, que ces règles de l'art soient les plus grands mystères du monde; et cependant ce ne sont que quelques observations aisées, que le bon sens a faites sur ce qui peut ôter le plaisir que l'on prend à ces sortes de poèmes: et le même bon sens qui a fait autrefois ces observations les fait aisément tous les jours, sans le secours d'Horace et d'Aristote.[35]

The young satirist in his intense admiration for Molière doubtless hung on his words, and it is not surprising to find that, following the comic poet's example, he incorporated in a satire this fling against the authority of the Stagirite's doctrine. Boileau's serious apprenticeship in Aristotelian studies had not yet begun.

At the end of 1664 [36] Boileau wrote the *Dissertation sur la " Joconde,"* in which there are seven apposite references to Horace. He has faith in the rules. He praises Virgil and Terence and cites a witticism of Quintilian. There are two allusions to Aristotle. But the first—an assertion that Aristotle considered the *Odyssey* " un ouvrage comique " [37]—shows a complete misunderstanding of the passage of the *Poetics* dealing with the early divergence of poetry into serious and comic.[38] When he mentions him again it is merely to remark that it would be as impossible

[33] *Satire IV*, vss. 5-6 and 9-10.

[34] Cf. *supra*, p. 42.

[35] *Critique de l'École des Femmes*, scene 6. Cf. also the *Préface* to *les Précieuses Ridicules*.

[36] Cf. *supra*, pp. 15-16.   [37] Chap. IV.   [38] *Œuvres*, III, 9.

a task to indicate all the faults of Bouillon's *Joconde* as to analyse a song of the Pont-Neuf according to the rules of Aristotle.

He was soon to feel another influence. It was that of a choice gathering of men of letters at the home of the premier président de Lamoignon, a " passionné admirateur de tous les bons livres de l'antiquité." [39] We have seen that, according to Boileau's written testimony, it was at the time when his *Satires* " faisaient le plus de bruit " that he became acquainted with Lamoignon, and that access to the latter's distinguished salon did much to counteract the reputation for libertinage and " mauvaises mœurs " that clung to him.[40] It was, then, about 1666 [41] that the *premier président* accepted Despréaux into the inner circle of his acquaintances. Gui Patin has left two brief accounts of the meetings held on Mondays from five to seven o'clock at Lamoignon's house. The physician tells of attending a supper at the *président*'s " après qu'on fut sorti de son académie de belle littérature." Also present were " seize autres honnêtes gens qui composent cette compagnie." [42] One would conclude from this statement that the academy was a more or less closed circle. We shall see, however, that outsiders sometimes took part in the literary colloquia. The leading spirit of these assemblages was Père Rapin, an erudite Jesuit, who during the last quarter of the century enjoyed great renown as a Latin poet, classical scholar, and historian.[43] This man, whose cultured mind lent its luster to Lamoignon's salon, was to become the life-long friend of Racine and Boileau. Rapin's

[39] *Second Avis au Lecteur* of *le Lutrin*. (*Œuvre*, II, 283.) This *Avis* was originally a part of the general *Préface* to the 1683 edition of Boileau's works.

[40] *Loc. cit.*

[41] Revillout (*RLR*, XXXVII, 150) favors the date 1663 on account of Lamoignon's long association with Jérôme Boileau, *greffier de la grand' chambre*, who would presumably have presented his brother to the *président* before 1666. Boileau's statement is, however, specific and refers doubtless to the time of the first edition of his *Satires*.

[42] *Lettres de Gui Patin*, III, 659. The letter is dated Aug. 12, 1667.

[43] His fame in England once rivalled that of Boileau, *les Réflexions sur la Poétique d'Aristote* having been translated into English by Rymer in the same year in which it appeared in France (1674). Dryden maintains in his *Apology for Heroick Poetry* (1677) that Rapin " is alone sufficient, were all other critics lost, to teach anew the rules of writing." (Cited in *Cambridge Hist. of Eng. Lit.*, VIII, 428.)

deference to Chapelain [44] seems not to have stood in the way of their friendship. Louis Racine,[45] in enumerating the men of letters whom his father and Boileau frequented after the former's retirement from the theater, mentions along with Rapin another distinguished member of Lamoignon's academy. It was Père Bouhours, author of the highly esteemed *Entretiens d'Ariste et d'Eugène*.[46] Pellisson, present on one occasion, spoke learnedly of history and historians.[47] Bossuet, although not a regular member, gave a discourse on the eloquence of the prophets.[48] Lamoignon would himself elaborate sometimes for half an hour on the conference of the day.

It is certain that in these gatherings Aristotle's doctrines were discussed and clarified. In the dedicatory letters of Rapin's critical dissertations, we read the acknowledgment of Lamoignon's part in these works. The latter have not only grown out of the learned discussions carried on in his academy, but are often the development of subjects suggested by the *président* himself. In addressing to him the *Comparaison de Platon et d'Aristote*, Rapin testifies that it is the "troisième volume des Ouvrages que j'ay faits sur les matières que vous avez proposées vous-mesme en cette illustre Assemblée de Sçavans, qui se tient toutes les semaines dans votre maison." [49] Rapin's *Réflexions sur la Philosophie*, likewise dedicated to Lamoignon, was the sixth of the volumes for which the inspiration had come to him from

---

[44] Chapelain, in a letter of Aug. 20, 1663, to M. Le Fèvre of Saumur calls Rapin his "ami intime." (*Lettres*, II, 323.)

[45] "Ceux qu'ils (Racine and Boileau) voyoient le plus souvent étoient les PP. Bourdaloue, Bouhours, et Rapin, le comte de Tréville, MM. Nicole, Valincour, la Bruyère, la Fontaine, et Bernier." (*Mémoires*, Mesnard, I, 310.)

[46] Sébastien Mabre-Cramoisy brought out this work in 1671. His *opus magnum* was *les Remarques sur la Langue française* (1675). He also gave in 1687 his platonic dialogue, *De la manière de bien penser dans les Ouvrages de l'esprit*. Bouhours, while inveighing against the preciousness of the Italians seems to have frequently fallen into similar faults of taste and merited for himself the title of "Empeseur des Muses." (Vigneul-Marville's *Mélanges*, 2nd ed. (1702), I, 78, cited by Revillout, *RLR*, XXXVII, 172.)

[47] *Lettres de Gui Patin*, III, 775. The letter is dated Jan. 14, 1671.

[48] Revillout, *RLR*, XXXVII, 174.

[49] *Œuvres*, I, 272. The *Épistre is dated* Aug. 20, 1678.

these learned conferences.[50] The printer informs us that the *Comparaison de Pindare et d'Horace* was originally a conference requested of Rapin on the subject that had been under discussion in that assembly.[51] In the work itself, addressed directly to Lamoignon, Rapin speaks of the blind obedience he owes to a command of the *président* and gives forthwith the results of his research on the two poets.[52] Again he reminds Lamoignon that it is by his order that he defends the interests of Virgil against a distinguished gentleman who had upheld those of Homer.[53] These indications, together with the fact that Rapin brought out his learned *Réflexions sur la Poétique* in the same year in which Boileau's *Art Poétique* appeared, are evidence that Lamoignon's academy was especially preoccupied with questions of poetics during the years when Boileau was composing his work and that the latter gained much from contact with a man whose treatises are quite generally conceded to show even finer nuances than his own.[54] It is significant that, according to Rapin, Boileau's masterpiece was not the *Art Poétique*, but the *Traduction de Longin,* " qui a plus l'air d'original que de traduction." [55] Both men are persuaded that genius does not go far without the aid of rules; [56] the same apotheosis of nature [57] and " bon sens " [58]

[50] The dedication dated May 10, 1676. (*Œuvres*, II, p. 325, in this edition wrongly numbered 227.)

[51] *L'Imprimeur au Lecteur.* (*Œuvres*, I, 435.)   [52] *Ibid.*, I, 437.

[53] *Épistre*, Oct. 10, 1668, preceding *la Comparaison d'Homère et de Virgile.* (*Œuvres*, I, 96.)

[54] Cf. Bédier et Hazard, *Hist. de la litt. fr. illustrée*, II, 29. Boileau's work, although more cursory in its treatment, was destined by virtue of its epigramatic style, piquant allusions, and vigorous tone to have the greater influence.

[55] *Du Grand ou du Sublime dans les Mœurs.* (*Œuvres*, II, 502.)

[56] " On ne peut plaire sûrement que par les règles." (*Réflexions sur la Poétique*, chap. XI; *Œuvres*, II, 118.)

[57] " A bien considérer ces regles, on trouvera qu'elles ne sont faites que pour reduire *la Nature en methode*, pour la suivre pas à pas, et pour n'en laisser échapper aucun trait." (*Ibid.*, chap. XI, *Œuvres*, II, 120.) In speaking of comedy, Rapin exhorts the poet to stay close to nature " car il faut bien se mettre dans l'esprit, que les traits les plus grossiers de la Nature, quels qu'ils soient, plaisent toûjours davantage, que les traits les plus délicats, qui sont hors du naturel " (*Ibid.*, chap. XXV, *Œuvres*, II, 198).

[58] " Enfin c'est par ces règles que tout devient juste, proportionné,

runs through their works. Boileau's marked devotion to Horace [59] may be due, at least in part, to the influence of Rapin, who venerated the author of the *Epistula ad Pisones* as the "premier Interprète d'Aristote." [60] A letter of Racine's [61] indicates that Boileau, as well as the dramatist, might also have gained something by way of poetics from his contacts with Père Bouhours. In sending him one of his plays,[62] Racine asks this "excellent master of the language" to note down not only linguistic errors, but those "d'une autre nature," if he finds any. He is to pass it on to Père Rapin if the latter can take a few minutes to read it.

Was Boileau a regular member of Lamoignon's select coterie? Dejob [63] thinks that he was not. We know certainly that Despréaux was an assiduous visitor at Lamoignon's house and that he found there especial favor with the host.

An incident [64] occurring in 1667 is proof that Despréaux was confident of being very firmly established in the good graces of

naturel, étant comme elles sont fondées sur le bon sens et sur la Raison, plus que sur l'autorité & sur l'exemple" (*ibid.*, chap. XI, *Œuvres*, II, 120). Cf. also *le Dessein de cet Ouvrage* where Rapin recommends the works of the ancients as "les sources les plus pures . . . d'où se forme le bon sens, & d'où naist ce discernement admirable, par lequel on distingue le vray d'avec le faux dans les beautez de la nature, auxquelles il faut s'attacher pour bien sentir celles de l'art. . . . Il n'y a rien de faux dans leur (the ancients) esprit, rien d'égaré dans leurs manières, rien d'affecté dans leur caractère: tout y va au bon sens pour lequel ils avoient un goût si seur, que ces expressions brillantes, qui éblouïssent les gens du commun, & tout cet attirail de beaux sentimens, & de belles pensées leur estoient entièrement inconnuës." (*Œuvres*, I, 2 verso-3 verso.)

[59] Cf. *Préface* for the 12mo editions of 1674 and 1675. Despréaux ironically thanks his critics who have noised abroad that his *Art Poétique* is merely the translation of Horace's, "car, puisque dans mon ouvrage, qui est d'onze cents vers, il n'y en a pas plus de cinquante ou soixante, tout au plus, imités d'Horace, ils ne peuvent pas faire un plus bel éloge du reste qu'en le supposant traduit de ce grand poète; et je m'étonne après cela qu'ils osent combattre les règles que j'y débite."

[60] *Réflexions sur la Poétique*, chap. VII. (*Œuvres*, II, 115.)

[61] Mesnard, VI, 528-529.

[62] *Phèdre*, if Mesnard's dating is correct. (*Loc. cit.*)

[63] *De Renato Rapino*, Parisiis, ap. Thorin, 1881, p. 16. The content is given by Revillout, *RLR*, XXXVII, 172.

[64] We are following the version given in Brossette's *Mémoires* written after a conversation with Boileau on Nov. 9, 1702. (Laverdet, 564-565.)

the *premier président*. The latter was charged with the admini-
stration and police of Paris while the king was away on his
campaign in Flanders. Before his departure, Louis XIV at the
behest of Madame [65] had authorized the public performance of
Tartuffe. It was played accordingly on August fifth. The *premier
président*, deeming the play dangerous, forthwith forbade the
performance announced for the following day. One of the
officers of Madame, who was, of course, piqued by the magistrate's
action, undertook to speak to Lamoignon in behalf of Her Royal
Highness, but " il gâta tout et compromit Madame avec M. de
Lamoignon." She had been so rebuffed that when the *président*
paid her a visit a few days afterward in order to conclude the
affair, she did not dare to broach the question of *Tartuffe* : neither
did he mention it, and the matter was dropped. That *démarche*
failing, Molière had recourse to Boileau, asking him to intercede
with Lamoignon in the interests of the play. Despréaux, however, counselled Molière to speak in his own behalf and offered
to introduce him to the *président*. They went together to see
Lamoignon. The latter, mingling his reproaches with highest
praise of the actor and of the man, told Molière that it was
nevertheless unseemly that comedians should attempt to instruct
men in Christian morals and religion, and " par un refus
gracieux " he gave him to understand that the suspension would
not be revoked. Molière " demeure entièrement déconcerté, de
sorte qu'il lui fut impossible de répondre à M. le premier président." Attempting to defend his comedy, " il ne fit que
bégaier et ne put point calmer le trouble où l'avoit jeté Monsieur
le premier président." It is true that Despréaux seems not to
have had on this occasion the courage to speak out in favor of
his friend, but under the circumstances to have dared present
the poet to Lamoignon was at once a proof of his affection for
Molière and of the security that he felt in regard to his standing
with the *président*. The latter's kindly disposition toward
Despréaux doubtless had much to do with the graciousness of
the refusal that Molière received in contrast to the snub previously
dealt the princess.

We have seen [66] that in November of the following year Boileau,
because he enjoyed the protection of the *premier président*,

---

[65] Henriette d'Angleterre, first wife of Monsieur.
[66] Cf. *supra*, pp. 75-76.

succeeded in getting an injunction forbidding the performance
of Boursault's *Satire des Satires*. The sale of the printed play
was stopped in a like manner.

According to tradition Lamoignon was much amused by the
mischievousness of Boileau's *Arrêt Burlesque* in 1671. It is said
that the greffier Dongois, Despréaux's nephew, presented this
Arrêt together with some other documents to the *président* for
his signature. The magistrate, who read everything before sign-
ing it, discovered the travesty and exclaimed to Dongois: " Ah!
voilà un tour de ton oncle! " [67]

Boileau, in what was originally the general *Préface* for the
collective edition of his works in 1683, sums up his relations
with the *premier président*, whom he portrays as Ariste in the
poem:

> J'eus donc le bonheur de ne lui être pas désagréable. Il m'appela à
> tous ses plaisirs et à tous ses divertissements, c'est-à-dire à ses lectures
> et à ses promenades. Il me favorisa même quelquefois de sa plus
> étroite confidence, et me fit voir à fond son âme entière. . . . Je fus
> sincèrement épris de tant de qualités admirables; et s'il eut beaucoup
> de bonne volonté pour moi, j'eus aussi pour lui une très forte attache.[68]

Now it is to be noted that Boileau in his *Avis* does not mention
the academy as such although he had two excellent occasions of
doing so: one in the passage just cited, the other in the eulogy of
Lamoignon's erudition and, in particular, of his devotion to
the ancients.[69] A remark in the first *Avis au Lecteur* in 1674
is the only allusion to anything like the academy that Boileau
himself makes. In regard to the genesis of his poem, the author
says:

> Il n'y a pas long-temps que *dans une assemblée* où j'étais, la conversa-
> tion tomba sur le poème héroïque. Chacun en parla suivant ses
> lumières. A l'égard de moi, comme on m'en eut demandé mon avis, je
> soutins ce que j'ai avancé dans ma poétique: qu'un poëme héroïque,

---

[67] Saint-Marc questions the authenticity of this anecdote. It does not
jar, however, with what we know of the gayety of both Boileau and
Lamoignon. Cf. *infra*, p. 101, n. 71.

[68] *L'Avis au Lecteur* for the 1701 edition of *le Lutrin*. (II, 283-284.)

[69] " C'était un homme d'un savoir étonnant, et passionné admirateur
de tous les bons livres de l'antiquité; et c'est ce qui lui fit plus aisément
souffrir mes ouvrages, où il crut entrevoir quelque goût des anciens."
(*Loc. cit.*)

pour être excellent, devait être chargé de peu de matière, et que c'était
à l'invention à la soutenir et à l'étendre. La chose fut fort contestée.[70]

The argument having subsided, the conversation turned to a
genial discussion of how easy it is to get wrought up over trifles.
Someone happened to tell of the altercation that arose in a small
church *in the provinces* between the treasurer and the precentor,
who differed in their opinions as to where the lectern should be
placed. Everyone agreed that this was indeed trivial matter for
a quarrel, and by way of rallying Boileau for what he had just
said in regard to the epic someone asked him if such a squabble
were a sufficiently meager subject for a heroic poem. Without
reflecting, he replied that it was quite suitable; then, in order
to make good his boast, he set to work on *le Lutrin* that very
night.

Now what was the assembly of which Boileau spoke in the
Préface to his poem? The subject treated, the vivacity of the
arguments, as well as the sprightly banter,[71] are in keeping with
what we know of the gatherings held at the home of the *premier
président*. His letter to Brienne [72] mentioned above is proof,

---

[70] *Ibid.*, II, 280.

[71] There is abundant evidence that Lamoignon, magistrate though he
was, liked gayety in his intellectual diversions. According to the
Ménagiana, " ce fut pour divertir M. le premier président de Lamoignon
plus que pour autre chose, que M. Boileau (probably Gilles) parodia
quelques endroits du *Cid* sur Chapelain, Cassagne et la Serre " (1694
ed., p. 44, cited by Revillout, *RLR*, XXXVII, 150). We have seen that
he was much amused by the *Arrêt Burlesque*. Brossette tells of a practical joke he is said to have played on Chapelain. He was delighted
with Boileau's quatrain against the author of *la Pucelle*:

> Maudit soit l'auteur dur, dont l'âpre et rude verve,
> Son cerveau tenaillant, rima malgré Minerve;
> Et, de son lourd Marteau martelant le bon sens,
> A fait de méchants vers douze fois douze cents.

Lamoignon, after reading it, sent to Billaine's bookshop for a copy of
la Pucelle, inscribed on the first page of it these verses of Despréaux,
and then returned the book to Billaine (Brossette's remarks on *Épigramme VIII*). Boileau himself said that, although Lamoignon's piety
was very sincere, " elle étoit aussi fort gaie, et n'avoit rien d'embarras-
sant (*Avis au Lecteur* for the 1701 edition of *le Lutrin*, originally a
part of the general *Préface* to the collective edition of 1683 (*Œuvres*,
II, 283).

[72] *Œuvres*, IV, 3-4.

moreover, that Despréaux, while the poem was yet in its early stages, gave a reading of *le Lutrin* in Lamoignon's house, quite likely for the delectation of the group that had seen its small beginnings.

That Boileau in his first *Avis* referred to an assembly at Lamoignon's home becomes reasonably certain in the light of what he wrote in the general *Préface* to the collective edition of his works in the year 1683. A part of this *Préface* was later detached and became the *Second Avis* for the edition of *le Lutrin* in 1701. We shall speak of it as the *Second Avis,* bearing in mind, however, that it was composed in 1683. Boileau admits in this later preface that there is no longer any use denying that the quarrel celebrated in his poem took place in one of the best known churches [73] of Paris. What he said, then, in the first *Avis* about a provincial's relating the dispute as having happened in his own province was evidently calculated to throw the reader off the track as regards the persons portrayed in the poem. In truth, to keep people from identifying his characters with their originals still seems to be the rather futile preoccupation of the author in the *Second Avis.* Now in the latter preface, Boileau does not mention an assembly where epic poetry was under discussion, nor does he go into any detail concerning the origin of the poem except to say that M. de Lamoignon had a part in it. This information, moreover, serves principally as a pretext for a long encomium on his friend. He wrote:

Je ne dirai point comment je fus engagé à travailler à cette bagatelle *sur une espèce de défi,* qui me fut fait en riant par feu M. le premier président de Lamoignon, qui est celui que j'y peins sous le nom d'Ariste. Ce détail, à mon avis, n'est pas fort nécessaire. Mais je croirais me faire un trop grand tort, si je laissais échapper cette occasion d'apprendre à ceux qui l'ignorent, que ce grand personnage, durant sa vie, m'a honoré de son amitié.[74]

Now what of the detailed account of Boileau's inspiration as given in the first *Avis?* Some, thinking the entire preface was intended to gull the reader, are inclined to discount it in gross. It seems quite possible, however, to reconcile the two versions.

---

[73] La Sainte-Chapelle.   Cf. *Mémoires* of Brossette, Nov. 2, 1702. (Laverdet, 561.)

[74] *Œuvres*, II, 282-283.

Boileau in the first account would have substituted "un pro-vincial" for M. de Lamoignon, thus contriving to put the reader on the wrong scent. Why should he have changed the version later on? There are two probable reasons. In the first place, the ecclesiastical quarrel in Paris having leaked out meantime, there was no use trying to keep up the pretense that he was burlesquing an incident that occurred in the provinces. Besides, M. de Lamoignon had died in the interval between the two *Avis*. Boileau would naturally feel more at liberty to cite his name, and he took that opportunity of turning the *Second Avis* into a eulogy of his friend.

We should say, in conclusion, that "une espèce de défi qui me fut fait en riant par feu M. le premier président" harmonizes perfectly with everything said in the first *Avis* except the name of the person who related the quarrel. Boileau had at that time good reasons for not wishing to divulge information that would give an inkling as to whom his characters were patterned after. The other details including the assembly where the epic was being discussed and Boileau's presence there are very probably true. Despréaux, if not a regular member of the academy, was, then, at least an occasional guest in that restricted circle where he must have come under a strong Aristotelian influence.

Despréaux's enthusiasm for a work of Aristotle is attested by a notice inserted in the second edition [75] of the *Traité du Sublime*. The *Préface* announced a forthcoming translation of the *Rhetoric* by M. Cassandre, the friend and secretary of Patru. After vouching for the clarity and fidelity of the translation, Boileau wrote this extravagant praise of the work that we know to contain illuminating passages on tragic pity and fear:

C'est un Ouvrage d'une extrême utilité pour moi, j'avoue franchement que sa lecture m'a plus profité que tout ce que j'ai jamais lu en ma vie.[76]

Although this announcement, deleted in later editions, was cal-culated to aid a deserving friend,[77] there can be no doubt of Boileau's sincere admiration for Aristotle's work.

[75] Cf. *supra*, p. 88, n. 2.   [76] Magne, I, 229-230.

[77] Brossette got this information from Boileau in a conversation re-corded in his *Mémoires* on Oct. 8, 1702. After speaking of the dire poverty in which Cassandre (the original of Damon in *Satire I*) lived, Brossette wrote: "M. Despréaux dans une de ses éditions, à la fin de

The *Bolœana* is responsible for two anecdotes which, if they were known to be exact, would show how ready Boileau was to flaunt his knowledge of Aristotle in the face of impertinent dilettanti, or even of more formidable adversaries, if the occasion arose. Monchesnay [78] relates how Despréaux, curious to get a look at Chapelain, begged Racine to take him incognito to pay a visit to the famous author of *la Pucelle*. The satirist, disguised as the Bailli de Chevreuse, accompanied Racine to Chapelain's house. During the visit the host nettled Boileau by contending that the comedies of Ariosto surpassed those of all the ancients and moderns. To Despréaux's persistent question, "What of Terence?" Chapelain would only answer that the Latin poet's style was pure; then he would straightway revert to Ariosto. Boileau all but flew into a rage. He was on the point of forgetting that he was, for the time being, the Bailli de Chevreuse, and of proving to Chapelain " par Aristote qu'il étoit éloigné de la droite raison." M. Racine saved the day, however, by rising suddenly and taking leave before Boileau had given himself away by an imprudent advertence to Aristotle. Although there are details in this anecdote that appear to be inexact.[79] the main

la préface de Longin, a parlé avantageusement d'une traduction que Cassandre avoit faite de la poëtique (Brossette is in error here) d'Aristote: et M. Despréaux ne le fit que par charité pour faire vendre le livre de Cassandre, afin que le libraire fît quelque gratification à ce pauvre auteur, et cela réussit sur le suffrage de M. Despréaux." (Laverdet, 524.)

[78] *Bolœana*, pp. 135-136.

[79] The incident would have occurred between the meeting of Racine and Boileau in 1663-1664 and the publication of the *Satires*, as it is improbable that Chapelain would not have recognized Boileau after that event. We have seen that, according to a letter of Chapelain written on March 13, 1665, the latter knew neither the "person" or the "name" of Despréaux at the time when he first attacked him. Now it is quite impossible that between the years 1663 and 1666 Racine and Boileau were on sufficiently intimate terms to plot the imposture in question. Racine respected Chapelain too much to dupe him in that manner. Boileau might, however, have had a somewhat similar adventure with someone besides Racine. We are already quite familiar with the tendency of anecdotists to interpolate Racine's name in their accounts of incidents that happened to Boileau and vice versa. It is also quite unlikely that Chapelain should prefer Ariosto to Terence. Cf. nevertheless his enthusiastic praise of La Fontaine's *Contes* written in the manner of Ariosto, *supra*, p. 24, n. 48.

point, namely, that in order to confound Chapelain Boileau was
tempted to invoke Aristotle's authority, bespeaks, if it is true,
not only an intimate knowledge of the rules, but even a certain
audacity on the part of the younger man who would venture to
lock horns with the author of *les Sentiments de l'Académie
française sur le " Cid."*

According to the second anecdote vouched for by Monchesnay,
Boileau, unhampered this time by any disguise and bridling in
his knowledge of Aristotle, quite overwhelmed no less a personage
than M. de Seignelay [80] by leveling at him six of the Stagirite's
most important precepts. The incident, if the details are exact,
would have occurred in 1679.[81] After a dinner at Seignelay's
house, the host, knowing that Despréaux had collaborated with
Thomas Corneille on the *Bellérophon,* was haggling him for
what he considered a want of verisimilitude in the piece. The
details, and in particular Boileau's assertion that *la Poétique* had
always been his principal preoccupation, are pertinent to our
study. The critic is reported to have said:

Après m'avoir harcelé par plusieurs raisons qui n'étoient pas tré-
buchantes, croiant m'avoir mis au pied du mur, il me dit avec un sourire
amer & dédaigneux: Répondez, répondez à cela. Comme je vis que la
chose étoit poussée avec une hauteur qui ne me convenoit pas, j'eus le
courage de lui dire: Monsieur, *j'ai toujours fait ma principale étude
de la Poétique,* tout le monde convient même que j'en ai écrit avec assez
de succès; si vous voulez que je vous réponde, il faut que vous consentiez
que je vous instruise au moins trois jours de suite. Après cela je lui
décochai six préceptes des plus importans d'Aristote. Il se sentit battu.
Toute la compagnie rioit dans l'âme, & Monsieur Racine en sortant me
dit: O le brave homme que vous êtes! Achille en personne n'auroit pas
mieux combattu que vous.[82]

Boileau recalled, during a conversation with Brossette, how
he had quelled a certain M. de Beaumont, with whom he was discussing the relative merits of Racine's and Pradon's *Phèdre.*
During the course of a supper at Mme de Broglio's, de Beaumont
declared that Pradon's play was more regular than Racine's.
Boileau, in defending his friend's tragedy, wittingly made use

[80] Boileau was on intimate terms with Colbert's son, having dedicated
to him his *Épître IX* (1675).

[81] The opera was performed in February, 1679. Cf. Mesnard, I, 272,
n. 2.

[82] *Bolœana,* pp. 8-9.

of technical terms unintelligible to his adversary, thus proving
that de Beaumont, in the actual state of his knowledge, had no
business even to talk about the rules:

Hâ! ce n'est donc plus des règles que vous parlez, lui dit M. Despréaux.
Or je m'en vais vous faire voir par les règles mêmes, combien vous vous
trompez. La péripétie et l'agnition se doivent rencontrer ensemble dans
la tragédie: et c'est ce qui arrive dans la Phèdre de M. Racine, et qui
n'est point dans celle de Pradon. . . . M. de Beaumont interrompit M.
Despréaux pour lui demander ce que c'étoit que *la péripétie* et *l'agnition*.[83] Hà, hà, lui répondit M. Despréaux, vous voulez parler des règles,
et vous n'en entendez pas même les termes. Apprenez à ne pas vouloir
disputer d'une chose que vous n'avez jamais apprise.[84]

From the examples of Boileau's familiarity with the ancients
that we have adduced thus far, it is evident that he leaned especially toward the critical works of antiquity. There will be
occasion later on in this study to consider in detail his especial
indebtedness to Horace. He undertook for his own instruction
a translation of *le Traité du Sublime* and, according to the
Préface of 1674 and 1675, brought it out as a sort of appendage
to the *Art Poétique*:

J'ai fait originairement cette traduction pour m'instruire, plutôt que
dans le dessein de la donner au public; mais j'ai cru qu'on ne serait pas
fâché de la voir ici à la suite de la *Poétique*, avec laquelle ce traité a
quelque rapport, et où j'ai même inséré plusieurs préceptes qui en sont
tirés.[85]

A eulogy of Sophocles in the *Art Poétique*,[86] although an addition to the parallel passage in Horace,[87] and a few scattered and

---

[83] The italics are Brossette's.
[84] Brossette's *Mémoires* written on Nov. 9, 1702. (Laverdet, p. 566.)
[85] Preface for the 4to ed. of 1674 and the 12mo ed. of 1674 and 1675.
(*Œuvres*, I, 6-7.)
[86] After giving the contributions of Thespis and Æschylus, Boileau
concludes his history of the development of Greek tragedy with these
verses:
> Sophocle enfin, donnant l'essor à son génie,
> Accrut encor la pompe, augmenta l'harmonie;
> Intéressa le chœur dans toute l'action;
> Des vers trop raboteux polit l'expression;
> Lui donna chez les Grecs cette hauteur divine
> Où jamais n'atteignit la faiblesse latine.
> > (*Chant III*, vss. 75-80.)
[87] *Ars Poetica*, vss. 275-280.

vague references to Sophocles and Euripides in works occasioned
by the quarrel of the Ancients and Moderns [88] are not sufficient
proof to convince us that Boileau had anything like the same
long and familiar intercourse with the Greek dramatists that we
know Racine to have enjoyed.

Racine's Familiarity with Greek Tragedy and with Aristotle

When we come to consider the case of Racine, we are at once
impressed by the insistence with which his devotion to Sophocles
and Euripides is recalled by nearly all contemporary witnesses.
Despréaux in his *Épître VII* addresses his friend thus:

> Toi donc, qui t'élevant sur la scène tragique,
> Suis les pas de Sophocle, et, seul de tant d'esprits,
> De Corneille vieilli sais consoler Paris . . . [1]

Ten years later,[2] in some verses to be inscribed below a portrait of
his friend, it is no longer a question of his imitating the ancients.
Racine's art, he tells us, vies with that of Sophocles and
Euripides:

> Du théâtre français l'honneur et la merveille,
> Il sut ressusciter Sophocle en ses écrits;
> Et, dans l'art d'enchanter les cœurs et les esprits,
> Surpasser Euripide, et balancer Corneille.[3]

In the famous letter to Perrault written the year after Racine's
death, Boileau, by grace of circumstances, sets at naught his own

---

[88] Cf. his suspended judgment on the relative greatness of Corneille
and Racine: "La postérité jugera qui vaut le mieux des deux; car je
suis persuadé que les écrits de l'un et de l'autre passeront aux siècles
suivants. Mais jusque-là ni l'un ni l'autre ne doit être mis en parallèle
avec Euripide et avec Sophocle, puisque leurs ouvrages n'ont point encore
le sceau qu'ont les ouvrages d'Euripide et de Sophocle, je veux dire
l'approbation de plusieurs siècles." (*VIIᵉ Réflexion, Œuvres*, III, 247.)

[1] Vss. 40-42.

[2] The first verse, which is a take-off on a line of Perrault's *Poème du
Siècle de Louis le Grand*, indicates that Boileau's poem was composed
in 1687 or shortly after that date.

[3] According to Brossette, Boileau first wrote "Balancer Euripide et
surpasser Corneille." He altered the verse in favor of the admirers of
Corneille's theater, but would not be sorry if some critic would later on
restore the original version.

prerogatives and puts this question to the advocate of the moderns: " Pouvez-vous ne pas convenir que ce sont Sophocle et Euripide qui ont formé M. Racine? " [4]   Valincour who said he had spent " la plus belle partie de mes jours " [5] with Racine, having been for nearly twenty years his " ami de toutes les heures," recalls to the academicians in his reception discourse how Racine spent entire days in the woods around Port-Royal reading Homer, Sophocles, and Euripides, whose language was already as familiar to him as his own.[6] Again in his letter to d'Olivet,[7] Valincour asserts the same fondness of Racine for the Greek poets:

Les tragédies de Sophocle et d'Euripide l'enchantèrent à un tel point qu'il passoit les journées à les lire et à les apprendre par cœur, dans les bois qui sont autour de l'étang de Port-Royal.[8]

Louis Racine in the *Mémoires* [9] and J.-B. Racine in the *Avant-Propos* prepared for an edition of his father's correspondence strengthen Valincour's assertion, the elder son adding, to the credit of Racine's prodigious memory, that in later life he " récitoit quelquefois en grec des scènes entières de Sophocle et d'Euripide qu'il avoit apprises dans sa jeunesse." [10] Louis Racine draws upon Valincour's letter to d'Olivet [11] for an example of the

---

[4] *Œuvres*, IV, 90.

[5] *Histoire de l'Académie française*, II, 327-328.

[6] The discourse is cited by Parfaict, *op. cit.*, X, 209.

[7] It was written at the request of d'Olivet for the article " Racine " in the *Hist. de l'Acad. fr.* It occupied some thirteen pages in the edition of 1730. In a letter to the président Bouhier, dated Dec. 1, 1729, Valincour says he dictated it at Fontainebleau " *stans pede in uno*, et étant fort tourmenté de mon rheumatisme." He sent it off without re-reading it, never dreaming that it would be printed " ainsi tout cru et sans avoir été retouché." (Edited in *RHLF* (1924), XXXI, 401.)

[8] *Hist. de l'Acad. fr.*, II, p. 329.

[9] " Au milieu de ces occupations (his studies), son génie l'entraînoit tout entier du côté de la poésie, et son plus grand plaisir étoit de s'aller enfoncer dans les bois de l'abbaye avec Sophocle et Euripide, qu'il savoit presque par cœur " (Mesnard, I, 219). In speaking of *Britannicus*, L. Racine says: " Cette pièce fit connoître que l'auteur n'étoit pas seule-ment rempli des poëtes grecs, et qu'il savoit également imiter les fameux écrivains de l'antiquité " (*Mémoires*, Mesnard, I, 253).

[10] The *Avant-Propos* is cited by Mesnard, VI, 382-383, footnote to *Lettre* 2.

[11] *Hist. de l'Acad. fr.*, II, 335-336

poet's elation while reading Sophocles aloud. In a gathering at Auteuil, M. Nicole and Valincour being present among others, someone spoke of Sophocles, whereupon Racine took up a Greek text and read the *Œdipus* turning it into French as he went. Louis Racine wrote of the incident as follows:

On vint à parler de Sophocle, dont il étoit si grand admirateur qu'il n'avoit jamais osé prendre un de ses sujets de tragédie. Plein de cette pensée, il prend un Sophocle grec, et lit la tragédie d'Œdipe, en la traduisant sur-le-champ. Il s'émut à tel point, dit M. de Valincour, que tous les auditeurs éprouvèrent les sentiments de terreur et de pitié dont cette pièce est pleine. " J'ai vu, ajoute-t-il, nos meilleures pièces représentées par nos meilleurs acteurs : rien n'a jamais approché du trouble où me jeta ce récit; et au moment que j'écris, je m'imagine voir encore Racine le livre à la main, et nous tous consternés autour de lui." [12]

Before passing to a detailed study of Racine's library and of his annotations on the Greek tragedies, we may profitably recall the impassioned devotion to the ancients expressed in his first letter to Nicole in the year 1666. He mocks Nicole's effete denunciation of poets, nothwithstanding which

Sophocle, Euripide, Térence, Homère et Virgile nous sont encore en vénération, comme ils l'ont été dans Athènes et dans Rome. Le temps, qui a abattu les statues qu'on leur a élevées à tous, et les temples mêmes qu'on a élevés à quelques-uns d'eux, n'a pas empêché que leur mémoire ne vînt jusqu'à nous. Notre siècle, qui ne croit pas être obligé de suivre votre jugement en toutes choses, nous donne tous les jours les marques de l'estime qu'il fait de ces sortes d'ouvrages, dont vous parlez avec tant de mépris; et malgré toutes ces maximes sévères que toujours quelque passion vous inspire, il ose prendre la liberté de considérer toutes les personnes en qui l'on voit luire quelques étincelles du feu qui échauffa autrefois ces grands génies de l'antiquité.[13]

We shall see in the course of this study [14] that Racine's *Préfaces* abound in tributes to the ancients and in generous acknowledgments of his indebtedness to them. Let one example suffice at this point. Although obliged to depart from Euripides in the dénouement of *Iphigénie,* he owns having followed him closely in the matter of the passions. It was indeed a goodly number

---

[12] *Mémoires, ibid.*, I, 307-308.

[13] *Lettre à l'Auteur des* Imaginaires. (Mesnard, IV, 285-286.)

[14] Cf. *infra*, pp. 121 *et sqq.*

of passages exactly imitated from the Greek that had won for
him the most hearty approval on the French stage:

J'avoue que je lui dois un bon nombre des endroits qui ont été les plus
approuvés dans ma tragédie.   Et je l'avoue d'autant plus volontiers,
que ces approbations m'ont confirmé dans l'estime et dans la vénération
que j'ai toujours eu pour les ouvrages qui nous restent de l'antiquité.[15]

That Racine's devotion to Euripides and Sophocles was not
to the detriment of his knowledge of the critical works of the
ancients will appear in the course of this investigation.   Valincour, in his reception discourse at the French Academy, wishing
to pay due honor to Boileau, avers that he often heard Racine
say that the success of most of his plays was due as much to the
judicious counsels of his friend as to the precepts of Horace and
Aristotle.[16]   In vouching for the quality of his father's translation of the *Poetics,* Louis Racine says:

Ce traducteur devoit entendre Aristote, *dont il avoit si bien profité.*[17]

Paul Bonnefon made an exhaustive study [18] of the books included in Racine's library.   He used as a starting point an inventory drawn up for Racine's heirs.[19]   It was discovered by M. le
vicomte de Grouchy and published in 1892 in the *Bulletin du
Bibliophile.*   Of the 1539 volumes that figure in this "état
estimatif," 319 exact titles are given, the rest being simply
included in the grand total.   Bonnefon found in various libraries
seventy-seven additional books belonging to Racine and for some
reason not included in the inventory.   This bibliographer considers that about fifteen of these books may be identified with
works designated somewhat vaguely in the inventory.   We know
the titles, then, of about 380 works possessed by Racine.   Holy
Scripture, books of exegesis, and biblical commentaries abound.
As one would expect, the historiographer's library is especially
complete as regards books dealing with the history of France.
Modern works treating Roman history are more numerous than

[15] *Préface* (1675) to *Iphigénie.*
[16] Cited by the frères Parfaict, *op. cit.,* X, 214.
[17] *Traité de la Poésie Dramatique,* chap. IV.   (*Œuvres,* VI, 377.)
[18] Published in *RHLF,* V (1898), 169-219.
[19] The books were listed, and their value was estimated, e. g.,
      "Bible de Sacy, 25 vol. in-8   50 francs."

those on Greek history. Among these historical works, Bonnefon notes the large number of costly illustrated volumes. Racine probably found in them the plastic form necessary to his dramatic conceptions.[20] Latin authors, though well represented in Racine's library, are less numerous than Greek. Now as regards the Greek dramatists, the " état estimatif " is wholly inadequate, listing as it does only one edition each of Æschylus,[21] Sophocles,[22] and Euripides.[23] Bonnefon, however, succeeded in finding another annotated copy of Æschylus,[24] four more editions of Sophocles [25] known to have belonged to Racine, and an additional annotated copy of Euripides.[26] Some editions have certainly been lost. This must be especially true of Euripides, the dramatist most frequently imitated by Racine.

The inventory includes by way of critical treatises the complete works of Aristotle,[27] a separate edition of the *Rhetoric*,[28] one of the *Poetics*,[29] Pietro Vettori's *Commentarii*,[30] to which was joined *la Poétique* of Scaliger, and the first edition of *la Pratique du Théâtre*.[31] He owned, in addition to the critical works listed there, Cassandre's French translation of the *Rhetoric* [32] and Heinsius' dissertation on poetics, which included the

[20] " Ces documents graphiques lui donneront l'aspect extérieur de ses personnages, comme la lecture des poètes anciens lui fournira, pour ainsi dire, l'âme dont il les animera. Ce sont là les deux parties d'un même ensemble." (*Op. cit., RHLF*, V, 219.)

[21] London: Thomas Stanley, 1613. For Racine's notes in this edition now at the library of Toulouse, cf. Mesnard, VI, 219-221.

[22] Geneva: Paulus Stephanus, 1603. It is preserved at the library of Toulouse.

[23] Coloniæ Allobrogum: Paulus Stephanus, 1602. It belongs to the library of Toulouse. For Racine's annotations cf. Mesnard, VI, 260-265.

[24] Paris: ex officina Adrian Turnebi, 1552.

[25] (1) Venice: Aldus, 1502 (at *Bib. Nat.*); (2) Paris: Turnebus, 1553 (at *Bib. Nat.*); (3) Henric. Stephanus, 1568 (at *Bib. royale* de Bruxelles); and (4) Heidelbergæ: Commelinun, 1597 (belonged to M. Armand Durand and listed in his catalogue under *n°* 265).

[26] Venice: Aldus, 1503. It is to be found at the *Bib. Nat.*

[27] Paris: Duval, 1629 (3 vols.).

[28] London: Griffinus, 1619. This book is now at the library of Toulouse.

[29] London: 1623.   [30] Florence: 1573.

[31] Paris: Sommaville, 1657. This book is at the library of Toulouse.

[32] Cf. *supra*, p. 103.

Greek text of Aristotle and a Latin translation thereof.[33]
Although no trace of the work has been found among the books
owned by Racine, we know from the *Préface* to *la Thébaïde*
written in 1676 that Racine was familiar with another critical
work of Heinsius:[34] an edition of Seneca published with the
author's critical remarks at Leyden in the year 1611. There
is no Horace listed in the inventory, and the briefly annotated
Quintus Horatius Flaccus[35] that belonged to M. le duc de Broglie
does not furnish any indications concerning Racine's study of
the *Epistula ad Pisones*. We know, however, that Racine was
thoroughly conversant with the work. To take a few of the many
allusions to the Latin treatise, we mention his refuting d'Aubignac's assertion that the Romans had no satyric drama by writing
in the margin of *la Pratique* a verse[36] of the *Ars Poetica* implying that the contrary was true; his transcription of thirteen
verses of the same epistle on the verso of the first page of his
Remarques sur l'Odyssée d'Homère;[37] and finally, two important
references to Horace's dramatic precepts embodied in the
Préfaces.[38]

Mesnard believes that from Racine's handwriting it is impossible to determine with any degree of certainty the date of the
marginalia.[39] Basing his opinion on the lack of archaisms[40]

[33] Leyden: Elzevir, 1643.

[34] Racine agrees with Heinsius in his opinion that the *Phœnician
Women* should not be attributed to Seneca.

[35] *Daniel Heinsius ex emendatissimis editionibus expressit, et repræ-
sentavit. Editio nova.* Leyden: Elzevir, 1653. The notations may be
found in Mesnard, VI, 327-330.

[36] "Silvis deducti caveant, me judice, Fauni, etc." (vs. 244). Cf.
ibid., VI, 359.

[37] Vss. 140-152. (*Ibid.*, VI, 56.) The *Remarques* are dated April,
1662.

[38] Cf. *la Première Préface* to *Andromaque* in which Racine invokes
Horace's counsel in regard to preserving the internal *bienséance* of characters (*Ars Poetica*, vss. 119-124) and *la Préface* to *Bérénice* where the
author, in setting forth his views on a simple subject for tragedy, leans
hard on Horace's dictum: "Denique sit quodvis simplex duntaxat et
unum" (*Ars Poetica*, vs. 23).

[39] Mesnard, V, 433; and VI, 218.

[40] Some letters that date from Racine's stay at Uzès contain such old
forms as "treuver," "Menelaüs," etc. Of his plays *la Thébaïde*, and
that only in the first edition, is the only one to have the old forms of
"trouver." (*Lexique*, Mesnard, VIII, 536.)

found therein, he maintains that they were written after the sojourn at Uzès and, quite obviously, before Racine's retirement from the theater. It would then be while the poet was actually engaged in the composition of his tragedies that he studied and annotated for his own benefit the Greek plays and treatises on poetics. In the latter his absorbing interest lies naturally enough in those parts dealing with drama. We shall see that his comments on the tragedies often call attention to the fact that in a particular passage a formal precept is being applied. These remarks reveal an important trait of Racine's mind that is seldom fully recognized: the scholarly and critical bent of his temperament that is again in the ascendant in the *Préfaces* to his plays.

La Pratique du Théâtre in its first edition is one of the three critical dissertations bearing annotations in Racine's handwriting. It contains a few marginal remarks [41] in which Racine takes haughty exception to some assertions made by d'Aubignac. He voices a protest against the *abbé*'s praise of the *Pastor Fido* and points out discrepancies in the latter's estimate of the number of verses in the average Greek tragedy. On the grounds of verisimilitude, he objects to d'Aubignac's suggestion that in *Rodogune* the spectator should be prepared for the swiftness of Cleopatra's death by previous mention of the unusual efficacy of the poison used. He maintains that a Latin satyric drama, the existence of which is denied by the *abbé,* is hinted at in the *Ars Poetica*. Finally, he corrects a mistake in regard to the respective ages of Sophocles and Æschylus, insinuating that the author misunderstood the Greek text from which he got his information.

The first part of *Dan. Heinsii de Tragœdiæ constitutione liber . . . cui et Aristotelis de Poetica libellus . . . accedit* shows underlining and brief indications as to the subject treated on various pages of Heinsius' treatise. On page 187 Racine thus stigmatizes the author's Latin translation of a passage of the *Electra*: " Impertinente version." The margins of the Greek text contain twenty-two brief notes [42] giving the gist of the corresponding passage of the *Poetics* as, for instance, " Temps de la tragédie et du poème épique.—Tour d'un soleil "; or " Quatre choses à observer dans les mœurs. Boni, convenientes, similes,

---

[41] They are published in Mesnard, VI, 358-359.
[42] *Ibid.*, VI, 289-290.

8

æquales." It is significant that all the notations are on passages apropos of the theater.

Racine's fragmentary translation of Aristotle's *Poetics*[43] is reproduced by Mesnard in the *Œuvres de J. Racine,* where it takes up pages 477 to 489 of the fifth volume. Frequent paraphrasing of the text and the interpolated explanatory comments included in this translation with no special indications imply that the poet undertook the translation merely for his own instruction. His translation of the passages on tragedy in general, poetic versus historical truth, recognition, character, *hamartía,* tragic action, and katharsis will be referred to later in connection with his treatment of those subjects in the *Préfaces.* A few examples of Racine's added comments will show the precision with which he interpreted the texts of Aristotle. According to the *Poetics,* the fourth thing to be aimed at in the portrayal of characters is consistency, and, though the character be inconsistent, still he must be consistently inconsistent. Racine enlarges upon the idea of such a character as the latter by adding that it is necessary " qu'il soit toujours le même dans le fond, que tout parte d'un même principe."[44] To Aristotle's definition of tragedy as " the imitation of an action that is serious, complete, and of a certain magnitude; . . . through pity and fear affecting the proper purgation of these emotions,"[45] Racine adds his interpretation of katharsis:

C'est-à-dire qu'en émouvant ces passions (pity and fear), elle (tragedy) leur ôte ce qu'elles ont d'excessif et de vicieux, et les ramène à un état modéré et conforme à la raison.[46]

The corrections [47] noted by Racine in his copy of Cassandre's translation of the *Rhetoric* [48] attest his thorough knowledge of the original.

---

[43] It is written in the margins of Racine's copy of *Petri Victorii Commentarii in librum Aristotelis de Arte Poetarum* (2a ed., *Florentiæ, in officina Juntarum,* 1573). The book is preserved at the *Bib. Nat.*

[44] Mesnard, V, 485.

[45] Butcher's translation, p. 23.

[46] Mesnard, V, 477.

[47] On page 37 and at the end of the volume he wrote a few lines correcting two passages which had been inexactly rendered by Cassandre. (Bonnefon, " La Bibliothèque de Racine," *RHLF*, V, 191.)

[48] Cf. *supra,* p. 103.

Racine's marginalia on the several copies of the Greek tragedies in his possession attest not only the studious habits of the poet,[49] but also his precise method of grasping the actual stage-craft of the ancients. The notes are those of a person trying to visualize the action, to experience the emotions called forth by the successive dramatic situations, and to see into the inner workings of the minds that created those masterpieces. His notes are frequent, occurring for the most part at intervals of four or five lines. Although in the main they are merely the summary of the thoughts expressed by the actors, there are notes of a technical character sufficiently numerous to construct a fairly complete poetics. As he examines the procedure of the ancient masters, Racine's poetic impulse is held somewhat in reserve, and we see the functioning of a mind that is at once critical, ratiocinative, and above all extremely practical.

Racine, following Horace,[50] divides the Greek plays into five acts and each act into a number of scenes generally determined by the entrance of an important character.[51] He frequently notes down that a character gives the reason for his entrance or exit.[52] That Racine consciously carried over this practice into his own plays is evident from the *Première Préface* to the *Alexandre*. Racine, defending his tragedy, asks what his critics have to find fault with when the scenes are " bien remplies," linked according to the rule of necessity, and when the " acteurs ne viennent point sur le théâtre que l'on ne sache la raison qui

[49] Louis Racine, writing the *Mémoires* for the benefit of his son, urges the latter to emulate Jean Racine in his habits of study. He adds: " Je vous ai montré des livres tout grecs, dont les marges sont couvertes de ses apostilles, lorsqu'il n'avoit que quinze ans (an evident exaggeration)." (Mesnard, I, 212.)

[50] *Ars Poetica*, vss. 189-190.

[51] Cf. the *Notes sur " Electra,"* vss. 1, 77, 120 and 325: " Acte 1er, scène 1re. Le Pédagogue explique le lieu de la scène, le temps et le sujet même. . . . Scène 2. Electra vient seule, et ils s'en vont pour n'être point vus. . . . Scène 3e. Chœur de filles qui viennent pour la consoler. . . . Scène 4ème. Chrysothemis vient." (Mesnard, VI, 224 *et sqq.*)

[52] Cf. note on the *Ajax*, vs. 328: " Raison pourquoi elle (Tecmessa) est sortie sur la scène." (*Ibid.*, VI, 238.) Cf. also the notes on the *Electra*, vss. 1404 and 1407-1408: " Electra sort pour n'être pas présente à la mort de sa mère.—Raison pourquoi Electra est dans la maison. Elle prépare ce qu'il faut pour les funérailles d'Oreste." (*Ibid.*, VI, 232.)

les y fait venir." The exact staging for the death scene in the
Ajax is visualized and written down in the margin.[53] Racine
remarks that it is the only time in Greek tragedy that the chorus
goes off the stage once it has entered. In the *Electra* he makes
this observation on the acting at a certain point:

Il y a apparence qu'Electra est dans un coin du théâtre ne prenant point
de part à ce que dit le Chœur.[54]

As regards the exposition, Racine commends the dramatist
on several occasions for the swiftness with which he acquaints
the spectator with the name of the actor and the place represented by the scene.[55] He notes that the subject of Euripides'
Medea is set forth, in beautiful verse by a *nourrice* conversing
with the *pœdagogus*; "mais je doute que Sophocle eût voulu
commencer une tragédie par de tels personnages." [56]
Racine indicates several times the pleasure he derives from
reversals and especially from what Aristotle considers the most
powerful elements of emotional interest in tragedy: peripeteia

---

[53] " Elle (Tecmessa) sort, et tout le monde sort comme elle. Le Chœur
se sépare en deux bandes; et ainsi le théâtre demeure vide, afin qu'Ajax
s'y puisse tuer aux yeux des spectateurs, sans que personne l'en puisse
empêcher.—Il n'y a point changement de scène, je veux dire du lieu de
la scène.—Voilà le seul endroit des tragédies grecques où le Chœur sort
de la scène, depuis qu'il y est entré; et c'est un bel artifice du poète,
parce que les dernières paroles d'Ajax étoient trop considérables pour
les cacher au spectateur." (*Ibid.*, VI, 241.)
    [54] Note on vs. 1077. (*Ibid.*, VI, 230.)
    [55] *Notes sur " Electra*," vss. 1-4 and vs. 2 in particular: " Il explique
dès les quatre premiers vers et le nom du principal acteur et le lieu de
la scène. . . . Voilà, ô fils d'Agamemnon, ces mêmes lieux que vous avez
tant désiré de voir.—Sophocle a un soin merveilleux d'établir d'abord le
lieu de la scène. Il se sert ici d'un artifice très-agréable, en introduisant
un vieillard qui montre les environs du palais d'Argos à Oreste, qui en
avoit été enlevé tout jeune. Le *Philoctète* commence à peu près de
même: c'est Ulysse qui montre à Pyrrhus tout jeune l'île de Lemnos,
où ils sont, et par où l'armée avoit passé. L'*Œdipe Coloneen* s'ouvre
par Œdipe aveugle qui se fait décrire par Antigone le lieu où il est.
Ces trois ouvertures, quoique un peu semblables, ne laissent pas d'avoir
une très-agréable diversité et des couleurs merveilleuses." (*Ibid.*, VI,
246.) Cf. also the note on vs. 3 of the *Ajax:* " Il établit d'abord le lieu
de la scène auprès des tentes d'Ajax, qui sont les dernières du camp des
Grecs." (*Ibid.*, VI, 237.)
    [56] Note on vs. 49. (*Ibid.*, VI, 254.)

and recognition.[57]   The poet was extremely sensitive to the beauty of such a change of situation as is implied in the imprecations of Œdipus against the slayer of Laius.[58]   He also commends this reverse in the *Electra*:

Au milieu de la douleur d'Electra et des regrets qu'elle fait sur la mort d'Oreste, Chrysothemis vient lui dire qu'il (Orestes) est venu.   Cela fait un fort bel effet.   Car les regrets d'Electra sont interrompus, et [59] sa douleur n'en devient que plus violent.   Ainsi la pitié va toujours en s'augmentant.[60]

He praises the remarkable example of peripeteia occurring in the same play when Ægisthus, expecting to find the dead body of Orestes, insolently orders the door to be flung open.   This haughtiness, according to Racine, not only marks his character, but at the same time prepares for the spectators the pleasure of seeing Ægisthus' surprise when, instead of the body of Orestes, he discovers that of his wife, Clytemnestra.[61]   As for recognitions, Racine considers that there is nothing more beautiful in drama " que de voir Electra pleurer son frère mort en sa (Orestes') présence, qui en étant lui-même attendri, est obligé de se découvrir." [62]   He notes carefully the double recognition that ensues, praising especially the second [63] as being

merveilleusement pathétique et bien amenée de parole en parole, en se répondant tous deux fort naturellement et tendrement.[64]

---

[57] *Poetics*, chap. VI.

[58] Note on vs. 241 of *Œdipus the King*.   (Mesnard, VI, 234.)

[59] Electra, however, having weighty reasons for discrediting the good news brought by her sister, resumes her mourning.

[60] Note on vs. 868 (Mesnard, VI, 229).   Racine in his comments on this incident fails to call attention to one of the most beautiful examples of peripeteia found in the Greek tragedies.   Chrysothemis came as a messenger of joy.   Her mission produced the opposite effect, however, and the outcome of it was that she herself was saddened, and the woes of Electra were increased.   Chrysothemis expresses the reverse clearly: " Oh, hapless that I am! And I was bringing such news in joyous haste, ignorant, it seems, how dire was our plight; but now that I have come, I find fresh sorrows added to the old." (*Tragedies of Sophocles* translated by Jebb, p. 254.)

[61] Note on vss. 1474-1487 of *Electra*.   (Mesnard, VI, 233.)

[62] Note on vs. 1095.   (*Ibid.*, VI, 230.)

[63] The first recognition was brought about by the chorus' naming Electra.   Orestes, in the second, makes known his identity by showing to his sister his father's ring.

[64] Note on vss. 1188 *et sqq.*   (*Ibid.*, VI, 231.)

The poet frequently calls attention to the observance of three of Aristotle's requirements for tragic characters.[65]

He apparently takes Aristotle's precept that characters should be " good " [66] to mean good in a moral sense and often points out in this connection that pity is increased by bringing to the fore the good traits in the tragic hero. Sophocles makes Œdipus a prince who loves his people " afin qu'il fasse plus de pitié." [67] Even his ill temper manifested toward Tiresias does not derogate from the favorable opinion we have of him because in his anger he speaks only for the public good. Racine remarks that this tragic flaw even increases our compassion for Œdipus in that, by his very arrogance, he forces the soothsayer to foretell the woes that are to fall upon him.[68] Racine notes in the margins of two other plays Sophocles' insistence on the " goodness " of a character. " Minerva praises Ajax at the opening of the tragedy in order to predispose the spectator in his favor." [69]   Orestes mitigates the horror that his design would inspire in the spectator and the odium that would attend him as a result by revealing that it is a command of the oracle.[70]

We notice several allusions to the characters' being true to type. A certain discourse of Jocasta in the *Phœnician Maidens* is " bien convenable à une mère." [71]   Racine also points out in his notes on the *Electra* of Sophocles that young persons are naturally imprudent and unguarded in their speech. Electra and Orestes, immoderate in their joy at finding each other, are talking loud enough to be overheard. The governor of Orestes reproaches them for their want of caution. Racine jots down

[65] Cf. Racine's summary of Aristotle's passage in Heinsius, pp. 282-283: " Quatre choses à observer dans les mœurs. *Boni, convenientes, similes, œquales.*" (*Ibid.*, VI, 290.)

[66] Cf. Butcher, *op. cit.*, pp. 337 *et sqq.*, for a discusion of *ethos* and *dianoia.*

[67] Note on vs. 58 of *Œdipus the King.* (Mesnard, VI, 234.)

[68] Note on vs. 383. (*Ibid.*, VI, 235.)

[69] Note on vs. 119. (*Ibid.*, VI, 237.)

[70] Note on vs. 36. (*Ibid.*, VI, 225.)

[71] Note on vs. 531 of Euripides' play. (*Ibid.*, VI, 262.) He notes likewise that the questions, vss. 390-391, are not necessary to the subject, adding that they are nevertheless " tendres et du caractère d'une mère." (*Ibid.*, VI, 261.)

this note insisting at once on their trueness to type and on a point of verisimilitude scored by the old man's rebuke:

Sophocle a voulu marquer l'imprudence des jeunes gens, qui ne peuvent se contenir dans leurs passions, et afin que le spectateur ne trouve point étrange qu'on ne les a point entendus de la maison, il fait que ce vieillard, plus sage qu'eux, a fait sentinelle à la porte.[72]

Again he comments on a verse of *Electra* justifying the poet for what would seem at first sight a violation of Aristotle's precept in regard to characters' being true to type:

Ce vers est un peu cruel pour une fille; mais c'est une fille depuis longtemps enragée contre sa mère.[73]

He questions, apropos of a passage in the *Trachiniæ,* " si une esclave ose se mêler de donner des conseils." [74]

As for consistency in a character, we have the example of Ulysses' expressing his compassion for Ajax at the opening of the tragedy. Racine comments that it is a " sentiment honnête " and that the character will be consistent in this respect throughout the piece:

Ce caractère d'Ulysse est soutenu jusqu'à la fin; car c'est lui qui fait accorder la sépulture à Ajax, quoiqu'il fût celui qu'Ajax haïssoit le plus.[75]

On the other hand, the character of Creon in Euripides' *Phœnician Maidens* is blamed for a want of consistency:

Créon est méchant inutilement, lui qui ne l'est point dans le reste de la pièce.[76]

Racine, in his marginal notes, takes into account the *bienséances* to be observed in the drama. Alongside the passage in which Tecmessa tells that she is covering the body of Ajax, the poet notes that this is an artifice to prevent the spectator from seeing blood.[77] The dramatist has carefully contrived the death

---

[72] Note on vs. 1330. (*Ibid.,* VI, 232.)
[73] Note on vs. 1426. (*Ibid.,* VI, 232-233.)
[74] Note on vs. 52. (*Ibid.,* VI, 247.)
[75] Note on vs. 121. (*Ibid.,* VI, 237.)
[76] Note on vs. 1583. (*Ibid.,* VI, 264.)
[77] Cf. *ibid.,* VI, 242, for Racine's note on vss. 923-925, which are thus rendered by Jebb:
No eye shall look on him: nay, in this enfolding robe I will shroud him

of Clytemnestra so as not to offend propriety, obviating at the
same time the necessity of a *récit*.[78]   Racine also observes that
Ægisthus enters the palace so as not to be killed on the stage.

We find that Racine, occasionally at variance with Euripides,
labels a scene of his "languissante" [79] and useless.[80]   Three times
in the *Phœnician Maidens,* he condemns the action because the
rule of necessity is violated.[81]   Twice he notes, without serious
protest, however, that the passage in question is more comic than
tragic.[82]

We have seen that Racine's comments are of a very practical
nature.   They represent his serious efforts to understand the
procédés of the ancient poets very likely at a time when he himself was practising their art.   Despite the technical knowledge
that prompted many of the remarks, they are, like Molière's
observations, notably free of pedantry.[83]   As he marked his copies,

wholly; for no man who loved him could bear to see him, as up to nostril
and forth from red gash he spirts the darkened blood from the self-dealt
wound.   (*The Tragedies of Sophocles*, p. 205.)

[78] "Electra sort (from the palace) pour n'être pas présent à la mort
de sa mère.—Elle dit ce que l'on fait en dedans."   "Raison pourquoi
Clytemnestre est dans la maison.   Elle prépare ce qu'il faut pour les
funérailles d'Oreste."   "Il rend raison pourquoi Electra sort.—Pour
empêcher qu'Égisthe ne les surprenne."   "Cris de Clytemnestre, afin
que, *sans voir cette mort*, le spectateur ne laisse pas d'y être comme
présent, et pour épargner un récit."   (Notes on vss. 1404, 1407-08, 1410-
11, and 1414, *ibid.*, VI, 232.)

[79] Notes on the *Phœnician Maidens,* vss. 697 and 1493.   (*Ibid.*, VI,
263-264.)

[80] Notes on vss. 697, 1215, 1290.   (*Loc cit.*)

[81] Notes on vss. 697, 841, and 949-955.   This last note reads: "Causes
trop recherchées pour faire mourir Ménécée.   Ce peu de nécessité rend
froide une action très-belle."   (*Ibid.*, VI, 263.)

[82] "Tout cela est plus comique que tragique, quoique beau et bien
exprimé."   (Note on the *Medea*, vss. 238-251, *ibid.*, VI, 255.)   Racine
also labels "comique" a part of Hippolytus' diatribe against women
(*Hippolytus*, notes on vss. 634-635, *ibid.*, VI, 264).

[83] Racine, from the very outset of his career, had an aversion for
pedants with a superstitious and narrow devotion to the rules.   As early
as 1666 he takes a fling at spectators who flaunt their knowledge of
Aristotle: "Mais je n'aurois jamais fait si je m'arrêtois aux subtilités
de quelques critiques, qui prétendent assujettir le goût du public aux
dégoûts d'un esprit malade, qui vont au théâtre avec un ferme dessein
de n'y point prendre de plaisir, et qui croient prouver à tous les specta-

he was more than the critic of stern intellect. That he was appreciably moved as he read the Greek tragedies is frequently attested by such annotations as " cette ouverture de la scène est magnifique," [84] " fort tendre et fort noble," [85] and " ceci est pathétique." [86]

Racine derived much profit from his careful reading of the ancient tragedies as is evinced by some twenty direct references in the *Préfaces* to Euripides, Sophocles, and Æschylus. It is most frequently as a controversialist justifying his own practice that he adverts to the Greek plays. When critics condemned the subject of *Bérénice* as too scanty for tragedy, Racine appealed to the taste of the ancients:

Ils (anciens) ont admiré l'*Ajax* de Sophocle, qui n'est autre chose qu'Ajax qui se tue de regret, à cause de la fureur où il étoit tombé après le refus qu'on lui avoit fait des armes d'Achille. Ils ont admiré le *Philoctète*, dont tout le sujet est Ulysse qui vient pour surprendre les flèches d'Hercule. L'*Œdipe* même, quoique tout plein de reconnoissances, est moins chargé de matière que la plus simple tragédie de nos jours. . . .[87]

In the *Première Préface* to *Britannicus,* Racine maintains that Junie's reappearance on the stage after the death of Britannicus and the few words she exchanges with Nero [88] have their counterpart in the ancient tragedies:

teurs, par un branlement de tête et par des grimaces affectées, qu'ils ont étudié à fond la *Poétique* d'Aristote " (*1ère Préface* of *Alexandre*). Although due allowance must be made for the patent flattery in the *Dédicace* of *Andromaque*, Racine here shows that he is not slavish in his devotion to the rules, especially as they are rigidly upheld by savants. Addressing his tragedy to Henriette d'Angleterre, he writes: " La cour vous regarde comme l'arbitre de tout ce qui se fait d'agréable. Et nous, qui travaillons pour plaire au public, nous n'avons plus que faire de demander aux savants si nous travaillons selon les règles. La règle souveraine est de plaire à Votre Altesse Royale." Cf. also the *Au lecteur* of *les Plaideurs*.

[84] Note on vs. 1 of *Œdipus the King.* (*Ibid.*, VI, 234.)

[85] Note on vs. 1182 of the *Ajax*. (*Ibid.*, VI, 244.)

[86] Note on vs. 1437 *et sqq.* of the *Phœnician Maidens.* (*Ibid.*, VI, 264.)

[87] *Préface* (1671) to *Bérénice.*

[88] Racine, however, later suppressed the scene in question (Act V, scene 6, in the early performances and in the first edition). Junie crossed the stage and to the importunities of Nero answered:

J'aimais Britannicus, Seigneur: je vous l'ai dit.
Si de quelque pitié ma misère est suivie,

Tous les anciens font venir souvent sur la scène des acteurs qui n'ont autre chose à dire, sinon qu'ils viennent d'un endroit, et qu'ils s'en retournent en un autre.

Censors were finding fault with the ending of *Britannicus* saying that the piece should stop with the *récit* of the poisoning of the hero. Racine, however, firmly vindicates his finishing off of the other characters by invoking Aristotle's definition of tragedy as the imitation of a *complete* action. Such is, furthermore, the practice of Sophocles:

C'est ainsi que Sophocle en use presque partout. C'est ainsi que dans l'*Antigone* il emploie autant de vers à représenter la fureur d'Hémon et la punition de Créon après la mort de cette princesse, que j'en ai employé aux imprécations d'Agrippine, à la retraite de Junie, à la punition de Narcisse, et au désespoir de Néron, après la mort de Britannicus.[89]

It was in part [90] the example of Euripides that emboldened Racine to change the age of Astyanax in the *Andromaque*.[91] Finally, the use of a modern subject in *Bajazet,* although not contrary to any rule, seemed to need some authorization. After endorsing the theory that in tragic subjects distance in space makes up for remoteness of time,[92] the poet reminds us that Æschylus treated a contemporary subject [93] and even introduced characters that were then living.[94]

Racine warmly acknowledges in several of his *Préfaces* his obligation to Euripides. We are told in the *Préface* to *Iphigénie* that what he has exactly imitated from Homer and Euripides

---

> Qu'on me laisse chercher dans le sein d'Octavie
> Un entretien conforme à l'état où je suis.
>
>   (Mesnard, II, 334, n. 1.)

[89] *Première Préface* (1670) to *Britannicus.*

[90] He invokes also the example of Ronsard who made Astyanax the hero of *la Franciade* and the progenitor of the ancient kings of France.

[91] " Combien Euripide a-t-il été plus hardi dans sa tragédie d'*Hélène*! Il y choque ouvertement la créance commune de toute la Grèce." The entire passage taken from the *Seconde Préface* (1676) is cited *infra*, p. 140.

[92] Segrais had stated it at the beginning of his *Nouvelles Françaises* (La Haye: 1741), I, 20. The sixth *nouvelle* of this collection is *Floridon ou l'Amour imprudent* which is thought by some scholars to be one source of Racine's tragedy.

[93] *The Persians.*   [94] *Seconde Préface.*

has always produced a good effect on the French stage, " bon
sens " and " raison " being the same in all ages. Paris was
touched by the same things " qui ont mis autrefois en larmes le
plus savant peuple de la Grèce." He then digresses with the
professed purpose of defending Euripides against those who were
condemning the *Alcestis,* thereby beginning a literary skirmish
that is now regarded as a prelude to the quarrel of the Ancients
and Moderns :

Il ne s'agit point ici de l'*Alceste.* Mais en vérité j'ai trop d'obligation
à Euripide pour ne pas prendre quelque soin de sa mémoire, et pour
laisser échapper l'occasion de le réconcilier avec ces Messieurs. Je
m'assure qu'il n'est si mal dans leur esprit que parce qu'ils n'ont pas
bien lu l'ouvrage sur lequel ils l'ont condamné. . . .

The last half of the *Préface* is devoted to overthrowing the
criticisms of Euripides' play made by Pierre Perrault in a
dialogue entitled *Critique de l'opéra ou Examen de la tragédie
intitulée Alceste, ou le Triomphe d'Alceste.*[95]
Racine tells us in the *Préface* to *Phèdre* that, although for the
" conduite de l'action " he follows a path somewhat different
from that of Euripides, he did not fail to enrich his piece with
what appeared to him most " éclatant " in the *Hippolytus.* He
is especially indebted to him for the character of Phèdre :

Quand je ne lui devrois que la seule idée du caractère de Phèdre, je
pourrois dire que je lui dois ce que j'ai peut-être mis de plus raisonnable
sur le théâtre.

In a passage full of acerbity toward Corneille and the censors
of *Britannicus,* whom he had good reason to believe were abetted
by the older dramatist, Racine flings aside their opinion and
proclaims the criteria by which he intends his work to be judged.
Although it would be an easy matter to please his critics—he
would have only to betray common sense, complicate his intrigue,
and write bombastic speeches making the actors say precisely the
opposite of what they should say—he would scruple to win
approval in this manner, for

que diroit cependant le petit nombre de gens sages auxquels je m'efforce
de plaire ? De quel front oserois-je me montrer, pour ainsi dire, aux

---

[95] It is the comparison between the Greek play and Quinault's opera.

yeux de ces grands hommes de l'antiquité que j'ai choisis pour modèles?
Car, pour me servir de la pensée d'un ancien, voilà les véritables spectateurs que nous devons nous proposer; et nous devons sans cesse nous
demander: "Que diroient Homère et Virgile, s'ils lisoient ces vers?
que diroit Sophocle, s'il voyoit représenter cette scène?" [96]

Racine's adaptation of this idea of Longinus [97] leaves no room for
doubt concerning either his regard for the ancient poets or his
conscious and painstaking imitation of their art.

---

[96] *Première Préface* to *Britannicus.*

[97] "Que penseraient Homère ou Démosthène de ce que je dis, s'ils
m'écoutaient? et quel jugement feraient-ils de moi?" (Boileau's translation of *le Traité du Sublime*, chap. XII, *Œuvres*, III, 336.)

A COMPARISON BETWEEN BOILEAU'S PRECEPTS AND THE DRAMATIC THEORY IN RACINE'S *PRÉFACES*

The Subject

The next part of this investigation will be a comparison between the formal precepts enunciated by Boileau and the critical remarks found in Racine's *Préfaces*. The subject, or as it was called by the seventeenth-century critics, the fable,[1] its relation to katharsis regarded as the function of tragedy, the characters, and the action will each in turn fall within our inquiry.

A few general observations, the truth of which will become more evident as this study advances, are not out of place at this point.

We note first the brevity of Boileau, who devotes not more than 159 verses of the *Art Poétique* to his discussion of the serious *genre*. This laconic treatment of tragedy is inherent in the nature of Boileau's work, which is a treatise on poetry in general. Moreover, it is written in verse and after the manner of Horace, whose praise of conciseness in such matters is well known:

> Quidquid præcipies, esto brevis, ut cito dicta
> percipiant animi dociles, teneantque fideles.[2]

The second point that we shall take pains to stress in our discussion of the *Art Poétique* is that here Boileau is in no wise an innovator. He advances nothing that has not previously been set forth by his predecessors or his contemporaries. We shall strengthen, by means of examples cited largely in the notes, M. Bray's statement that, except on the question of the " merveilleux chrétien," the poetics of Boileau is in the main that of his adversaries and that from the standpoint of doctrine the seventeenth century " fait bloc." [3]

---

[1] Rapin, *Réflexions sur la Poétique*, chap. XX. (*Œuvres*, II, 128.)

[2] *Ars Poetica*, vss. 335-336.

[3] *La Formation de la Doctrine Classique en France*, p. 363. Lanson expressed substantially the same opinion when he said that, despite all Chapelain's shortcomings, one sees the formula of the classical ideal take

Racine's *Préfaces*, which until 1672 were sharply polemical in their intent, seek to justify those *procédés* that have been the occasion of caviling criticism. After that date their tone changes. They become merely explanatory and aim to prepare the reader psychologically for the events set forth in the tragedy.[4]   They are documents of actuality that constitute a poetics at once more complete and less complete than that of Boileau. Racine treats only those points that seem to him to require explanation or authorization. On the other hand, the subjects which he does take up are considered in far greater detail and with more immediateness than in the corresponding passages of the *Art Poétique*. Instead of a theoretical dissertation on tragedy in general, we have the specialized study of a poet working with his own plays as a point of departure. After deducing from Racine's observations the principal tenets of his poetics, we shall compare them with those set forth more categorically in the *Art Poétique*. The study of the actual practice of Racine as evinced by lines of his plays will be reserved for a later work.

We shall examine first the tragic subject. Boileau opens *Chant III* of his poem with a restatement in verse of the doctrine of imitation underlying Aristotle's æsthetics. According to that philosopher, all the arts derive from imitation. Things imitated imply on our part a learning process, the pleasure [5] of

shape in his critical works. Chapelain placed side by side its two component terms: sovereignty of reason and respect for antiquity. (*Hist. de la Litt. fr.*, 4e Partie, Livre I, chap. III, 2.)

[4] Cf. *infra*, pp. 141-142.

[5] "The cause of this . . . is, that to learn gives the liveliest pleasure, not only to philosophers but to men in general; whose capacity, however, of learning is more limited. Thus the reason why men enjoy seeing a likeness is, that in contemplating it they find themselves learning or inferring, and saying perhaps, 'Ah, that is he!'" (*Poetics*, chap. IV, Butcher's translation.)   The pleasure resulting from learning is treated more explicitly in the *Rhetoric*. To grasp Aristotle's idea, we must keep in mind his definition of pleasure: the settling down of the soul into its natural state after a period of disturbance. A change, then, is pleasant, the pleasure being occasioned by a return to the normal. Learning and admiring are likewise satisfying in that the latter "implies the desire to learn, so that what causes admiration is to be desired (the disturbance), and learning implies a return to the normal (i. e., to true knowledge, the highest condition of the intellect, its normal or settled state)." (*Rhetoric*, Bk. I, chap. XI, J. H. Freese's translation.)

which is universal. In order to strengthen his assertion, Aristotle appeals to our experience, citing what he obviously considers an extreme case:

Objects which in themselves we view with pain, we delight to contemplate when reproduced with minute fidelity: such as the forms of the most ignoble animals and of dead bodies.[6]

Again in a passage of the *Rhetoric*, explaining how learning and admiring afford pleasure, he instances

a work of imitation such as painting, sculpture, poetry, and all that is well imitated, even if the object of imitation is not pleasant; for it is not this that causes pleasure or the reverse, but the inference that the imitation and the object imitated are identical, so that the result is that we learn something.[7]

Every treatise [8] on poetics repeated Aristotle's dictum regarding the efficacy of art, which by the process of imitation can render ugly objects beautiful. It is interesting to note that at the hand of seventeenth-century commentators, Aristotle's expression "ignoble animals," gained much by way of precision. Vauquelin mentioned a "singe" and a "dragon écaillé" as worthy of imitation.[9] Vossius added the particular case "draconum et monstrorum," which is doubtless the source of Boileau's "serpent" and "monstre." Despréaux, then, began his *Chant III* with a doctrine already consecrated by long tradition:

> Il n'est point de *serpent*, ni de *monstre* odieux,
> Qui, par *l'art imité*, ne puisse plaire aux yeux;
> *D'un pinceau délicat l'artifice agréable*
> Du plus affreux objet fait un objet aimable.[10]

Boileau then makes an adroit transition into the *genre* he is about to treat. The imitation of the "most ignoble animals

---

[6] *Poetics*, chap. IV.   [7] Bk. I, chap. XI.

[8] Heinsius, Desmarets, and Vossius are cited by M. Bray, p. 153.

[9]   " Et nous plait en peinture une chose hideuse,
          Qui seroit à la voir en essence fâcheuse.
          Comme il fait plus beau voir un singe bien pourtrait:
          Un dragon écaillé proprement contrefait,
          Un visage hideux de quelque laid Thersite,
          Que le vray naturel qu'un sçavant peintre imite."
                    (*Art Poétique*, Livre I, vss. 191-196.)

[10] *Art Poétique*, *Chant III*, vss. 1-4.

and of dead bodies," applicable to the fine arts and to poetry
in a general way, is not Boileau's affair. Translating Aristotle's
idea into terms of tragedy, he continues:

> Ainsi, pour nous charmer, la Tragédie en pleurs,
> D'Œdipe tout sanglant fit parler les douleurs,
> D'Oreste parricide exprima les alarmes,
> Et, pour nous divertir, nous arracha des larmes.[11]

It is highly significant that, notwithstanding a transitional
" donc," these verses have a very slender bearing [12] on the direct
precepts which follow. They seem indeed little more than a
bookish defense of the ancient fables that we know appeared
quite unpalatable to a certain over-refined taste of that period.
Heinsius, moreover, had expressed the same idea as early as
1611 in his *De Tragœdiæ Constitutione*. He could have had
no thought of French tragedy when he wrote:

Omnes mores imitatur tragœdia, neque minus Atrei aut Thyeste quam
Tiresiæ aut Ajacis; neque magis nos delectat, cum hos exprimit quam
illos.[13]

We are inclined to agree with M. Bray who sees in the opening lines of *Chant III* merely a " lieu commun à portée très
restreinte." [14] Some critics,[15] however, regard these verses as
legitimatizing all nature as a fit subject for artistic treatment.
They see in them the virtual manifesto of a naturalistic school.
In order to give this passage the significance that to all intents
and purposes Boileau meant it to have, we must look at it from
his angle of vision, that is, from the viewpoint of the Aristotelian doctrine of imitation with its two-fold application: (1)
imitation of a harmonized, ideal nature stripped of what is
momentary or accidental and (2) imitation of the ancients who
have already realized this transmutation of facts into truths.

---

[11] *Ibid.*, vss. 5-8.

[12] The idea of the pleasure derived from the tears called forth by
the stories of Orestes and Œdipus is indeed slight enough pretext for
Boileau to launch into his discussion of what everyone knew to be the
secret of both immediate and lasting success on the stage of Paris,
namely, " de plaire et de toucher."

[13] Cited by M. Bray, p. 154.

[14] *Ibid.*, p. 153.

[15] M. Albert Cahen's review of *la Formation de la Doctrine Classique
en France*, *RHLF*, XXXV (1928), 269.

Poetic truth, while not contradicting facts and experience, goes beyond them and completes nature's unfulfilled intentions. Poetry being confined to the realm of the universal has therefore a higher subject matter than history which deals merely with the particular.[16] Few critics have grasped more firmly than Boileau the relation in which imaginative truth stands to the wantonly disordered and baffling experiences of real life, and no one has embodied in clearer poetic form the Aristotelian doctrine that " it is not the function of the poet to relate what has happened, but what may happen—what is possible according to the law of probability or necessity."[17] Boileau, enjoining the dramatist to avoid the improbable, gives warning that

Le vrai peut quelquefois n'être pas vraisemblable.[18]

In thus excluding from poetic treatment actual truth that does not square with the probable,[19] Boileau sides with Aristotle, who preferred even probable impossibilities to improbable possibilities.[20] This rule of probability laid down by Aristotle[21] and repeated with much critical acumen by Boileau[22] is not the

[16] Rostagni points out (la Poetica di Aristotele, p. xxxv) that this is not a pivotal point in the Poetics, but rather Aristotle's attempt to refute one of Plato's arguments against poetry. The latter had claimed that poetry, imitating as it does, not the idea, which is the real domain of philosophy, but a mere phenomenon, is therefore three removes from Truth. Aristotle tried to justify poetry by establishing its universal, almost philosophical character in the famous distinction between the particular truth of history and the universal truth of poetry.

[17] Aristotle's Poetics, chap. IX. On this subject cf. also chaps. XXIV and XXV and Butcher's chapter on " Poetic Truth," op. cit., pp. 163-197.

[18] Art Poétique, Chant III, vs. 48.

[19] Almost no line in the Art Poétique has lent itself to so many varied interpretations as this verse on verisimilitude or poetic truth. Brunetière even chose to see in it a gibe at Corneille, who had said that " le sujet d'une belle tragédie doit n'être pas vraisemblable." (Œuvres Poétiques de Boileau ed. by Brunetière, p. 208, n. 5.)

[20] Poetics, chap. IX.

[21] The idea of keeping fictions " proxima veris " and of rejecting what is incredible is found in the Ars Poetica, vss. 188 and 338-339. Nowhere, however, does Horace give the pure Aristotelian conception of verisimilitude as conformity to an ideal rather than to an actual truth.

[22] Lanson (Hist. de la Litt. fr., 4e Partie Livre III, chap. II, 3), however, held that Boileau's intention was " l'équivalence de l'image à

narrow *vraisemblance* advocated by the older French critics. They interpreted it as a requirement that there should be an identical likeness between the image and the object imitated. It was this desire to approximate to a likeness extending not only to the action and characters, but to the stage representation as well, that is the rational basis of the unities.[23] What in Scaliger had been a simple counsel [24] becomes the very foundation of Chapelain's poetics:

Je pose pour fondement . . . que l'imitation en tous poèmes doit être si parfaite qu'il ne paraisse aucune différence entre la chose imitée et celle qui imite.[25]

We have seen on the other hand that Boileau, in the matter of verisimilitude, was true not only to the spirit, but also to the letter of Aristotle. The only clearer expression in the seventeenth century of the pure Aristotelian concept of poetic truth is found in the works of Père Rapin.[26] To recapitulate, Boi-

l'objet." He cites as proof two verses of the *Art Poétique* in which Boileau praises the truth of Terence's characters:

> Ce n'est plus (*sic*) un portrait, une image semblable:
> C'est un amant, un fils, un père *véritable*.
>
> (Chant III, vss. 419-420.)

These lines, however, apply to comedy in which, according to Aristotle, the more rigorous rule of probability is not prescribed. (*Poetics*, chap. IX.)

[23] Cf. Rapin's eulogy of the rules: "Ce n'est que par ces régles, qu'on peut établir la vrai-semblance dans la fiction, qui est l'ame de la Poësie: car s'il n'y a point d'unité de lieu, de tems, & d'action dans les grands Poëmes, il n'y a point de vrai-semblance." (*Réflexions sur la Poétique*, chap. XI, *Œuvres*, II, 120.)

[24] "Quam proxime accedant ad veritatem," cited by Arnaud, *Étude sur la Vie et les Œuvres de l'abbé d'Aubignac*, p. 140. The similarity with Horace's "proxima veris" should be noted. Cf. *infra*, p. 129, n. 21.

[25] Cited by Arnaud, *loc. cit.* The citation is taken from the principal inedited dissertation of Chapelain (Nov. 29, 1630). He maintains therein that the likeness should "ôter aux regardants toutes les occasions de douter de la réalité de ce qu'ils voient."

[26] "Outre que la vrai-semblance sert à donner de la créance à ce que la Poësie a de plus fabuleux, elle sert aussi à donner aux choses que dit le Poëte, un plus grand air de perfection, que ne pourroit faire la vérité même, quoy que la vrai-semblance n'en soit que la copie. Car la vérité ne fait les choses que comme elles sont; & la vrai-semblance les fait comme elles doivent être. La vérité est presque toûjours défectueuse,

leau's viewpoint in recommending unpleasant subjects as fit for poetic treatment is not that of the practical observer noting down what is going on about him, but rather that of a follower of a well-established literary tradition. That he does not propose all nature for imitation is evidenced by the fact that he understood and endorsed the purely Aristotelian doctrine of poetic truth.

Turning again to the opening verses of *Chant III*, we see that the imitative process is, according to Boileau, an " artifice agréable" wrought by a "pinceau délicat." Surely these are not the words of a naturalist! Boileau states clearly under what conditions the "serpent" or the "monstre odieux" become pleasing: "par l'art imité." [27] Later on apropos of the *récit*, he speaks of "l'art judicieux," [28] implying clearly that there must be a choice in the things imitated.

Monchesnay tells us that Homer was "la belle passion" of Despréaux. One of the qualities he admired most in him was

le talent qu'il a d'exprimer noblement les plus petites choses. C'est là, disoit-il, où consiste l'art; car les grandes choses se soutiennent assez d'elles-mêmes.[29]

Boileau, then, does not exclude from poetry the trivial realities of life, but he does require that they be expressed nobly. He makes art indeed to consist in this. Monchesnay's testimony is

par le mélange des conditions singuliéres, qui la composent. *Il ne naît rien au monde, qui ne s'éloigne de la perfection de son idée en y naissant.* Il faut chercher des originaux & des modèles dans la vrai-semblance, & dans les principes universels des choses: où il n'entre rien de materiel et de singulier, qui les corrompe." (*Réflexions sur la Poétique,* chap. XXIV, *Œuvres,* II, 132.)

[27] Cf. also *Art Poétique, Chant III,* vs. 44: "Nous voulons qu'*avec art* l'action se ménage."

[28]　　　"Mais il est des objets que l'art judicieux
　　　　Doit offrir à l'oreille et reculer des yeux."
　　　　　　　　　　　　　　　　(*Chant III,* vss. 53-54.)

[29] *Bolœana,* p. 91. Rapin expressed precisely the same idea in his *Réflexions sur la Poétique,* chap. VIII: "Homère est agreable jusques dans la description de la cabane du porcher de Laërte en son Odyssée: & Virgile plaît jusques dans le fumier & dans les chardons de ses Georgiques, de la maniére dont il en parle. Car tout devient beau, fleury, & agréable entre les mains d'un Poëte qui a du génie." (*Œuvres,* II, 116.)

pertinent at this point as it stresses what we believe to be the real import of the opening lines of *Chant III,* namely, Boileau's insistence on the necessity of art.

Even if Despréaux's own text left any doubt in the matter, we have Brossette's singularly rich commentary proving that Boileau had a very clear notion of the difference that exists between a work of art and the object imitated. Brossette composed his remarks on these verses after notes jotted down on October 22, 1702, following a conversation with Boileau. There is only one important change [30] between the rough notes and the *Éclaircissement* as it appeared in 1716. That variation, consisting in Brossette's suppression of the examples " crapaut " and " couleuvre," is, however, significant. The first draft shows Boileau's preoccupation, even in 1702, with what had become the traditional amplification of Aristotle's " most ignoble animals." It was evidently Brossette who did not like the idea of " toads " and " snakes." We give Brossette's original version of this part of the conversation:

M. Despréaux m'a encore parlé d'Aristote, qui dit que la force de l'imitation est telle sur l'esprit de l'homme, que les choses les plus horribles lui plaisent quand elles sont bien imitées.

M. Despréaux a ajouté qu'*il faut que cette imitation ne soit pas en tout semblable à la nature même*: que trop de ressemblance feroit avoir autant d'horreur pour la chose faite par imitation, que pour la chose même qu'on auroit imitée.   Par exemple: l'imitation parfaite d'un cadavre, représenté en cire avec toutes les couleurs, sans aucune différence sensible, cette imitation ne seroit pas supportable; de même d'un *crapaut*, d'une *couleuvre*, etc.

Et c'est pourquoy les portraits que *Benoît* faisoit en cire, n'ont pas réussi: parce qu'ils étoient trop ressemblans.   Mais que l'on fasse la même chose en marbre d'une seule couleur, ou en platte peinture: ces imitations plairont d'autant plus qu'elles approcheront de la vérité, parce que quelque ressemblance qu'on y trouve, les yeux et l'esprit ne laissent pas d'y apercevoir d'abord une différence telle qu'elle doit être nécessairement entre l'art et la nature.[31]

Brossette's testimony is conclusive.   Boileau, comprehending the idea of creative activity inherent in the Greek word imitation,

---

[30] Stylistic changes are, however, quite frequent.   For instance, the awkward sentence at the beginning of the second paragraph of the citation reads in the published version as follows: " M. Despréaux disait pourtant qu'il ne faut pas que l'imitation soit entière."

[31] *Mémoires* of Brossette, Oct. 22, 1702.   (Laverdet, p. 537.)

was fully aware of the distance that separates the object imitated from the copy. This conversation with Brossette is more than sufficient to clear him of the imputation of naturalistic tendencies in art. Whatever the bent of his native disposition, in the field of high art[32] Despréaux held to the Aristotelian concept of an " ideal " imitation.

We are not surprised to find that Boileau's passage on imitation has no equivalent in the *Préfaces* of Racine. The latter doubtless took Aristotle's theory for granted and considered it more immediately applicable to fine art than to tragedy. Racine never showed a purely philosophical turn of mind;[33] doubtless he preferred to study the artistic creations of Sophocles and Euripides rather than to indulge in what would seem to him idle speculation concerning the doctrine of imitation. It is a very telling fact that in his fragmentary translation of the *Poetics*, Racine skipped the three preliminary chapters on imitation, the fourth on the origin and development of poetry, and the fifth treating of the ludicrous. He began his translation in Chapter VI with Aristotle's definition of tragedy. The practical dramatist bent on the immediate success of his plays could not stop long on a subject that is, after all, mainly a bookish one. His copy of Heinsius bears only this succinct notation on the passage in question: " L'homme aime l'imitation."[34]

[32] Boileau would never have dreamed of including here either the *Satires* or the *Lutrin*, the works in which critics have rightly pointed out strong realistic tendencies on the part of the author of the *Art Poétique*. In an undated letter to Brienne written sometime during the composition of *le Lutrin*, Boileau contradicts the rumor that religious scruples have made him destroy his poem. He adds, moreover, that " si quelque raison me le fait jamais déchirer, ce ne sera point la dévotion, qu'il ne choque en aucune manière, mais le peu d'estime que j'en fais, aussi bien que de tous mes autres ouvrages (satires and early epistles), qui me semblent des bagatelles assez inutiles " (IV, 4). Although we may doubt Boileau's sincerity in everything he wrote to Brienne, it is evident that he does not place the *Satires* or *le Lutrin* on the same artistic level as tragedy, where the application of Aristotle's doctrine of ideal imitation is most rigorous.

[33] As far as we know, the subjects he studied at Port-Royal were literary in character. Cf. *supra*, p. 108, n. 9. His letters dated at Uzès and the *Abrégé de l'Histoire de Port-Royal* show a marked aversion for philosophical and theological controversy.

[34] Mesnard, VI, 289.

An interesting anecdote indicates that Racine agreed with Boileau on the point at issue in the opening verses of *Chant III*: a thing repulsive in itself, when imitated according to art, becomes an "objet aimable." The story is told by the abbé de Saint-Pierre,[35] who got it from Mme de la Fayette. In a conversation at which she was present,

Racine soutint qu'un bon poëte pouvoit faire excuser les plus grands crimes, et même inspirer de la compassion pour les criminels. Il ajouta qu'il ne falloit que de la fécondité, de la *délicatesse*, de la *justice d'esprit* pour diminuer tellement l'horreur des crimes de Médée ou de Phèdre, qu'on les rendroit *aimables* aux spectateurs *au point de leur inspirer de la pitié pour leurs malheurs.*

The rest of the anecdote appears very doubtful. The poet's interlocutors laughed at his assertion, and it was in order to prove he was right that Racine undertook *Phèdre*, "où il réussit si bien à faire plaindre ses malheurs que le spectateur a plus de pitié de la criminelle belle-mère que du vertueux Hippolyte." Although we cannot ascribe to a salon altercation the conception of the tragedy in the mind of Racine, it is quite possible that the first part of the anecdote is true. He was perhaps already working on *Phèdre* at the time of the incident. That he succeeded in rendering his heroine "aimable" is attested by Boileau, who foretells that future ages will praise

> . . . . la douleur *vertueuse*
> De Phèdre, malgré soi perfide, incestueuse.[36]

Although Racine in the *Préfaces* chose to overlook the doctrine of imitation, he treats fully and consistently the matter of verisimilitude, which in Aristotle is an important appendage to the former. We have seen that, according to the Stagirite, the possible is the subject of art, "for what is possible is credible."[37] This precept was not meant to preclude the poet's choice of a subject that was true. On the contrary, historical fidelity may even enhance a subject, for "what has not happened we do not at once feel sure to be possible: but what has happened is manifestly possible."[38] Aristotle states precisely

---

[35] *Anecdotes dramatiques de l'abbé de la Porte*, II, 57-58, cited by Mesnard, III, 263.

[36] *Épître VII* vss. 79-80.

[37] *Poetics*, chap. IX.   [38] *Ibid., loc. cit.*

that "there is no reason why some events that have actually
happened should not conform to the law of the probable and
possible," [39] and by virtue of that quality, rather than by virtue
of their truth, they become fit subjects for poetry. In other
words, if it conforms to certain conditions, Aristotle regards
the true as a higher form of the possible. Up to this point
Aristotle seems to use the words "possible" and "probable"
quite interchangeably. That he considers the "probable" as a
third category of facts comes to light when he says that he
prefers a probable impossibility to an improbable possibility.[40]
The probable, then, is placed above the possible as it is capable
of redeeming even the impossible, while the opposite is also
true: improbability can vitiate the possible. Now the criterion
of possibility is an affirmative answer to the question: Is this
thing scientifically possible? Verisimilitude, on the other hand,
rests on public opinion or the belief on the part of the spectators that the event is likely to happen.[41] Now it is to be
noted that no French theorist or dramatist takes much interest
in the "possible" although Aristotle's expression is repeated
unconvincingly in a few critical dissertations. French poets
and doctrinaires lean to the *vraisemblable*, virtually setting at
naught "le possible." [42] D'Aubignac states clearly his viewpoint, which will also be that of Boileau and Racine:

Le vrai n'est pas le sujet du théâtre, parce qu'il y a bien des choses
véritables qui n'y doivent pas être vues. . . . Le possible n'en sera pas
aussi le sujet, car il y a bien des choses qui se peuvent faire . . . , qui
pourtant seraient ridicules et peu croyables, si elles étaient représentées.
. . . Il n'y a donc que le vraisemblable qui puisse raisonnablement fonder,
soutenir et terminer un poème dramatique: ce n'est pas que les choses

[39] *Ibid., loc. cit.*

[40] *Poetics*, chap. XXIV.

[41] Deimier, Mareschal, Chapelain, and others reversed the very nature
of Aristotle's precept by confining its application to average reality
and to the trivial round of everyday affairs. Cf. Bray, pp. 197-199.

[42] The question became an issue during the quarrel of the *Cid*. The
incidents being historically true were "possible" in the Aristotelian
sense and therefore a proper subject for tragedy. They were none the
less *invraisemblables*, it was objected: "Si le possible est la propre
matière de la poésie, il ne l'est pourtant que lorsqu'il est vraisemblable
ou nécessaire" (*Sentiments de l'Académie sur la tragi-comédie du "Cid"*
in Gasté's *la Querelle du "Cid,"* p. 364).

véritables et possibles soient bannies du théâtre, mais elles n'y sont reçues qu'autant qu'elles ont de la vraisemblance.[43]

The seventeenth century, then, was preoccupied by and large, not with the possible, but with the true and above all with the probable.

If we turn to the *Préfaces*, we shall see that Racine's position was precisely that of d'Aubignac. He builds his tragedies on *vraisemblance*, at the same time making capital use of "le véritable." The connection between these two is a close one: "What has happened is manifestly possible," said Aristotle; what has happened is more or less firmly ingrained in people's minds and is consequently, from their standpoint, *vraisemblable*, implies Racine. Rapin is at one with him on this point, affirming that "le vrai-semblable est tout ce qui est conforme à l'opinion du Public."[44] This last point is, we believe, the very kernel of Racine's dramatic system.

In answering the strictures on the simplicity of action in *Bérénice*, the poet has recourse to the law of verisimilitude. He makes the probable the only matter for tragedy:

Il n'y a que le vraisemblable qui touche dans la tragédie. Et quelle vraisemblance y a-t-il qu'il arrive en un jour une multitude de choses qui pourroient à peine arriver en plusieurs semaines.[45]

The pains Racine takes to give the exact sources of the history or legend he is treating seem at first sight to jar with his insistence on verisimilitude. We shall see, however, that the contradiction is more apparent than real.

In 1676 the poet points out that in scarcely any other tragedy has he followed history more faithfully than in *Alexandre*, the subject of which is taken from the eighth book of Quintus Curtius. Even the love episode is not of his invention; the authority of the latter historian is on this point corroborated by the testimony of Justin.[46]

The *Seconde Préface* to *Britannicus* would have to be cited in its entirety to give an adequate idea of the meticulous pains

[43] *La Pratique du Théâtre* cited by M. Bray, p. 200.

[44] Rapin's *Réflexions sur la Poétique*, chap. XXIII, *Œuvres*, II, 131.

[45] *Préface* to *Bérénice*. Cf. also the *Première Préface* to *Britannicus*, where the poet had said the same thing.

[46] *Seconde Préface*.

Racine takes to establish the truth of his characters. He adduces, citing directly, eleven passages from the *Annales* to show how authentic is the portrayal of character in the play that he considers in 1676 the most "solide" and praiseworthy thing he has done. In telling how closely he has adhered to Tacitus, he does so, not by way of duly acknowledging an indebtedness or of expressing his devotion, as we have seen him do in regard to Euripides, but in order to stress the solidity of the piece. Tacitus has given "support" to his representation of Nero's court:

A la vérité j'avois travaillé sur des modèles qui m'avoient extrêmement soutenu dans la peinture que je voulois faire de la cour d'Agrippine et de Néron. J'avois copié mes personnages d'après le plus grand peintre de l'antiquité, je veux dire d'après Tacite. Et j'étois alors si rempli de la lecture de cet excellent historien, qu'il n'y a presque pas un trait éclatant dans ma tragédie dont il ne m'ait donné l'idée. J'avois voulu mettre dans ce recueil un extrait des plus beaux endroits que j'ai tâché d'imiter, mais j'ai trouvé que cet extrait tiendroit presque autant de place que la tragédie. Ainsi le lecteur trouvera bon que je le renvoie à cet auteur, qui aussi bien est entre les mains de tout le monde; et je me contenterai de rapporter ici quelques-uns de ses passages sur chacun des personnages que j'introduis sur la scène.

The subject of *Bajazet* is "très-véritable" and vouched for by no less a personage than M. de Césy, a former ambassador to Constantinople,[47] who with his own eyes saw Bajazet several times as he used to walk up and down "à la pointe du Serrail sur le canal de la mer Noire." Several persons of quality, among them the chevalier de Nantouillet, still remember hearing the story told by the legate on his return to France. Racine likewise acknowledges his indebtedness to Césy's successor, a certain M. de la Haye, who enlightened the poet on all the difficulties proposed to him.[48]

Most of the *Préface* to *Mithridate* deals with the trueness to life of the characters and belongs to another section of our study. The character of Mithridate is, however, inseparable from his death, which is the "action of the tragedy." Racine claims that excepting a rapprochement of dates allowed by

---

[47] He held this position from 1618 to 1641, with the exception of a short interval in 1631.

[48] Cf. *Première Préface* (1672) and *Seconde Préface* (1676).

poetic license "tout le monde reconnoître aisément que j'ai
suivi l'histoire avec beaucoup de fidélité." No name is "plus
connu" than that of Mithridate. Although most of the facts
of his life are matters of general information, there is one less
known, which Racine found rich in dramatic possibilities:

> La seule chose qui pourroit n'être pas aussi connue que le reste, c'est
> le dessein que je lui fais prendre de passer dans l'Italie. Comme ce
> dessein m'a fourni une des scènes qui ont le plus réussi dans ma tragédie,
> *je crois que le plaisir du lecteur pourra redoubler, quand il verra que*
> *presque tous les historiens ont dit ce que je fais dire à Mithridate.*
> Florus, Plutarque et Dion Cassius nomment les pays par où il devoit
> passer. Appien d'Alexandrie entre plus dans le détail. . . . . .
> Ainsi elle (the enterprise) fut en partie cause de sa mort, qui est l'action
> de ma tragédie.[49]

It is for our purposes extremely important to note how much
Racine is counting on the information in the minds of his
readers. Their pleasure, he believes, will be enhanced by the
conviction that all is historically true. It is deeply significant
that he protests strongly the historical accuracy of a play of
which he invented the plot and the sentimental complications
and of which only two characters have a precise historical basis
that Racine really utilized.[50]

In the *Préface* to *Iphigénie* the author cites recondite sources
for the changes he has introduced into the legend. Pausanias[51]
is his authority for introducing another Iphigenia, a daughter
whom Helen had secreted before her marriage to Menelaus. His
testimony furnished Racine with a dénouement that had verisimilitude:

---

[49] *Préface* to *Mithridate*.

[50] Monime and Xipharès, although historical in names and in their
relationships to Mithridate are virtually Racine's creations. For
Xipharès, according to Appian, did not survive infancy. Of Monime
we know from Plutarch (*Life of Lucullus*) only that she was beautiful
and virtuous and that, although the favorite among several wives of
Mithridate, she was unhappy and lonely, and finally welcomed the king's
order that she should die. It was indeed only "en partie" after this
portrait that Racine built his character. Cf. *la Préface.*

[51] A note of Racine refers the reader to p. 125 of the *Corinthiaques*
(Hanau: 1613), where Pausanias says that Euphorion of Chalcidice,
Alexander of Pleuron, and Stesichorus, as well as the Argives in general,
were of the opinion that Iphigenia was the daughter of Theseus.

J'ai rapporté tous ces avis si différents, et surtout le passage de Pausanias, parce que c'est à cet auteur que je dois l'heureux personnage d'Ériphile, sans lequel je n'aurois jamais osé entreprendre cette tragédie. . . . Et il ne faut que l'avoir vu représenter pour comprendre quel plaisir j'ai fait au spectateur, et en sauvant à la fin une princesse vertueuse pour qui il s'est si fort intéressé dans le cours de la tragédie, *et en la sauvant par une autre voie que par un miracle, qu'il n'auroit pu souffrir, parce qu'il ne le sauroit jamais croire.*

Racine was careful not to tax the credulity of his audience by a *deus ex machina* ending. As a matter of fact he was so intent upon solving the problem of verisimilitude that he was even willing to do implicit violence to his sources in order to establish in the minds of the readers a belief that there were two Iphigenias. Stesichorus and Pausanias merely allege a different parentage for Iphigenia making her, not the daughter of Agamemnon and Clytemnestra, but the offspring of Theseus and Helen. The latter, before marrying Menelaus, was supposed to have secretly entrusted her child to Clytemnestra. This does not, of course, imply that there were two Iphigenias as Racine intends us to infer.

The *Préface* also affirms that Achilles' expedition to Lesbos, where a princess fell passionately in love with him, is well grounded in history:

Euphorion de Chalcide, poète très connu parmi les anciens et dont Virgile et Quintilien font une mention honorable, parloit de ce voyage de Lesbos. Il disoit dans un de ses poèmes, au rapport de Parthenius, qu'Achille avoit fait la conquête de cette île avant que de joindre l'armée des grecs, et qu'il y avoit même trouvé une princesse qui s'étoit éprise d'amour pour lui.

It would be tedious to cite further examples of how Racine invokes history or legend as a basis for the characters and action in his plays. From the evidence already given we are inclined at first to conclude that the true, not the *vraisemblable*, is Racine's main concern. That it is not mere respect for secular history [52] or legend that makes him so scrupulously exact is evident, however, from such passages as the following:

Il est vrai que j'ai été obligé de faire vivre Astyanax un peu plus

---

[52] According to the *Préface* to *Esther*, any alteration of Sacred Scripture would be a sort of sacrilege.

qu'il n'a vécu; mais j'écris dans un pays où cette liberté ne pouvoit pas être mal reçue. Car, sans parler de Ronsard, qui a choisi ce même Astyanax pour le héros de sa *Franciade*, qui ne sait que l'on fait descendre nos anciens rois de ce fils d'Hector, et que nos vieilles chroniques sauvent la vie à ce jeune prince, après la désolation de son pays, pour en faire le fondateur de notre monarchie?

Combien Euripide a-t-il été plus hardi dans sa tragédie d'*Hélène*. Il y choque ouvertement la créance commune de toute la Grèce. Il suppose qu'Hélène n'a jamais mis le pied dans Troie; et qu'après l'embrasement de cette ville, Ménélas trouve sa femme en Égypte, dont elle n'étoit point partie. Tout cela fondé sur une opinion qui n'étoit reçue que parmi les Égyptiens, comme on le peut voir dans Hérodote.

Je ne crois pas que j'eusse besoin de cet exemple d'Euripide pour justifier le peu de liberté que j'ai prise. Car il y a bien de la différence entre détruire le principal fondement d'une fable, et en altérer quelques incidents, qui changent presque de face dans toutes les mains qui les traitent. . . . Et c'est à propos de quelque contrariété de cette nature qu'un ancien commentateur de Sophocle [53] remarque fort bien, " qu'il ne faut point s'amuser à chicaner les poètes pour quelques changements qu'ils ont pu faire dans la fable; mais qu'il faut s'attacher à considerer l'excellent usage qu'ils ont fait de ces changements, et la manière ingénieuse dont ils ont su accommoder la fable à leur sujet." [54]

The passage carries even greater weight when we know that Racine, in citing the commentator of Sophocles, distorts somewhat the import of his text to make it fit more appropriately into his scheme. What Camerarius said was: " We should not presume to search out anxiously such historical inaccuracies (as those found in verses 540 to 542 of the *Electra*),[55] but rather notice ' illa pulcherrima exempla bonarum artium et præcepta optima vitæ et memorabiles sententias morum atque sapientiæ.' " [56] Although it is evident from this *Préface* written in 1676 that, in theory, Racine allowed the poet considerable freedom in changing the facts of history, in practice, he had far more regard for public opinion than did Euripides in writing his *Helen*. He obviously cited this as an extreme case, almost

[53] Camerarius, a German scholar of the sixteenth century, whose commentaries on Sophocles are published in Paul Estienne's edition of the Greek dramatist given in 1603.

[54] *Seconde Préface* to *Andromaque* (1676).

[55] In giving to Menelaus two children, Sophocles is going against Homer, who says Hermione was an only child.

[56] Cited by Mesnard, II, 39-40.

a *reductio ad absurdum* of what he really considered were the rights of a poet.[57]

As we read the *Préfaces* through from that of *Alexandre* to the last one written in 1691, we are impressed, not indeed with Racine's respect for history, but with his respect for what his public knows of history. A few examples will suffice to prove this cardinal point. In the *Seconde Préface* to *Andromaque*, Racine explains how his subject differs from that of Euripides: in the latter's play Andromaque feared for the life of Molossus, a son by Pyrrhus; in the French play, however, there is no question of Molossus, Andromaque having no other husband than Hector and no son except Astyanax. Racine then tells, in what is the crucial passage of his critical writings, why he changed the legend. It was because

j'ai cru en cela me conformer à l'idée que nous avons maintenant de cette princesse. La plupart de ceux qui ont entendu parler d'Andromaque, ne la connoissent guère que pour la veuve d'Hector et pour la mère d'Astyanax. *On ne croit point* qu'elle doive aimer ni un autre mari, ni un autre fils. Et je doute que les larmes d'Andromaque eussent fait sur l'esprit de mes spectateurs l'impression qu'elles y ont faite, si elles avoient coulé pour un autre fils que celui qu'elle avoit d'Hector.

In a passage added to the *Préface* of *Bajazet* in 1676,[58] he tells us what was his intention in representing the mores and politics of the Turks:

Je me suis attaché à bien exprimer dans ma tragédie *ce que nous savons* des mœurs et des maximes des Turcs.

We see, then, that the opinions and belief of the public play an absolutely preponderant rôle in Racine's poetics. He takes stock of what the public knows and builds his play with that in mind. Occasionally, as in the story of Bajazet or in Mithridate's plan for a campaign in Italy, he thinks the audience not sufficiently informed to give ready credence to an incident. Then with the professed purpose of adding to the common knowledge, he carefully adduces the less-known sources, thus gradually bringing the reader to admit the authenticity of the point in question. The *Préface* to *Athalie* is a long disquisition designed for those

[57] Cf. *Préface* to *Mithridate*: " Excepté quelque événement que j'ai un peu rapproché par *le droit que donne la poésie.* . . . "

[58] It was suppressed in 1687.

" à qui l'histoire de l'Ancien Testament ne sera pas assez présente." It is very evident that he believes the pleasure derived from his plays is dependent upon the spectators' willingness to accept them as true. The purpose of the *Préfaces*, especially in proportion as the polemical tone diminishes, seems to be to prepare the way for this psychological attitude in the audience.

A few examples in the opposite direction will show the same tendency to *vraisemblance*, or to what Rapin defined as conformity to the belief of the public.[59] What are Racine's considerations when he goes counter to history or legend? There are two: he is changing a fact little known to the general public; the change has so much plausibility that it will readily be believed. The character of Junie is an example of the first kind of change. She is in the play far more " retenue qu'elle n'étoit," but Racine defends the departure from Seneca and Tacitus saying,

Je n'ai pas ouï dire qu'il nous fût défendu de rectifier les mœurs d'un personnage, *surtout lorsqu'il n'est pas connu.*[60]

He demurs, however, when it comes to doing violence to what is common opinion. Everyone knows the characters in *Andromaque*, " aussi n'ai-je pas pensé qu'il me fût permis de rien changer à leurs mœurs." [61] The age of Britannicus is so well known that the poet dares not represent him otherwise than as a very young prince.[62] The same play furnishes an excellent example of the second kind of alteration that Racine is willing to make in history. Aulus Gellius states explicitly that no one above ten years of age can become a vestal virgin. Racine, however, defends his ending on the grounds of plausibility. The Roman people, in consideration of Junie's high birth, her virtues, and above all her utter bereavement, might dispense her from the age prescribed by law just as had been done so often in the case of worthy men seeking after the consulship.[63] This

---

[59] Cf. *supra*, p. 136.

[60] *Première Préface* to *Britannicus*.

[61] *Première Préface* to *Andromaque*.

[62] *Seconde Préface*, in which Racine renounces making him a seventeen-year-old hero, as he had at first tried to do.

[63] *Ibid.*

is an instance where Racine lets probability supersede the truth
of history. Another change that Racine makes in history is the
prophecy he puts into the mouth of Joad. Although Holy
Scripture does not expressly ascribe to him the gift of seeing
into the future, the poet considers that it is in keeping with
what the Old Testament says of the man who is there represented as filled with the spirit of God. Besides, by virtue of
his office of high priest, Joad would be likely to prophesy.[64] It
is therefore on the grounds of plausibility that the poet makes
this addition to the character of Joad, his great reverence for
the sacred text notwithstanding. Using history as an adjunct
to verisimilitude, he stays close to it in those matters on which
his audience is well informed. He departs from historical facts
and deals in the *vraisemblable* when the spectators are willing
to believe something contrary to history and when the change
serves a dramatic purpose.

Moreover, to substantiate these conclusions which we have
drawn from scattered examples in the *Préfaces*, we have Racine's
own statement. It occurs in the *Préface* to *Phèdre*. Plutarch
tells how Theseus made a trip to Epirus near the mouth of the
Acheron in order to help his friend Pirithoüs in an amatory
undertaking that proved to be the latter's undoing. Theseus
himself was made prisoner by the offended king and held for
a long time. There is also a legend that Theseus once descended
into the lower world to carry off Proserpina. Racine adroitly
combines the two episodes, one historical, the other fabulous.
Besides serving the plot,[65] this device enriches the poetic value
of his tragedy:

Ainsi j'ai tâché de conserver la vraisemblance de l'histoire sans rien
perdre des ornements de la fable, qui fournit extrêmement à la poésie.[66]

" La vraisemblance de l'histoire " clinches the foregoing argument concerning the relation of truth to the *vraisemblable* in
Racine's tragedies. This elliptical expression, meaning the air

---

[64] *Préface* to *Athalie.*

[65] " Et le bruit de la mort de Thésée, fondé sur ce voyage fabuleux,
donne lieu à Phèdre de faire une déclaration d'amour qui devient une
des principales causes de son malheur, et qu'elle n'auroit jamais osé
faire tant qu'elle auroit cru que son mari étoit vivant." (*Préface.*)

[66] *Ibid.*

of truthfulness that history imparts to a subject, is simply
another way of expressing Aristotle's dictum: " What has happened is manifestly possible: otherwise it would not have happened." [67] Racine based his tragedy on *vraisemblance*, the criterion of which is the belief of the public. The latter believes
more readily what it knows to have happened, hence the large
place that Racine accords to history.

On the point of verisimilitude Racine and Boileau are at one.
The critic forbade poets to offer the spectator anything " incroyable," adding in true Aristotelian fashion that what is true
is not by that fact verisimilar.[68] He then repeats in poetic form
precisely what Racine has said in the *Préface* to *Bérénice*: " Il
n'y a que le vraisemblable qui touche dans la tragédie." Boileau
affirms that

> Une merveille absurde est pour moi sans appas;
> L'esprit n'est point ému de ce qu'il ne croit pas.[69]

The other considerations in regard to tragic subjects can be
disposed of more summarily. Was there disparity between the
views of the two poets on the matter of religious drama?
Boileau's castigation of the " troupe grossière " and " sottement
zélée " that

> Joua les Saints, la Vierge, et Dieu, par piété [70]

is well known. To his great satisfaction, knowledge finally
came dispelling the ignorance that had fostered the religious
theater of the middle ages, and happily

> On vit renaître Hector, Andromaque, Ilion.[71]

This verse harking back to the praise of ancient fables found
at the beginning of his treatment of tragedy makes it clear what

[67] *Poetics*, chap. IX.

[68] There is a curious remark to this effect in Racine's account of the
Campagnes de Louis XIV. After relating the capitulation of Nimwegen
and other Dutch towns that gave the French a prodigious number of
prisoners, the historiographer makes this comment: " Par là on peut voir
qu'il y a quelquefois des choses vraies qui ne sont pas vraisemblables
aux yeux des hommes, et que nous traitons souvent de fabuleux, dans
l'histoire, des événements qui, tout incroyables qu'ils sont, ne laissent
pas d'être véritables." (Mesnard, V, 250.)

[69] *Art Poétique, Chant III*, 49-50.

[70] *Ibid.*, vs. 86.   [71] *Ibid.*, vs. 90.

are the subjects of Boileau's predilection. Even in the sketch bringing the history of the theater up to his day, he thinks only in terms of Greek heroes. Admitting the preponderance of *tendresse* on the modern stage, he counsels

> Qu'Achille aime autrement que Tircis et Philène.[72]

Apropos of the exposition, Boileau says he would brook a character's saying outright, " Je suis Oreste, ou bien Agamemnon." [73] In telling how characters should be portrayed, the critic is still preoccupied with the traditional traits of Agamemnon and Æneas.[74]

There is nothing in the *Art Poétique*, however, to justify our saying that Boileau condemned religious subjects as such.[75] His contempt for the *mystères* is due to the clumsiness of the actors, their " simplicité," and their presumption in preaching " sans mission." He also alleges the " dévote imprudence " of their undertaking.[76] Boileau could have known little or noth-

---

[72] *Ibid.*, vs. 99.   [73] *Ibid.*, vs. 34.

[74] *Ibid.*, vss. 105-112. Cf. also vss. 238-240 where, in speaking of the epic, he praises the sound of names which " semblent nés pour les vers ":

> Ulysse, Agamemnon, Oreste, Idoménée,
> Hélène, Ménélas, Pâris, Hector, Enée . . .

[75] For Boileau's ideas on a religious subject for the epic, see *Art Poétique, Chant III,* vss. 160-236. The case is quite different from that of tragedy. The epic, he tells us,

> Se soutient par la fable et vit de fiction.

The poet here " s'égaye," embellishing his poem with personifications, allegory, and mythological imagery. Without these " ornements " his verse languishes, and he himself becomes a cold historian. Boileau then launches into the discussion of the " merveilleux chrétien," his main contention being that the awful mysteries of faith

> D'ornements égayés ne sont point susceptibles

and that mingling the " merveilleux chrétien " with sacred truths tends to give to the latter the semblance of fiction. Even for the epic he admits of a Christian subject, as is implied in this gibe at Ariosto:

> Ce n'est pas que j'approuve *en un sujet chrétien*
> Un auteur follement idolâtre et païen. . . .

[76]   " De pélerins, dit-on, une troupe grossière,
> En public, à Paris, y monta la première,
> Et, sottement zélee en sa simplicité,
> Joua les Saints, la Vierge, et Dieu, par piété.
> Le savoir, à la fin dissipant l'ignorance,

ing of the medieval drama; predisposed as he was in favor of
Aristotle and the rules, he would have found nothing good
therein.   That he was not opposed to a religious subject when
treated according to the rules of art is evident from the high
regard he professed for *Polyeucte* which, according to Monchesnay, he considered Corneille's masterpiece.[77]

Turning to Racine we find that the *Préfaces* to *Esther* and
Athalie written fifteen and seventeen years, respectively, after
the publication of the *Art Poétique* show a lively interest in
religious subjects possessing high dramatic possibilities.   When
the poet, in response to Mme de Maintenon's request for a
sacred poem with chorus and action, proposed the subject of
Esther, the mistresses of Saint-Cyr saw in the story excellent
lessons of the love of God and detachment from the world.
Racine, however, was viewing it from his angle:

Et je crus *de mon côté* que je trouverois assez de facilité à traiter ce
sujet; d'autant plus qu'il me sembla que sans altérer aucune des circonstances tant soit peu considérables de l'Écriture sainte, . . . je
pourrois remplir toute mon action avec les seules scènes que Dieu lui-
même, pour ainsi dire, a préparées.[78]

As Racine worked, he came to realize that he was carrying out
a plan that had often passed through his mind.   It was

de lier, comme dans les anciennes tragédies grecques, le chœur et le
chant avec l'action, et d'employer à chanter les louanges du vrai Dieu
cette partie du chœur que les païens employoient à chanter les louanges
de leurs fausses divinités.[79]

We may question whether Racine entertained thoughts of composing a religious drama before his retirement from the theater
in 1677.   In any event, the commission of Mme de Maintenon
is said to have thrown the poet, still chary of his fame, into a
" grande agitation."[80]   For a courtier, refusal was out of the
question.   Boileau, whom he consulted, " décida brusquement
pour la négative."   Racine, nevertheless, after some reflection

---

    Fit voir de ce projet la dévote imprudence.
    On chassa ces docteurs prêchant sans mission.
    On vit renaître Hector, Andromaque, Ilion."
       (*Art Poétique, Chant III*, vss. 83-90.)

[77] *Bolœana*, p. 131.   [78] *Préface.*   [79] *Ibid.*
 [80] *Souvenirs de la Marquise de Caylus*, p. 164.

came upon the subject of Esther. Despréaux was delighted with
it and urged the poet to go on with the tragedy as eagerly as
he had previously sought to turn him away from it.[81]

Racine seems to have turned eagerly to another religious subject after the success of *Esther*:

Ce grand succès mit Racine en goût; il voulut composer une autre
pièce; et le sujet d'Athalie . . . lui parut le plus beau de tous ceux
qu'il pouvoit tirer de l'Écriture sainte. Il y travailla sans perdre de
temps; et l'hiver d'après, cette nouvelle pièce se trouva en état d'être
représentée.[82]

Boileau was even more impressed with the beauty of this piece.
When Racine, disheartened at the reception it got, thought he
had been unhappy in his choice of subject, it was Boileau who
reassured him saying that *Athalie* was his masterpiece. "'Je
m'y connois, lui disoit-il, et le public y reviendra.'"[83] Whatever may have been Boileau's—or Racine's—attitude toward
religious subjects at the time of the *Art Poétique*, we know
that the former was completely won over by the success Racine
had in treating two biblical subjects at the end of his career.

Boileau says nothing of the feasibility of taking subjects from
modern history. Racine, while he decries the imitation of an
action in modern times if it took place in the country where
the play is to be given, and if the majority of spectators have
known the characters in real life, considers nevertheless that
"l'éloignement des pays répare en quelque sorte la trop grande
proximité de temps" and that the dignity of tragic characters
will not suffer if this precept is followed. The reason given is
in line with what we have already said of his serious concern
for what the public knows or thinks is true:

Car le peuple ne met guère de différence entre ce qui est, si j'ose ainsi
parler, à mille ans de lui, et ce qui en est à mille lieues. C'est ce qui
fait, par exemple, que les personnages turcs, quelque modernes qu'ils

---

[81] *Ibid.*, p. 165.

[82] *Ibid.*, p. 168.

[83] *Mémoires* of L. Racine, Mesnard, I, 325. Brossette (*Recueil des
Mémoires touchant la vie et les ouvrages de Boileau-Despréaux*, p. 496,
cited by Mesnard, I, 325, n. 2) says that Boileau placed *Phèdre* first
among Racine's plays and *Andromaque* second. Mesnard suggests that
at the time he was perhaps leaving the religious tragedies out of consideration.

soient, ont de la dignité sur notre théâtre. *On les regarde de bonne heure comme anciens.*[84]

Racine, moreover, finds a precedent in the *Persians* of Æschylus. The latter, despite the modernity of his subject, succeeded in imparting to his characters the glamour necessary to tragic personages by placing his action in a far-off country.

Not a line in the *Art Poétique* gives us an inkling of Boileau's taste in regard to the structural nature of the subject. He endorses neither the simple nor the complex subject according to Aristotle's classification;[85] neither does he expressly approve any of the types of subject noted by d'Aubignac: those of intrigue,[86] of passion (simple), and those of intrigue and passion mixed.[87] Dubos' anecdote telling how Despréaux disapproved of the simplicity of the subject and, except for an absence from Paris, would have prevented his friend from undertaking *Bérénice* would be enlightening if we knew it were trustworthy. We have seen, however, that it has many of the earmarks of a spurious account.[88]

Racine, on the other hand, does not mince words in defending " cette même simplicité que j'avois recherchée avec tant de soin." [89] We have already seen [90] how he twice tartly maintains that a multiplicity of events is contrary to verisimilitude, it being unlikely that many incidents should occur in one day. In the *Préface* to *Alexandre* he flings at critics the retort that a simple subject is according to the taste of the ancients, with which they are apparently little conversant. Again in the *Préface* to *Bérénice* he invokes the practice of the Greek dramatists. Of those who consider simplicity a sign of poor invention,[91] he says:

[84] *Seconde Préface* to *Bajazet.*
[85] Aristotle divides tragedy into the Complex, the Pathetic, the Ethical, and the Simple. (*Poetics*, chap. XVIII.)
[86] For the vogue of subjects of intrigue see M. Mornet's noteworthy " Introduction " to his *Racine, Théâtre*, pp. 11-16.
[87] D'Aubignac, *la Pratique du Théâtre*, pp. 85-86.
[88] Cf. *supra*, pp. 76-77.
[89] *Préface* to *Bérénice.*   [90] Cf. *supra*, p. 136.
[91] Segrais' remark (cited by Le Bidois, *la Vie dans la Tragédie de Racine*, p. 10) is characteristic: " La matière lui manque et il dit des choses très communes pour donner à ses scènes la longueur qu'elles

Ils ne songent pas qu'au contraire, toute l'invention consiste à faire quelque chose de rien, et que tout ce grand nombre d'incidents a toujours été le refuge des poëtes qui ne sentoient dans leur génie ni assez d'abondance ni assez de force pour attacher durant cinq actes leurs spectateurs par une action simple, soutenue de la violence des passions, de la beauté des sentiments et de l'élégance de l'expression.[92]

The *Préface* of *la Thébaïde* tells how he limited his subject, although, there, he is perhaps more concerned with unity than with simplicity of subject. In both *Préfaces* to *Andromaque*, after citing eighteen verses of the *Æneid*, Racine announces:

Voilà, en peu de vers, *tout le sujet de cette tragédie*. Voilà le lieu de la scène, l'action qui s'y passe, les quatre principaux acteurs, et même leurs caractères.

A few words of Suetonius were the inspiration and subject of *Bérénice*. For the benefit of anyone doubting that the separation of two lovers is sufficient matter for a tragedy, he alleges the most touching story ever treated by poets: the separation of Dido and Æneas in Virgil. What was matter for an entire canto in which the action lasted several days is surely sufficient for the subject of a tragedy " dont la durée ne doit être que de quelques heures." [93]   The question of action treated in a later part of this study will throw further light on the simplicity Racine sometimes sought in tragic subjects.   Let it suffice, moreover, to say at this point that a careful analysis of his plays will show that he departs several times from the simplicity which he consciously effected in *Bérénice*.

The one definite expression of Racine's idea of love as a tragic subject is found in the *Préface* to *la Thébaïde*. It was written for the collective edition of 1676 and therefore postdates by two years the publication of the *Art Poétique*. Looking back upon a play that he puts definitely among his *juvenilia,* Racine observes that love, " which ordinarily plays such an important part in tragedies," has almost no place in this piece. If he had it to do over again, however, he doubts that he would give to it any more prominence. The famous hatred that possessed these two brothers crowded out all other interests.   In

doivent avoir. Il y a plus de matière dans une seule scène de Corneille que dans toute une pièce de Racine."

   [92] *Préface* to *Bérénice*.   [93] *Ibid.*

truth the story of the house of Œdipus with its incests, parri-
cides, and other horrors leaves scant room for either the *tendresse* or the jealousy of lovers. He notes, moreover, that love
when relegated to secondary characters produces only a mediocre
effect. From this statement, which by virtue of its date is fairly
definitive, it is evident that Racine thinks that love, if it is to
be portrayed in tragedy, should be the all-absorbing passion of
the principal characters. Louis Racine says as much in the
Mémoires:

D'ailleurs il étoit persuadé que l'amour, à moins qu'il ne soit entièrement tragique, ne doit point entrer dans les tragédies.[94]

The only other time that Racine speaks of love as a tragic
subject is in the last paragraph of the *Préface* to *Phèdre*. His
statement is then so entangled in the curious and unprecedented
plea for a utilitarian purpose in tragedy that it loses much of
its force. Without going into the motive of this part of the
Préface—it will be studied under the heading of the function
of tragedy [95]—we shall merely cite what he says about love:

Les *foiblesses de l'amour y passent pour de. vraies foiblesses;* les passions n'y sont présentées aux yeux que pour montrer tout le désordre
dont elles sont cause; et le vice y est peint partout avec des couleurs
qui en font connoître et haïr la difformité.

This may perhaps be regarded as an implication that love, if it
occurs at all, should be a perverting and fatal passion. When
we recall, however, that this passage was likely calculated to be
the means of the poet's reconciliation with Port-Royal, it seems
to smack too much of opportuneness for us to attach it directly
to his æsthetics.

There is one passage which, although bearing essentially on
character,[96] throws some light on the kind of love that Racine

---

[94] Mesnard, I, 263.   [95] Cf. *infra*, pp. 166 *et sqq.*

[96] There are other passages where he speaks of love, but it is in connection with characters. With the professed purpose of giving him a
tragic flaw and the evident purpose of rendering him human, he changes
the traditional Hippolytus into a lover. " J'appelle foiblesse la passion
qu'il ressent malgré lui pour Aricie, qui est la fille et la sœur des ennemis mortels de son père." It is to be noted that the " foiblesse " is not
so much in his loving as in his loving against the command of his
father. Racine seems to be dissembling in this passage. Hippolytus'

considered proper to tragedy. According to the author, critics had found Pyrrhus too violent to suit their taste. They complained

> qu'il s'emportât contre Andromaque, et qu'il voulût épouser cette captive à quelque prix que ce fût. J'avoue qu'il n'est pas assez résigné à la volonté de sa maîtresse, et que Céladon a mieux connu que lui le parfait amour. Mais que faire? Pyrrhus n'avoit pas lu nos romans. Il étoit violent *de son naturel. Et tous les héros ne sont pas faits pour être des Céladons.*[97]

Tragic love, then, should be in keeping with the character's natural disposition and quite free from the mawkishness that mars that sentiment in pastoral novels.

We shall find that in the matter of love Boileau is more explicit than Racine. The critic remarks, along with everyone else,[98] that

> Bientôt l'amour, fertile en tendres sentiments,
> S'empara du théâtre ainsi que des romans.[99]

He judges it the surest way of moving the spectator, and this

scorn for Venus was clearly his tragic flaw in Euripides' play. In making him a lover, Racine was more likely guided by the external *bienséance* of an age enamoured of *tendresse* and most of all by the inherent possibility of intensifying Phèdre's passion under the lash of jealousy. Cf. *infra*, pp. 194-196.

[97] *Première Préface* to *Andromaque*. Cf. also the *Ière Préface* to *Alexandre*, in which he scoffs at those critics who " croient qu'un héros ne doit jamais faire un pas sans la permission de sa maîtresse."

[98] Corneille in the *Avis au lecteur* prefixed to *Sophonisbe* (1663) fleers the "goût de nos délicats, qui veulent de l'amour partout." Saint-Évremond in the *Discours sur l'Alexandre* (1666), Guéret in *le Parnasse Réformé* (1668), La Fontaine in the *Préface* to *les Amours de Psyché et de Cupidon* (1669), Rapin in his *Réflexions sur la Poétique*, chap. XX (*Œuvres*, II, 186-187), and Chappuzeau in the *Théâtre français* (1674), p. 41, all writing during the period covered by Boileau's observation, bear witness to the preponderance of *tendresse*. Longepierre in his *Parallèle* (1686) calls love the very soul of the modern theater (cited by Parfaict, *op. cit.*, X, 242). Valincour (d'Olivet, *Histoire de l'Académie française*, II, 334), Fénelon (*Lettre sur les Occupations de l'Académie*), Dubos (*op. cit.*, I, 129-130), and Louis Racine (*Mémoires*, Mesnard, I, 263) all regret that Racine allowed himself to be carried along by the taste of the century.

[99] *Art Poétique, Chant III*, vss. 93-94.

he considers the very purpose of tragedy.[100] While approving of amorous heroes and "la sensible peinture"[101] of love, he warns poets against certain abuses that are all too prevalent. In precisely the same vein of irony as Racine's retort to those who censured Pyrrhus for being too violent and too little complaisant to the wishes of his mistress, Boileau insists that the love of tragic characters should be of a different caliber from that of "bergers doucereux."[102] He would not banish love like those "tristes esprits" who

> D'un si riche *ornement* veulent priver la scène.[103]

This last verse would make us suspect that Boileau, if he here weighed his words, did not grasp the full import of love as a tragic passion. In the lines that follow, however, he alleges the examples of Rodrigue and Chimène and of Dido. Surely Boileau did not consider their love an "ornement" in the sense of its being an accessory beauty. Although it is true that, in his discussion of the epic, Boileau uses the word "ornement" three times to designate an applied embellishment,[104] such a meaning

---

[100] Cf. vss. 15-16 of *Chant III*, where Boileau gives the secret of success on the stage:

> Que dans tous vos discours la passion émue
> Aille chercher le cœur, l'échauffe, et le remue.

Boileau was chided very vehemently for this view by Frain du Tremblay, an academician of Anjou: "Que n'était-il au moins aussi sage que les païens, qui n'ont jamais ni dit ni pensé que les pièces de théâtre ne puissent réussir sans l'amour." (*Discours IV*, p. 260, cited by Delaporte, *op. cit.*, III, 149.)

[101] *Art Poétique, Chant III*, vs. 95.

[102] *Ibid.*, vs. 98. Cf. also *Satire IX*, vss. 261-266, for his hatred of this affectation. Saint-Évremond in 1672 uttered the same complaint in his treatise, *De la Tragédie Ancienne et Moderne*: "Bien souvent nos plus grans héros aiment en bergers sur nos théâtres, & l'innocence d'une espèce d'amour champêtre leur tient lieu de toute gloire & de toute vertu." (*Œuvres*, I, 180.)

Even as early as 1664 in the *Dissertation*, Boileau had remarked ironically that Ariosto's Joconde, under certain exasperating circumstances, surpassed Céladon and Silvandre in their resolve to do nothing to displease their mistresses. He had also maintained that love should be conformable to the character of the lover. (*Œuvres*, III, 12-13.)

[103] *Art Poétique, Chant IV*, vs. 99.

[104] *Chant III*, vss. 189, 194, and 200.

in this context would violate not only the spirit, but even the letter of what Boileau says of love in other passages of the *Art Poétique* and elsewhere. Anyone who placed *Phèdre* first among Racine's secular dramas [105] was not likely to consider love a mere adjunct. If our interpretation is correct, " ornement " as used in verse ninety-seven of the *Art Poétique* must be taken figuratively to mean " ce qui sert à rendre plus recommendable," [106] or in this particular context that which lends beauty and glory to the theater. Despréaux's further comments on love as a tragic passion will bear out our interpretation.

Boileau expressly disavowed any scruples in regard to the suitableness of portraying love even as a disordered passion providing it be done " chastely ":

> L'amour le moins honnête, exprimé chastement,[107]
> N'excite point en nous de honteux mouvement.
> Didon a beau gémir et m'étaler ses charmes,
> Je condamne sa faute en partageant ses larmes.
> Un auteur vertueux, dans ses vers innocents,
> Ne corrompt point le cœur *en chatouillant les sens*; [108]
> Son feu n'allume point de criminelle flamme.[109]

That Boileau was not squeamish in such matters is further attested by what he says of the elegy. To excel in this *genre* treating of the sorrows and joys of love, the poet must fall back on an emotional experience of his own:

[105] " M. Despréaux nommoit aussi *Phèdre* la première, et *Andromaque* la seconde." (Brossette, *Recueil des mémoires touchant la vie et les ouvrages de Boileau Despréaux*. MS. appartenant à M. Feuillet de Conches, cited by Mesnard, I, 325, n. 2.)

[106] *Dictionnaire de l'Académie française* (1694). Examples given are: " La vertu est un grand ornement " and " La dignité de Duc et Pair est un grand ornement dans une maison." Furetière gives: " La science est l'ornement de l'esprit " and " La vertu et le savoir sont les plus beaux ornemens."

[107] Chapelain did not forbid the portrayal of " sales amours " if it was done " avec des paroles honnêtes." " Cela s'appelle envelopper les ordures " (*Lettres*, II, 685). Cf. also Chappuzeau, *le Théâtre français*, p. 43.

[108] This coming from Boileau, together with the admissions made by a man like Bossuet in his *Maximes et Réflexions sur la Comédie*, is among the most valid testimonies we have of the power of the French classic drama to stir men's souls.

[109] *Chant IV*, vss. 101-107.

> Mais, pour bien exprimer ces caprices heureux,
> C'est peu d'être poète, il faut être amoureux.[110]

Another qualification that Boileau demands is

> . . . que l'amour, souvent de remords combattu
> Paraisse une faiblesse, et non une vertu.[111]

Now this passage, along with the verse in which he says that, while sharing Dido's tears, he nevertheless " condemns " her " faute," has led many serious-minded scholars [112] into thinking that it was on moral grounds that he insisted that love, if it is to be represented at all, should be portrayed as a weakness and as something to be struggled against. This opinion, however, goes counter to everything that Boileau says of love. The *Dissertation sur la " Joconde,"* written in 1664, contains no word of blame for the licentious portrayal of love in La Fontaine's *conte*. In the *Art Poétique* he speaks tenderly of the love of Chimène and Rodrigue.[113] He commends Terence for showing a lover in such true colors that he is not a portrait nor a life-like image, but a lover " véritable." [114] Boileau, then, does not object to the presentation of love.

Going back to Boileau's dictum about love's being a " faiblesse," let us place it in its context. Its meaning then becomes clear, and it is quite consistent with what Boileau says elsewhere. Tragic heroes, if they are to be lovers, should be possessed by more than a maudlin sentiment. Achilles' love should not be patterned after that of Tircis. If love in a tragedy is to have all its efficacy, it must have the destructive and pitiable character of an ill-regulated passion, or, in the words of Boileau, it must be a " faiblesse," [115] not a virtue.

[110] *Ibid., Chant II*, vss. 43-44.   [111] *Ibid., Chant III*, vss. 101-102.

[112] Nisard, *Histoire de la Littérature*, II, 304; Brunetière, " l'Esthétique de Boileau," *Revue des Deux Mondes*, XCIII (1889), 681-682; and Morillot, *Boileau*, pp. 155-156. The latter carries his contention the farthest saying that even when Boileau recommended love he did so without realizing " le prix des conseils qu'il donnait." This precept, Morillot maintains, is out of harmony with his exaltation of reason, his personal experience, his slander of women in *Satire X*, and Monchesnay's report that he relegated love to comedy.

[113] *Chant IV*, vs. 100.

[114] *Chant III*, vss. 419-420.

[115] Cf. the derivation: *flebilem* > faible.

Most of the confusion in regard to what the critic really thought of love as a tragic passion arises from what Monchesnay reports that he said later in life and from a letter of Boileau written to the latter in September, 1707. In any attempt to clarify the matter, we must recall that some thirty-three years have elapsed since the *Art Poétique* appeared. Due allowance must be made, then, for a change in attitude brought about by age and circumstances and also for a certain amount of inconsistency that marks the utterances of most men.

In this letter to Monchesnay, Boileau refutes the latter's wholesale condemnation of the theater as dangerous to morals. He maintains that in itself it is indifferent providing love is chastely expressed. He even protests that a play not only does not inspire love in the spectator, but that it can do much to cure a person from the effects of this passion. He insists again, however, " qu'on n'y répande point d'images ni de sentimens voluptueux." [116] Thus far we see not only the corroboration of what he said in the *Art Poétique*, but the ascription to tragedy of a rather doubtful ethical function.

We come now to a passage in the *Bolæana* that has been widely misused.[117] It has usually been cut in two and then cited quite apart from its context. Monchesnay, who can be little suspected of partiality toward the theater in general or toward Racine in particular, reports that Despréaux used to say that

l'amour est un caractère affecté à la Comédie, parce qu'au fond il n'y a rien de si ridicule que le caractère d'un Amant, & que cette passion fait tomber les hommes dans une espèce d'enfance.[118]

He gives Terence's Phædria as an example of what a ninny love makes of a young man. Although Boileau considered a lover's petulant moods, unreal woes, and fretful joys the very quintessence of comedy, he held that " l'amour pris à la lettre n'étoit point du caractère de la Tragédie, à laquelle il ne pouvoit convenir "—but listen to the end of the sentence—" qu'entant

[116] Laverdet, p. 453.

[117] Brunetière, " Esthétique de Boileau," *Rev. des Deux Mondes*, XCIII (1889), 681-682; Morillot, *Boileau*, p. 156; and Delaporte, *op. cit.*, III, 149.

[118] P. 59.

qu'il alloit jusqu'à la fureur, et par conséquent devenoit passion tragique." [119] Certainly this sentence quoted in its entirety is no denial, but rather the full approval of love as a tragic resource. Monchesnay gives in the next breath precisely the example we anticipated when he said that certain aspects of love were particularly suited to comedy. It is Boileau's well-known criticism of Pyrrhus' question,

> . . . . Crois-tu, si je l'épouse,
> Qu'Andromaque en son cœur n'en sera pas jalouse? [120]

Such artlessness Boileau considered "puéril" and ill befitting the dignity of tragedy. We have seen,[121] moreover, that this idea was not original with Boileau and that apparently he did not discover the "flaw" in Racine's play until after the edition of the poet's works in 1697—perhaps not until after the latter's death. Rapin, on the other hand, as Delaporte points out,[122] had remarked as early as 1674 the trifling nature of love and its tendency to derogate from the gravity of the serious *genre*.[123] Monchesnay at last testifies that, although Boileau thus condemned Pyrrhus, he considered the lovers Oreste and Hermione to be truly tragic characters.[124]

Boileau's irritation at the love represented in the operas of Quinault and his followers has been for some a stumblingblock.

---

[119] This telling part of Monchesnay's testimony has usually been omitted in discussions on the subject.

[120] *Andromaque*, vss. 669-670.

[121] Cf. *supra*, p. 70.   [122] *Op. cit.*, III, 149.

[123] Rapin in discussing the taste for *tendresse* says regretfully: " C'est dégrader la Tragédie de cet air de majesté qui lui est propre, que d'y mêler de l'amour, qui est d'un caractère toujours *badin* & peu conforme à cette *gravité*, dont elle fait profession " (*Réflexions sur la Poétique*, chap. XX, *Œuvres*, II, 187). Boileau's words as reported by Monchesnay are almost identical: " De pareils sentiments . . . sont trop *badins*, . . . & *dérogent à la gravité* magnifique de la Tragédie " (*op. cit.*, pp. 59-60). Cf. also d'Olivet's objection to the love in Racine's plays. He deplores the poet's departure from the practice of the ancients, who understood that " l'amour n'a point assez de gravité, ou plutôt . . . que c'est quelque chose de trop *badin* pour entrer dans le tragique." (*Hist. de l'Acad. fr.*, II, 343.)

[124] Cf. this statement in the *Dissertation sur la " Joconde "*: " Il n'y a point de passion plus tragique et plus violente que la jalousie qui naît d'une extrême amour." (*Œuvres*, III, 12.)

His objections here are made on both artistic and ethical grounds.

He finds, first of all, that love in the operas does not have the ring of sincerity. No one ever talked more of love than Quinault, Monchesnay reports Boileau to have said, " mais il n'est point amoureux." [125] Brossette heard him say the same thing; he admitted that Quinault spoke prettily of love, " mais qu'il n'en avoit pas parlé en amoureux, c'est-à-dire comme la nature doit parler." [126] This double testimony is convincing and in harmony with what we have advanced thus far concerning Boileau's ideas on love.

He often takes a fling at the " morale lubrique " [127] of operatic choruses, in which one hears nothing except fulsome invitations to love while there is yet time.[128] Even this he could endure if it were only the language of passion, but it is nothing more nor less than the language of debauch. Modern choruses cut a sorry figure alongside those of antiquity, which despite the darkness of paganism always sang the praises of virtue. While he cannot brook a gratuitous devotion to love, he admits of it when it is required for purposes of plot:

> Je pardonnerois, disoit-il, toutes leurs dévotions à l'Amour dans un sacrifice *qu'on seroit forcé de faire à ce Dieu sur le Théâtre*; mais le Chœur de l'Opéra prêche toujours une morale lubrique.[129]

He voices a similar sentiment in 1710.[130] Considering the *romanesque* novels of the preceding century, he admits that the *Astrée* was held in high esteem by persons of discriminating

---

[125] *Bolœana*, p. 4.

[126] A conversation recorded in Brossette's *Mémoires* on October 22, 1702. (Laverdet, p. 535.)

[127] Cf. his letter of July 15, 1702, to Brossette (Laverdet, p. 113) and, for the most complete treatment of " ces lieux communs de morale lubrique," see *Satire X*, vss. 131-142.

[128] The example brought forward by Boileau is in this strain:

> Il faut aimer
> Il faut s'enflammer :
> La sagesse
> De la jeunesse,
> C'est de sçavoir jouir de ses appas.

[129] *Bolœana*, pp. 4-5.

[130] *Discours sur le Dialogue des Héros de Roman.* (Œuvres, III, 32.)

taste, " bien que la morale en fût fort vicieuse, ne prêchant que l'amour et la mollesse, et allant quelquefois jusqu'à blesser un peu la pudeur." He is ashamed of the pleasure he once took in the works of La Calprenède and of Mlle de Scudéry, and, without impugning the latter's character, he censures the " mauvaise morale " of her novels.

We come now to a remark made by Boileau that does, however, present real difficulty. In the letter to Monchesnay referred to above, Boileau writes that, providing there are " point d'images ni de sentimens voluptueux " in the play, the spectator should be able to see it without any harm coming to him. If he cannot, it is his own fault, for even religious paintings can awaken concupiscence in corrupt natures. Boileau would permit Monchesnay to condemn particular comedies and tragedies, for as a rule they are " vicieux," but he bids him not to condemn comedy and tragedy in general. He then concludes with this baffling concession to Monchesnay:

Du reste, je vous abandonne le Comédien, et la pluspart de nos Poëtes, et *mesme M. Racine en plusieurs de ses pièces.*[131]

Boileau, according to this indisputable testimony, would let Monchesnay decide for himself in regard to the morals of actors and of the majority of poets; furthermore he hints strongly that the morality of several of Racine's plays is at least problematic. This statement coming from Boileau himself is indeed disconcerting. M. Demeure expresses surprise that Boileau should, at an age when most persons become more indulgent, go against the opinions he had always held. We question, however, if, in such a matter as the morality of the theater, greater indulgence does come with age.[132] M. Demeure sees a solution. Monchesnay was in this instance Boileau's correspondent. The former's aversion for the theater being well known, Boileau would under the circumstances feel free to backbite more or less covertly his friend, then dead for eight years. Unless we exaggerate the

---

[131] Laverdet, p. 453.

[132] Brossette testifies that Boileau used to express to his friends his regret at having used his pen to defend a work like *la Joconde.* (Commentary on *Satire X,* vs. 52, composed after his notes of October 8, 1702.)

import of M. Demeure's hint,[133] he considers this a case in point
for his thesis " Racine et son Ennemi Boileau."

We would like to venture quite an opposite conjecture. We
do not believe that Boileau intended the tail of his remark to be
a " grave avowal " [134] or a serious indictment of several of his
friend's plays. " And *even* M. Racine " is a friendly gesture
and softens whatever incrimination the context implies. Indeed
it seems to us that it is with a certain pride that Boileau alludes
to Racine's powerful portrayal of the passion which

Est pour aller au cœur la route la plus sûre.[135]

His remark would then be in keeping with Racine's own smug
acknowledgment that dramatists were " empoisonneurs publics "
and that perhaps he had been the most dangerous of all.[136]
Despois [137] was right, we believe, in reading some pride into
this confession of the dramatist. Despréaux or anyone else
could scarcely overlook the fact that Racine's representation of
passion as a perverting force is of a saliency that remains un-
rivalled. That danger lurked therein is possible; that the tragedies contained images and sentiments that Boileau would call
" voluptueux " [138] is certain. We do not believe, however, that
even in his old age the critic who in 1674 admitted that a poet

Ne corrompt point le cœur en chatouillant les sens [139]

---

[133] " Notre embarras (what plays Boileau meant) serait bien grand si
nous ne connaissions la personne à qui Boileau faisait connoître ses
sentiments et qu'il invitait à poursuivre oralement la conversation entreprise sur ce sujet délicat: c'est . . . Monchesnay, l'auteur de ce *Bolæana* où se trouvent formulés, sur quelques tragédies de Racine, des
jugements d'une nature telle que Mesnard ne peut croire à leur au-
thenticité et en vient à écrire drôlement que Boileau est, pour Racine
' un ami si peu suspect de préventions hostiles.' Ne croirait-on pas
que Mesnard a vu le dessous des cartes? " (" Racine et son Ennemi
Boileau," *MF*, CCV (1928), 56.)

[134] Delaporte, *op. cit.*, III, 143.   [135] *Chant III*, vs. 96.

[136] *Mémoires* of L. Racine, Mesnard, I, 276. Saint-Surin in his edition of Boileau cites Monchesnay's answer to Boileau's letter: " Je vous
sais bon gré de m'abandonner le comédien et nos poëtes modernes, et
même M. Racine en plusieurs de ses pièces. Lui-même est convenu avec
moi que sa *Bérénice* étoit très dangereuse pour les mœurs." (Cited by
Amar in his edition of Boileau, IV, 462, n. 1.)

[137] *Le Théâtre français sous Louis XIV*, p. 274

[138] Cf. *supra*, p. 158.   [139] *Chant IV*, vs. 106.

had any serious misgivings in regard to the tragedies of his friend. His observation to Monchesnay would simply mean, then, that these plays, like many other good things, might be ethically dangerous for some persons. It is to be noted that the numerous variations in Boileau's works from edition to edition give no indication that his ideas on love as a tragic subject underwent any change as he advanced in years.

To summarize, we repeat that Boileau and Racine both enjoined verisimilitude in the name of æsthetic pleasure. They had the same theories concerning love as a tragic passion: they both flouted the mawkishness of that sentiment as it was represented in pastoral novels and maintained that love, if it was to be the subject of tragedy, must have the earmarks of a " faiblesse " or a destructive and pathetic force. In theory Racine upheld a starkly simple subject. Boileau did not commit himself on the matter.

The Function of Tragedy

We have noticed that both Racine and Boileau were guided in their discussion of subject matter by what they considered to be the function of tragedy. To recall an instance in point, Racine found the story of Bérénice an apt subject for the theater on account of the " violence des passions qu'elle y pouvoit exciter." Boileau is equally insistent that the spectator be moved. A consideration of the purpose of tragedy will constitute the next section of our study.

Renascence ideas regarding the function of tragedy persisted in France throughout the classical period. There were Aristotelians, who held that the end of tragedy is that pleasure " which comes from pity and fear through imitation "[1] and who adduced Aristotle's definition, which concludes with what they considered a more or less technical word for the pleasure proper to tragedy:[2] " the purgation of these emotions," namely,

[1] *Poetics,* chap. XIV.

[2] Rostagni points out (*la Poetica di Aristotele,* pp. xl-liii) the absurdity of thus confusing pleasure (ηδονή), a sentiment, with katharsis, which can not be a sentiment. He holds that Aristotle considers pleasure, not katharsis the end of art. Taking upon himself, however, to answer Plato's objection that the passions are stirred up by tragedy, Aristotle aims to show that they are, on the contrary,

pity and fear.[3] But of these the larger number, admittedly be-
fuddled or skeptical in regard to the actual working of katharsis,
were content to take from Aristotle's teaching the idea of
æsthetic pleasure as the principal, if not the only end of tragedy.
For a very much larger group of poets, however, Horace's recommendation to mingle the " utile dulci "[4] had become a byword,
and they were inclined, at least in theory, to make for their
literary works a moral claim. Moreover, Horace's precept,
although applicable to all the *genres*, seemed especially apposite
to tragedy inasmuch as it could be made to explain away some
of the difficulties inherent in the preponderant but elusive idea
of katharsis; and so under the influence of Horatian utility,
most seventeenth-century theorists, like their predecessors, gave
an ethical interpretation [5] to katharsis. It then came to mean,
among other things, a purgation of the passions in general or,

relieved, and he attributes the phenomenon to some sort of a kathartic
process. Rostagni thinks the latter must be in substance identical with
musical katharsis " un' operazione tra medica ed orgiastica mediante la
quale gli uomini trovano sfogo alle loro passioni e, in conseguenza di
ciò, si sentono alleggeriti ed allietati." Tragedy then provides a safe
outlet for passions which, if exercised in real life, might do harm. Thus
the whole idea of katharsis seems to have been developed as an answer
to one of Plato's objections to poetry. If such is the case, the æsthetic
interpretation of it is inadmissible.

   [3] *Poetics*, chap. VI.
   [4]   " Omne tulit punctum, qui miscuit utile dulci,
             lectorem delectando pariterque monendo."
                                 (*Ars Poetica*, vss. 342-343.)
In advocating a utilitarian purpose for art, Horace was following the
theory of Neottolemo of Pario and also the Augustan tendency to make
everything serve the state. Cf. Rostagni, *Arte Poetica di Orazio*, pp.
cx-cxii.
   [5] M. Bray (*op. cit.*, p. 75) points out that their treatment of the subject is gingerly and vague. Chapelain in 1623 (*Préface* to *l'Adonis*)
showed how essential verisimilitude was by pointing out that if the
spectators do not believe what they see represented " il n'y peut avoir
d'émotion et par conséquent de purgation ou d'amendement ès mœurs
des hommes *qui est le but de la poésie.*" Scudéry, writing at the instigation of Richelieu, considers that purgation, which he defined as a kind
of moral edification and a quieting of all the passions, is enough to
rehabilitate the theater in the minds of respectable people (*Apologie
des Spectacles*, 1639, discussed by Arnaud, *Étude sur la Vie et les
Œuvres de l'abbé d'Aubignac*, p. 192). La Mesnardière, Sarrasin, and,

11

as one commentator scrupulously specified, a purgation of the evil passions. But even as such, katharsis remained largely a matter for academic quibbling, and the more practical dramatists and theorists sought to rest the utility of the theater on firmer grounds.

In the light of these different opinions, it is interesting to see what Racine considered the function of tragedy. The main facts we have to take into consideration are these: (1) Racine translated and paraphrased Aristotle's definition of tragedy culminating in the idea of katharsis. (2) Racine's prefaces before 1677 stress the pleasure resulting from pity and terror as the end of tragic art. (3) The *Préface* to *Phèdre* on the contrary sets forth with striking emphasis the utilitarian function of tragedy.

In translating Aristotle's definition, Racine confines purgation to passions like pity and fear. He seems, moreover, to consider purgation as a purely medical metaphor. The explanation of katharsis inserted as a running commentary in the text of his translation reads as follows:

C'est-à-dire qu'en *émouvant* [6] ces passions elle leur *ôte* ce qu'elles ont

---

at the end of the century, Dacier (*la Poétique d'Aristote traduite en français avec des remarques*, p. 79) repeat the assertion that tragedy moderates pity and fear by familiarizing us with suffering. Corneille is skeptical in regard to the efficacy of katharsis (*II*[e] *Discours, Œuvres,* I, 53-57), and he favors admiration as having a more positively beneficial effect on the spectators. Saint-Évremond decries Aristotle's idea as impractical and foolhardy. He says that the Greek choruses with their tears and qualms had an enervating effect upon the Athenians; Aristotle was aware of it and tried to counteract it by a certain purgation, which neither he nor anyone else has fully grasped (*De la Tragédie Ancienne et Moderne*, 1672, *Œuvres* 1, 178). Rapin says at one time that the pleasure of tragedy consists in agitation, which is always " doux à l'âme " (*Réflexions sur la Poétique*, chaps. VI and XVIII); again he asserts that tragedy rectifies the passions " par les passions mêmes, en calmant par leur émotion le trouble qu'elles excitent dans le cœur (*ibid.*, chap. XVII). Dacier is even more at sea. He notes that tragedy, which " roule ordinairement sur des intrigues d'amour," ought to purge men of that passion, but it obviously " ne fait que peu de fruit " (*op. cit.*, p. 80).

[6] Louis Racine read " émoussant," and consequently his father's elaboration of katharsis is a conundrum to him. Cf. his *Traité de la Poésie Dramatique*, chap. IV. (*Œuvres*, VI, 393 and 397.)

d'excessif et de vicieux et *les ramène à un état modéré et conforme à la raison.*[7]

He thus distinguishes three steps in purgation: the excitation, purifying, and relief of the tragic passions. If we judge aright, his idea is that in the universalizing process of classic art, pity[8] and fear[9] are tempered and set free from the egoism, disquietude, and morbidness that characterize these emotions in real life. If he implies, as seems probable, that in the calm that ensues lies the pleasure[10] afforded by tragedy, he is here giving an æsthetic interpretation to purgation. In his prefaces Racine does not mention katharsis, but his making everything converge in pity and fear proves that he considers these emotions the source of the pleasure proper to tragedy.

Before studying the passages dealing directly with pity and fear, it will be well to recall what Racine says of pleasure as the end of tragic art. In the *Préface* to *Bérénice,* in defining the requisites of a tragedy, he does so leading up to its ultimate purpose, æsthetic pleasure. There is no need for bloodshed, he says:

il suffit que l'action en soit grande, que les acteurs en soient héroïques, que les passions y soient excitées, et que tout s'y ressente de cette tristesse majestueuse qui fait tout le plaisir de la tragédie.

He says, speaking of those who found fault with the simplicity of action in his play:

Je m'informai s'ils se plaignoient qu'elle les eût ennuyés. On me dit qu'ils avouoient tous qu'elle n'ennuyoit point, qu'elle les *touchoit* même

[7] Marginalia on Vettori's *Commentarii*, cited by Mesnard, V, 477.

[8] Cf. Aristotle's definition of pity in real life: " Let pity then be a kind of *pain* excited by the sight of evil, deadly or painful, which befalls one who does not deserve it; an evil which one might expect to come upon himself or one of his friends." (*Rhetoric*, Bk. II, chapter VIII.)

[9] Aristotle likewise describes fear as painful in real life: " Let fear be defined as a painful or troubled feeling caused by the impression of an imminent evil that causes destruction or pain." (*Ibid.*, Bk. II, chap. V.)

[10] Aristotle's definition of pleasure must be kept in mind: " Let it be assumed by us that pleasure is a certain movement of the soul, a sudden and perceptible settling down into its natural state, and pain the opposite." (*Ibid.*, Bk. I, chap. XI.)

en plusieurs endroits, et qu'ils la verroient encore *avec plaisir. Que veulent-ils davantage?*

" Que veulent-ils davantage? " Clearly, no moral aim. The poet then avers that " la principale règle est de plaire et de toucher," and he bids the spectators refrain from delving into the difficulties of Aristotle's *Poetics* and reserve for themselves " le plaisir de pleurer et d'être attendris." He says elsewhere that his extreme care to establish the verisimilitude of his characters and their actions was in the interests of the added pleasure that would be afforded the spectators if they knew that all was historically true.[11] He is gratified by the pleasure the audience had in seeing Iphigénie saved [12] and even measures the success of *Esther,* that " divertissement d'enfants," by the pleasure of the king and the great lords who were privileged to see it.[13]

Although in his dedications and prefaces before 1677 he admits striving to " please the public " [14] or, that failing, to please a " small number of sensible persons," [15] he makes no pretense of edifying anyone. That he looks upon tragedy solely as a work of art is evident from a passage in the first *Préface* to *Britannicus,* where he maintains that the criteria of a French tragedy should be the judgments that Homer and Vergil would pass on the verse and that Sophocles would pass on the action.

We now turn to what he says regarding pity and fear, which he claims are the " véritables effets de la tragédie." [16] It is principally in connection with the portrayal of character that he mentions the tragic emotions. Apropos of the violence of Pyrrhus' character, he sets forth Aristotle's theory of the tragic flaw,[17] which is expressly designed to produce pity in the spec-

---

[11] Cf. *supra*, pp. 136 *et sqq.*   [12] *Préface.*   [13] *Préface.*

[14] *Dédicace* of *Andromaque* to Henriette d'Angleterre.

[15] *Première Préface* to *Britannicus.*

[16] *Préface* to *Iphigénie.* Cf. *Poetics*, chap. XI, where Aristotle affirms that " actions producing these effects (pity and fear) are those which, by our definition, Tragedy represents "; and chap. XIII where we read that a perfect tragedy should " imitate actions which excite pity and fear, this being the distinctive mark of tragic imitation." Cf. also chap. XIV. Racine translated the last two passages in the margin of Vettori's *Commentarii.* (Mesnard, V, 480-482.)

[17] Since it is necessary that tragedy be " une imitation de choses terribles et dignes de compassion [car c'est là le propre de la tragédie],

tator. In the first *Préface* to *Britannicus,* he is again concerned with *hamartía.* The prince, with those youthful qualities which bring about his destruction, seems to the poet " very capable of exciting compassion." " Je n'en veux pas davantage," he asserts. Ériphile's jealousy is her undoing, although it does not render her "utterly unworthy of pity." [18] In making Hippolytus an amorous hero contrary to tradition, the poet alleges the necessity of giving him a tragic flaw, for, according to him,[19] the death of the Greek hero " caused much more indignation than pity." He is not surprised that the character of Phèdre had so much success both in the time of Euripides and in his own " puisqu'il a toutes les qualités qu'Aristote demande dans le héros de la tragédie, et qui sont propres à exciter la compassion et la terreur." [20]

Valincour in his reception discourse at the French Academy makes much of Racine's power to rouse the spectator to pity and fear. In contrast to Corneille, who called forth admiration,

M. Racine entra, pour ainsi dire, dans leur cœur, & s'en rendit le maître; il y excita ce trouble agréable, qui nous fait prendre un véritable intérêt à tous les événemens d'une fable que l'on représente devant nous; il les remplit de cette terreur et de cette pitié,[21] qui selon

---

il est clair premièrement qu'il ne faut point introduire des hommes vertueux qui tombent du bonheur dans le malheur; car cela ne seroit ni terrible ni digne de compassion, mais bien cela seroit détestable et digne d'indignation." (Racine's translation of the *Poetics,* chap. XIII, written on Vettori's *Commentarii,* reproduced by Mesnard, V, 480-481.) The part between brackets is Racine's interpolation.

[18] *Préface* to *Iphigénie.*

[19] For a discussion of Racine's sincerity in giving this reason for changing the character, cf. *infra,* pp. 193 *et sqq.*

[20] *Préface* to *Phèdre.* He had also learned not only from the *Poetics,* chap. XV, which he translated, but also from the Greek tragedies themselves, as his notes attest (cf. *supra,* p. 118) that good must be uppermost in the character if the maximum of pity is to be called forth by his ultimate destruction.

[21] Cf. Valincour's letter to the président Bouhier dated May 19, 1726. The idea of purging the passions by exciting them is a stumblingblock to Racine's friend. " Cette imagination m'a toujours paru si ridicule que je ne puis m'empêcher de croire que le passage d'Aristote qu'on nous cite à ce sujet ne soit altéré et même entièrement corrompu." The letter is published in *RHLF,* XXXI (1924), 381. Cf. also *ibid.,* 382, for a letter of June 3, 1726, on the same subject.

Aristote, sont les véritables passions que doit produire la Tragédie: il leur arracha ces larmes,[22] qui font le plaisir de ceux qui les répandent.[23]

We have seen that in all the *Préfaces* up to that of *Phèdre* æsthetic pleasure is given as the end toward which the poet is striving. Subject, plot, and character are expressly designed to produce the tragic passions, pity and fear.

We pass now to a different conception of the function of poetry set forth in the *Préface* of 1677. This is the only time that Racine attributes a ultilitarian aim to tragedy, and in nowise does he make it accessory or subservient to the pleasure element. After explaining at length the artistic procedure he has followed, the poet insinuates, with elegant reticence, that *Phèdre* is his best play.[24] Of its moral import he is certain:

[22] The Versailles public liked to weep at tragedy. Racine claims that *Bérénice* was "honorée de tant de larmes." Mme de Sévigné admits having shed more than six tears at *Andromaque* performed at Vitré by a country troupe (*Lettre* of Aug. 12, 1671, *Lettres*, II, 318) and more than twenty at *Bajazet* (*Lettre* of Jan. 15, 1672, *ibid.*, II, 470). The songs in *Esther* are "d'une beauté qu'on ne soutient pas sans larmes" (*Lettre* of Feb. 21, 1689, *ibid.*, VIII, 477-478). Mme de Coulanges telling of a performance of *Mithridate* testifies that "on y pleure" (Letter dated Feb. 24, 1673, and cited by Mesnard, III, 6). Robinet in his *Lettre en Vers* of Sept. 1, 1674, describes the effect that *Iphigénie* had on the court:

> . . . La cour, toute pleine
> De pleureurs, fit une autre scène,
> Où l'on vit maints des plus beaux yeux,
> Voire des plus impérieux
> Pleurer sans aucun artifice
> Sur ce fabuleux sacrifice.   (Cited by Mesnard, III, 105.)

Boileau says the same thing in his *Épître VII*, vss. 3-6:

> Jamais Iphigénie en Aulide immolée
> N'a coûté tant de pleurs à la Grèce assemblée,
> Que, dans l'heureux spectacle à nos yeux étalé,
> En a fait sous son nom verser la Champmeslé.

[23] Cited by Parfaict, *op. cit.*, X, 210-211.

[24] Racine has carefully explained the artistic *procédés* that he has used: making Phèdre less "*odieuse*" and Theseus more "*agréable*" than in the ancient tragedies, giving to Hippolytus the tragic flaw required by Aristotle, finding in history the character of Aricie, and, as regards the story of Theseus, the harmonizing of *vraisemblance* with the "ornement de la fable qui fournit extrêmement à la poésie." He then adds: "Au reste, je n'ose encore assurer que cette pièce soit en effet la meilleure de mes tragédies. Je laisse et aux lecteurs et au temps à décider de son véritable prix."

Ce que je puis assurer, c'est que je n'en ai point fait où la vertu soit plus mise en jour que dans celle-ci. Les moindres fautes y sont sévèrement punies. La seule pensée du crime y est regardée avec autant d'horreur que le crime même. Les foiblesses de l'amour y passent pour de vraies foiblesses; les passions n'y sont présentées aux yeux que pour montrer tout le désordre dont elles sont cause; et le vice y est peint partout avec des couleurs qui en font connoître et haïr la difformité. C'est là proprement le but que tout homme qui travaille pour le public doit se proposer; et c'est ce que les premiers poètes tragiques avoient en vue sur toute chose. Leur théâtre étoit une école où la vertu n'étoit pas moins bien enseignée que dans les écoles des philosophes. Aussi Aristote a bien voulu donner des règles du poëme dramatique; et Socrate, le plus sage des philosophes, ne dédaignoit pas de mettre la main aux tragédies d'Euripide. Il seroit à souhaiter que nos ouvrages fussent aussi solides et aussi pleins d'utiles instructions que ceux de ces poëtes. Ce seroit peut-être un moyen de réconcilier la tragédie avec quantité de personnes, célèbres par leur piété et par leur doctrine, qui l'ont condamnée dans ces derniers temps, et qui en jugeroient sans doute plus favorablement, si les auteurs songeoient autant à instruire leurs spectateurs qu'à les divertir, et s'ils suivoient en cela la véritable intention de la tragédie.[25]

This unprecedented disquisition on the morality of the theater containing a very patent exaggeration of the moral import of Greek plays is emphasized not only by its length, but also by its strategic position at the very end of the *Préface*. Its position and its nature make us strongly suspect, however, that it does not make one piece with the preceding treatment of the artistic *procédés* followed by the poet. Beside the brusque shift in emphasis, it contains a real inconsistency. His professed purpose in making the character of the heroine " less odious " than she was in the ancient plays and in giving her " des sentiments si nobles et si vertueux " [26] does not harmonize with what he says in the last paragraph of painting vice " in colors that make us know and hate its deformity." The moral function of the play seems to be an after-thought that agrees none too well with the first part of the *Préface* or with any previous tendency we have noticed in Racine.

[25] Dacier, without making any acknowledgment, incorporated these ideas in his *Poétique d'Aristote traduite en français avec des remarques,* pp. xv-xvi. The *Préface* (1669) to *Tartuffe* contained a similar passage on the dignity and morality of the ancient theater.

[26] Cf. the anecdote of Mme de la Fayette cited, *supra,* p. 134, which shows that Racine was fully aware of the poet's power to make great crimes excusable and to render " aimables " even such characters as Medea and Phædra.

How does it fit in with the facts bearing on the composition of the tragedy? We know that Racine spent two years writing *Phèdre*. Pradon, in the *Préface* to *Phèdre et Hippolyte,* takes the liberty of taunting his rival for his scrupulous polishing of the play. Pradon's verses, on which he spent only three months, are likely to contain errors

puis qu'on en trouve bien dans celles (pièces) qu'on a été deux ans à travailler et à polir.[27]

The fact that Racine sent his play to Bouhours and Rapin asking the former to point out errors in language and those " d'une autre nature " shows the care he had for the perfection of this work.[28] The superb artistry of the piece has its own significance here. Brossette testifies that it was the play that the poet himself preferred to all the others he had written.[29] For him to place *Phèdre* above *Britannicus,* which in 1676 was the play on which he had worked hardest and which he then considered his masterpiece,[30] was indeed high praise. Louis Racine also tells us that, despite Boileau's predilection for *Athalie,* his father was always convinced that " s'il avoit fait quelque chose de parfait c'étoit Phèdre." [31] If it is true that the tormented conscience of Phèdre borders upon a moral experience of the poet, as subsequent events would seem to indicate, it is even more likely that in seeking to universalize and give artistic expression to a poignant emotional crisis of his own, he was little concerned with the moral gain that might thereby accrue to others. These considerations all indicate that while Racine was actually composing his tragedy, he was dominated by artistic, rather than moral preoccupations.

There is, moreover, an abundance of testimony, both contemporary and modern, to show that the play is far from having the salutary effect promised in the last paragraph of the *Préface.* Vice, instead of being shown in all its horror, has perhaps never in all literature been made so beautiful and so excusable. Boileau

[27] Cited by Bussom, *The Life and Dramatic Works of Pradon*, p. 28.

[28] Cf. *supra*, p. 98.

[29] *Recueil des mémoires touchant la vie et les ouvrages de Boileau Despréaux,* cited by Mesnard, I, 325, n. 2.

[30] *Seconde Préface* to *Britannicus.*

[31] *Mémoires,* Mesnard, I, 325.

caught this at once and was quick to adduce to the honor of his friend

> . . . la douleur *vertueuse*
> De Phèdre, malgré soi perfide, incestueuse.[32]

The abbé de la Porte tells us frankly, and without any tone of disparagement, that " le spectateur a plus de pitié de la criminelle belle-mère que du vertueux Hippolyte." [33] J.-J. Rousseau pounced upon Racine for making heinous crimes " permis ou pardonnables à la faveur de je ne sais quelles commodes suppositions," and he acknowledges that it is difficult not to excuse Phèdre " incestueuse et versant le sang innocent." [34] Lemaître's reaction to the character is not different from that of Rousseau. She is a chaste and pitiable victim. " On l'aime, on l'adore, on la plaint, on la tient parfaitement innocente." [35] Lemaître, who was convinced of Racine's sincerity in adducing a moral intent for the play, testifies in an all the more striking fashion how wide of the mark it actually goes:

Tandis qu'il *pensait* nous démontrer la nécessité de la grâce, Racine n'est arrivé qu'à nous démontrer la fatalité terrible et *délicieuse* de la passion.[36]

If Racine did not write the play with the moral purpose uppermost, when and how does it usurp first place in the *Préface*? The answer lies, we believe, in the fact that *Phèdre* and, in particular, its *Préface* were the occasion of Racine's reconciliation with Port-Royal. While we are not ready to admit that Racine wrote *Phèdre* " avec l'intention avouée de se concilier Port-Royal," [37] we know that it was used to bring about the desired reconciliation. It would not be practical here to go into three very difficult questions however closely connected with our problem: Racine's " conversion," the reasons for his retirement from the theater, and the " Jansenism " of *Phèdre*. Let it suffice for us to indicate the tendency of the most thorough studies on

---

[32] *Épître VII* (1677), vss. 79-80.

[33] *Anecdotes dramatiques*, II, 57-58, cited by Mesnard, III, 263.

[34] *Lettre à d'Alembert sur les Spectacles*.

[35] *Impressions de Théâtre*, I, 77.

[36] *Jean Racine*, pp. 267-268.

[37] Lanson et Tuffrau, *Manuel Illustré d'Hist. de la Litt. fr.* (2e éd.), p. 274.

these subjects. Racine's " conversion " is extremely problematic, and, unless new documents are found, it is destined to remain largely a matter of conjecture. As for his retirement from the theater, scholars are attributing it in large part to absorption in his duties as father of a family and historiographer to the king.[38] If he was sincere in the *Préface* to *Phèdre* and thought it possible to reconcile tragedy with those persons " célèbres par leur piété et par leur doctrine " who condemned it, it was not religious scruples that made him that same year retire from the theater. Lastly, there seems to be no more necessity nor justification for bringing the question of Jansenism to bear upon *Phèdre* [39] than upon any other of Racine's tragedies.

[38] Boileau, in his *Préface* of 1683, says he has included in that edition five new *Épîtres* written " avant que d'être engagé dans *le glorieux emploi qui m'a tiré du métier de la poésie.*" Cf. also his letter to the baron de Walef (*Œuvres,* IV, 21-22). If Boileau's poetic production almost ceased at his becoming historiographer, there is all the more reason for Racine's writing to be seriously interrupted, as he worked in a *genre* that requires more sustained effort than do the shorter poems of Boileau.

[39] Voltaire (Letter to the Marquis Albergati Capacelli cited by Mesnard, III, 265), who says that in his youth he heard Phèdre accused of Jansenism not once but thirty times, and Sainte-Beuve (*Port-Royal,* V, 485) are the principal exponents of the Jansenism of Phèdre. Jean Cousin showed, however, the genesis of this unreliable tradition; their arguments rest on the *Préface* and were fortified by words of Arnauld and by the fact of the reconciliation. We cite his conclusions: " Il est incontestable que Racine, élève de Port-Royal, fut amené à porter son attention sur la faiblesse de l'homme plutôt que sur sa volonté; il est incontestable aussi que l'idée de la fatalité de la passion est janséniste, mais les fièvres, les obsessions, les hallucinations de Phèdre se trouvaient déjà dans les modèles de Racine. . . . Il y a dans le jansénisme, dans le théâtre d'Euripide, dans le drame de Racine une part très grande de vérité humaine; mais alors que Racine s'est étroitement inspiré des données antiques; alors qu'il a observé lui-même et vécu en partie la vie agitée de ses héros; alors, enfin, que l'explication janséniste supprimée, le drame est aussi facilement compréhensible, n'est-ce point faire une faute de raisonnement que de voir l'influence du jansénisme dans *Phèdre* sous prétexte que Racine a reçu l'enseignement de Port-Royal " (" Phèdre n'est point Janséniste," *RHLF*, XXXIX (1932), 391-396).

Contemporaries probably made apposite rapprochements that enriched the play. Cf. Racine's marking " De libero arbitrio," " Grace suffisante," etc., in the margins of Plutarch (Mesnard, VI, 299-301). Phèdre's sense of doom corresponds with the despair of a soul deprived of grace.

According to the *Mémoires*,[40] one of the first things that
Racine did after his marriage on June 1, 1677, was to conciliate
the *Messieurs* of Port-Royal. The last paragraph of the *Préface*
to *Phèdre* printed in March and addressed to those persons
" célèbres par leur piété et par leur doctrine qui l' (tragedy)
ont condamnée [41] dans ces derniers temps " was a move in that
direction. Louis Racine says expressly that it was the desire to
" se rapprocher de ses premiers maîtres " that made him speak in
this way.[42] As for the actual reconciliation, the *Mémoires* tell
us that Nicole received his former pupil with open arms. Arnauld
was less approachable, and Boileau, who was charged with the
affair, had always found him " intraitable." According to Louis
Racine, the plan that finally succeeded as well as the actual execution of it, was Boileau's:

Un jour il s'avisa de lui porter un exemplaire de la tragédie de *Phèdre*,
de la part de l'auteur. M. Arnaud demeuroit alors dans le faubourg
Saint-Jacques. Boileau, en allant le voir, prend la résolution de lui
prouver qu'une tragédie peut être innocente aux yeux des casuistes les
plus sévères; et ruminant sa thèse en chemin: " Cet homme, disoit-il,

---

Venus' implacable hate was a glimmer of predestination. When Phèdre
in her confusion implores Minos, begging, " *Pardonne*," the audience, as
Lemaître points out (*Impressions de Théâtre*, I, 80), saw a prayer to
the God of Racine. All this does not make Phèdre a Jansenist, however.
Scholars have been too prone to put to the account of Jansenism the
delicacy of conscience discernible in Phèdre. Eleanor Pellet adheres to
the Jansenism of Phèdre " shown in her struggle with her conscience,"
but she admits that this seems less of an innovation when one turns to
it after a study of Gilbert's *Hypolite*, in which the vacillating Phèdre
is " swayed this way and that by a sensitive conscience whose subtle
promptings are at times difficult to understand. Racine's Jansenist
Phèdre is preceded by Gilbert's Calvinist heroine " (*A Forgotten French
Dramatist: Gabriel Gilbert*, pp. 96-97). But as Euripides' play shows,
one need not be either a Jansenist or a Calvinist to be disturbed by a
sin like Phèdre's. In Christian teaching, sins of thought, e. g., the desire
or intention of sinning and consent to another's sin, even though tacit,
have always been considered quite as real as sins of deed. Cf. Christ's
sermon on the mount: " Whosoever shall look on a woman to lust after
her hath already committed adultery with her in his heart." (Matt.,
chap. V, vs. 28).

[40] Mesnard, I, 281.
[41] Nicole's *Traité de la Comédie* (1659) had been reprinted in 1675 in
the third volume of his *Essais de Morale*.
[42] *Mémoires*, Mesnard, I, 263.

aura-t-il toujours raison, et ne pourrai-je parvenir à lui faire avoir tort?
Je suis bien sûr qu'aujourd'hui j'ai raison: s'il n'est pas de mon avis,
il aura tort." Plein de cette pensée, il entre chez M. Arnaud, où il trouve
une nombreuse compagnie. Il lui présente la tragédie, et lui lit en même
temps l'endroit de la préface où l'auteur témoigne tant d'envie de voir
la tragédie réconciliée avec les personnes de piété. Ensuite, déclarant
qu'il abandonnoit acteurs, actrices, et théâtre, sans prétendre les soutenir en aucune façon, il élève sa voix en prédicateur, pour soutenir que
si la tragédie étoit dangereuse, c'étoit la faute des poëtes, qui en cela
même alloient directement contre les règles de leur art; mais que la
tragédie de *Phèdre*, conforme à ces règles, n'avoit rien que d'utile.
*L'auditoire, composé de jeunes théologiens, l'écoutoit en souriant, et
regardoit tout ce qu'il avançoit comme les paradoxes d'un poëte peu
instruit de la bonne morale.* Cet auditoire fut bien surpris, lorsque
M. Arnaud prit ainsi la parole: " Si les choses sont comme il le dit,
il a raison, et la tragédie est innocente." [43]

As for the moral purpose of tragedy set forth by Racine and
the " thesis " that Boileau " ruminated " on his way to Arnauld's
house, there was nothing novel about them except their application to *Phèdre*. Chapelain,[44] Scudéry,[45] d'Aubignac,[46] Saint-
Évremond,[47] Chappuzeau,[48] and Rapin [49] had been preaching the
Renascence doctrine of utility for more than half a century. We
note that the young theologians present were not taken in by
Boileau's " paradoxes." They evidently expected another reaction from Arnauld as they were " surprised " at his mild and
noncommittal response. A few days later Despréaux returned
to get Arnauld's opinion of the play which he had left him to
read. His decision was that

il n'y a rien à reprendre au caractère de sa Phèdre, puisque par ce
caractère il nous donne cette grande leçon, que lorsqu'en punition de
fautes précédentes, Dieu nous abandonne à nous-mêmes, et à la per-
versité de notre cœur, il n'est point d'excès où nous ne puissions nous
porter, même en les détestant. Mais pourquoi a-t-il fait Hippolyte
amoureux? [50]

---

[43] *Op. cit.*, Mesnard, I, 281.

[44] *Préface* to *Adonis*.

[45] *Observations sur le " Cid "* (1637) and *Apologie des Spectacles*
(1639).

[46] *La Pratique du Théâtre*, pp. 5 and 418.

[47] *De la Tragédie Ancienne et Moderne* (1672), *Œuvres*, I, 182.

[48] *Théâtre français* (1674), pp. 26, 29, 42, 48, and 97.

[49] *Réflexions sur la Poétique* (1674), chap. XVII. (*Œuvres*, II, 180.)

[50] *Mémoires*, Mesnard, I, 281-282.

The *Mémoires* then record the touching scene that took place on the following day when Racine and Arnauld were finally reconciled. It would appear from the foregoing account that Arnauld, at heart eager to make peace with Racine, did not press the matter of the morality of *Phèdre*. Indeed his comment after reading the piece seems to be a pious truism little applicable to the tragedy.[51] A later remark of Arnauld confirms our opinion that on this occasion he intentionally read a moral lesson into the play. In approving *Athalie,* he condemns, without alleging any example, a situation precisely like that of *Phèdre* :

Ce qu'on y (*Athalie*) fait dire aux gens de bien inspire du respect pour la religion et pour la vertu; ce que l'on fait dire aux méchans n'empêche point qu'on n'ait de l'horreur de leur malice; en quoi je trouve que beaucoup de poètes sont blâmables, mettant tout leur esprit à faire parler leurs personnages d'une manière qui peut rendre leur cause si bonne, qu'on est plus porté ou à approuver ou à excuser les plus méchantes actions qu'à en avoir de la haine.[52]

There is every reason to believe that the part of the *Préface* ascribing a moral function to tragedy and read to Arnauld with such eagerness as an initial step in the reconciliation was composed after the play was completed and perhaps even as an addition to the original draft of the *Préface*.[53] Internal evidence and the first part of the *Préface* show that the play was written according to Aristotelian principles with small regard for utility. The construction of the plot, the character of the heroine, and the changes introduced into the legend show a consistent regard for *bienséance* and verisimilitude to the end that the pity and terror aroused may produce the greatest amount of pleasure. The last paragraph of the *Préface* then becomes merely an expedient to bring about the desired reconciliation with Port-Royal.

[51] To what " fautes précédentes " of Phèdre is he referring?

[52] *Lettre* to Vuillard, Apr. 10, 1691, found in Lanson, *Choix de Lettres du XVIIe Siècle*, p. 188.

[53] It does not seem reasonable to suppose that Boileau should wait until June to show Arnauld the *Préface* published in March, when it contained a passage especially designed to placate him. Neither is it likely that Boileau and Racine should have been willing to let things take their natural course, trusting that sooner or later Arnauld would see the *Préface*, as he seems not to have been in the habit of reading tragedies (*Furetériana*, p. 64). There is no way of checking the accuracy of Louis Racine in dating the reconciliation.

It is consequently an occasional document that has no real bearing on Racine's æsthetics.[54]

We pass now to Boileau's idea of the function of poetry. That he considers pleasure the principal purpose of tragedy is evident from the following excerpts: " plaire aux yeux," [55] " artifice agréable," [56] " pour nous charmer," [57] " pour nous divertir nous arracher des larmes," [58] " agréable fureur," [59] " le secret est d'abord de plaire et de toucher," [60] " un divertissement," [61] and " il faut qu'en cent façons, pour plaire, il se replie." [62] In his treatment of style and versification, the critic still has pleasure as the end in view. He bids a poet be " simple avec art " and " agréable sans fard " [63] and offer the reader nothing except " ce qui peut lui plaire," [64] reminding him that even the most noble thought can not " plaire à l'esprit " [65] if the ear is offended.

We recall that certain passages apropos of *tendresse* reënforce the idea of pleasure and lead us to assume that Boileau believed tragedy should appeal to the feelings rather than to the will of the spectators. He enjoins poets to avoid " une scène savante " [66] and those " froids raisonnements " [67] which leave an audience unmoved. He urges

[54] The conclusion that we reached independently is also that of Truc, in *Le Cas Racine*, p. 36 (cf. also the earlier form of this study in *RHLF*, XVIII (1911), 569), and of Jean Cousin in his article " Phèdre n'est pas Janséniste " (*RHLF*, XXXIX (1932), 396).

[55] *Chant III*, vs. 2.
[56] *Ibid.*, vs. 3.
[57] *Ibid.*, vs. 5.
[58] *Ibid.*, vs. 8.
[59] *Ibid.*, vs. 17.
[60] *Ibid.*, vs. 25. It will be recalled that Racine had said the same thing in his *Préface* to *Bérénice:* " La principale règle est de plaire et de toucher." Cf. also La Fontaine's remark: " On ne considère en France que ce qui plaît; c'est la grande règle et pour ainsi dire, la seule (*Fables, Préface du Premier Recueil*). Cf. also the *Critique de l'École des Femmes*, scène VI: " Je voudrais bien savoir si la grande règle de toutes les règles n'est pas de *plaire*. . . . Pour moi, quand je vois une comédie, je regarde seulement si les choses me *touchent*; et, lorsque je m'y suis bien divertie, je ne vais point demander si j'ai eu tort, et si les règles d'Aristote me défendoient de rire."
[61] *Op. cit.*, vs. 32.
[62] *Ibid.*, vs. 151.
[63] *Chant I*, vss. 101-102. Cf. also *Chant III*, vs. 154.
[64] *Chant I*, vs. 103.
[65] *Ibid.*, vs. 112.
[66] *Chant III*, vs. 20.
[67] *Ibid.*, vs. 21.

Que dans tous vos discours la passion émue
Aille chercher le cœur, l'échauffe, et le remue,[68]
Le secret est d'abord de plaire et de toucher.
Inventez des ressorts qui puissent m'attacher.[69]

An absurd marvel has no attraction, for when verisimilitude is
wanting " l'esprit n'est pas ému." [70] Love is an apt subject for
tragedy because

De cette passion, la sensible peinture
Est pour aller au cœur la route la plus sûre.[71]

There is, however, a passage in *Chant IV* of the *Art Poétique*
in which Boileau alludes to a utilitarian function of poetry:

Voulez-vous faire aimer vos riches fictions?
Qu'en savantes leçons votre Muse fertile

---

[68] Cf. Horace's praise of the tragic poet
. . . meum qui pectus inaniter angit,
irritat, mulcet, falsis terroribus implet.
(*Epistulæ*, Liber II, I, vss. 211-212.)
Boileau's passage approximates vss. 99-100 of the *Ars Poetica:*
Non satis est pulchra esse poemata; dulcia sunto,
et, quocumque volent, animum auditoris agunto.
D'Aubignac, before Boileau, had condemned maxims and instructions
which " vont seulement à l'esprit et ne frappent point le cœur; ils
éclairent et *n'échauffent pas*; et quoy qu'ils soient souvent assez beaux
et bien exprimez, ils ne font que toucher l'oreille, sans émouvoir l'âme:
de sorte que l'Action du Theatre, où nous cherchons quelque chose qui
remuë nos affections, et qui fasse quelque impression sur nostre cœur,
nous devient peu sensible, et consequemment peu capable de nous divertir " (*op. cit.*, pp. 413-414). Rapin, who favors a utilitarian purpose
in poetry, admits nevertheless that one of the faults of contemporary
tragedy was that " on ne parle pas assez *au cœur* des Spectateurs, qui
est le seul art du theatre, où rien n'est capable de plaire, que ce qui
remuë les affections, et ce qui fait impression sur l'ame: on ne connoît
point cette Rhetorique, qui sçait développer les passions par tous les
degrez naturels de leur naissance et de leur progrès " (*Réflexions sur la
Poétique*, chap. XXI, *Œuvres*, II, 189). Longepierre in his *Parallèle*
testifies that Racine succeeded where Corneille often failed: " M. Racine
songe plus à donner de la passion à ses personnages, qu'à les faire
raisonner. Il sçait que la meilleure politique, le plus grand art qu'on
puisse étaler sur le Théâtre, est celui de *remuer les passions*. Chez lui,
les raffinemens, les délicatesses du cœur sont préférables à celle de
l'esprit; & il semble éviter avec soin tous ces ornemens ambitieux *qui
plaisent sans échauffer* " (cited by Parfaict, *op. cit.*, X, 241-242).
[69] *Chant III*, vss. 15-16 and 25-26.
[70] *Ibid.*, vss. 49-50.   [71] *Ibid.*, vss. 95-96.

> Partout joigne au plaisant le solide et l'utile.
> Un lecteur sage fuit un vain amusement,
> Et veut mettre à profit son divertissement.[72]

This restatement of Horace's precept to join the "utile dulci"[73] stands in striking contrast to the numerous passages in the *Art Poétique* stressing pleasure as the only end of poetry. It is to be noted that, even here, Boileau, in counselling poets to add "le solide et l'utile" to "le plaisant," implies that he can conceive of a work of art without the adjunct of morality. If beauty and utility were both present, however, he would agree with Horace that the work "omne tulit punctum";[74] it would be "loved" as well as admired from an æsthetic standpoint. Boileau could scarcely avoid this allusion to what we know was considered, at least in theory, the principal purpose of poetry up and down the seventeenth century.[75] He commended, on at least two occasions, the usefulness of Molière's comedies.[76] It is perhaps in a spirit of contradiction, however, that he alleges in his letter to Monchesnay[77] instances of the utility of tragedy. The critic tells this acknowledged adversary of the theater that after seeing *Britannicus,* in which Nero's passion to appear on the stage is "attaquée," "un très grand prince," who used to dance in ballets, resolved never to take part in these perform-

---

[72] Vss. 86-90. The same thing is stated inversely, vss. 93-96.

[73] *Ars Poetica,* vs. 343.

[74] *Loc. cit.* Boileau in a letter of July 29 [1687], to Racine, felicitates the latter on having combined utility and pleasure in a recent business trip to Maintenon made in company with the king and some charming courtiers. Boileau applies Horace's "omne tulit punctum" to the excursion. (Mesnard, VI, 579).

[75] M. Bray (p. 191) places it foremost in his alignment of classical traits. Cf. also *ibid.,* p. 355.

[76] Cf. his youthful admiration for the comic poet expressed in the *Stances à Molière* (1663):

> Ta Muse, *avec utilité,*
> Dit plaisamment la vérité;
> Chacun profite à ton école;
> Tout en est beau, tout en est bon,
> Et ta plus burlesque parole
> Et souvent *un docte sermon.*

Monchesnay tells that Boileau regretted that *le Docteur Amoureux* had been lost because there is always "*quelque chose de saillant et d'instructif* dans ses moindres ouvrages" (*Bolœana,* p. 31).

[77] Cf. *supra,* p. 155.

ances again and kept his resolution even in the time of the carnival. The truth of the story has been seriously questioned.[78] Even granting that this amendment in Louis XIV's life was due to a lesson gathered from Racine's play, it is still a reform of such slight consequence as to be better left uncited as far as the cause of the theater goes. Dubious as it is, it is perhaps the only one the critic could lay his finger on. That Boileau is here forcing the point is also apparent from his assertion that love chastely expressed on the stage does not inspire love, but rather serves " à guérir de l'amour les esprits bien faicts." [79] We then come to the real import of the letter, namely, that certain precautions being taken, " la comédie " is in itself indifferent, and its effect depends entirely upon the individual who sees it.

An anecdote told by Monchesnay indicates that what Boileau said occasionally in favor of the utility of poetry was said largely *pour la forme* and out of deference to the Horatian principle that had taken firm root in France. The author of the *Bolœana* records Boileau's retort to an intelligent but unlettered man who claimed that he would rather be able to " faire la barbe " than write a good poem. To his question, " Where does poetry ever get you? " the critic answered:

C'est en cela . . . que j'admire la Poésie, que *n'étant bonne à rien*, elle ne laisse pas de faire les délices des hommes intelligens.[80]

From the foregoing evidence we conclude that, according to Boileau, æsthetic pleasure is the foremost and practically the only end of art. If poetry possesses a moral value in addition to beauty, it is, however, doubly acceptable.

Did Boileau, like Racine, relate pity and fear to pleasure? Verse eight cited above, where " divertir " and " larmes " are placed in striking juxtaposition, implies that it is the emotion giving rise to tears that produces the pleasure proper to tragedy. The process is more fully described in the following verses:

Si d'un beau mouvement l'agréable fureur
Souvent ne nous remplit d'une *douce terreur*,
Ou n'excite en notre âme une *pitié charmante*,
En vain vous étalez une scène savante.[81]

---

[78] Cf. Mesnard, II, 235.
[79] Laverdet, p. 453.
[80] Pp. 52-53.
[81] *Chant III*, vss. 17-20.

12

Pity and terror are the tragic emotions without which it is futile to try to stir an audience. It is worth noting that "douce" and "charmante" are Boileau's elaborations on Aristotle's Terror and Pity.[82] They stress the pleasure element in these passions: "douce," originally applied to the satisfaction of the sense of taste, should be interpreted quite literally as "pleasurable"; "charmante" should be taken in its common meaning of "affording delight."

The proper balance of pity and terror has always been a difficult problem for the dramatist. Aristotle noted that "the terrible is different from the pitiable, for it drives out pity and often serves to produce the opposite feeling."[83] He also warns against arousing pity and fear by sheer spectacle.[84] The character of these tragic passions undergoes considerable change during the sixteenth and seventeenth centuries.[85] As attested by successive theorists translating Aristotle and by the tragedies written in conformity with the general tendency, there is a gradual attenuation in the element of fear accompanied by a proportional increase in pity. The Italian Renascence was prone to judge the excellence of a tragedy according to the cruelty of it, the assumption being that the greater the violence, the greater was the pity and "horror" produced. A tragedy of violence, then, was thought to give the greatest amount of æsthetic pleasure: "plus les tragédies sont cruelles, plus elles sont excellentes,"[86] as Laudun put it in 1598. The seventeenth century is less and less dominated by the idea of pity and horror in their Renascence acceptations. Heinsius admits the possi-

---

[82] Louis Racine objects to Boileau's thus qualifying the tragic emotions: "Ce n'est point une douce terreur dont les Atrées, les Œdipes, les Phèdres nous remplissent: ainsi l'on pourroit croire que Boileau, toujours si exact dans ses expressions, ne l'a point été dans ces deux vers" (*Traité de la Poésie Dramatique*, chap. IV, *Œuvres*, VI, 387). He seems not to be aware of the fact that Boileau has modern, not ancient tragedy, in mind. Cf. vs. 12, where he states that he is envisaging works

Où tout *Paris* en foule apporte ses suffrages.

[83] *Rhetoric*, Book II, chap. VIII, p. 229.

[84] *Poetics*, chap. XIV. Cf. the rustic's reluctance to bring a lion in before the ladies (*Midsummer Night's Dream*, Act III, scene 1).

[85] Cf. Bray, p. 318.

[86] *Art Poétique* cited by Bray, *loc. cit.*

bility of exciting only one of these passions.[87] M. Bray points out a significant change in terminology.[88] Isnard in his *Préface* to *la Filis de Scire*[89] and Scudéry in the *Préface* to *la Mort de César*[90] translate the Aristotelian φόβος by the word " horreur." La Mesnardière, in the name of the *bienséances,* enjoins " terreur," a milder emotion than horror. Both he[91] and d'Aubignac,[92] while recognizing the utility of terror, place it far below pity as a tragic passion. Corneille professes to depend more on admiration as the mainspring of his tragedy.[93] Racine's plays illustrate the tendency to increase pity at the expense of fear. In the *Première Préface* to *Britannicus*, the author maintains that love, frankness, and credulity in a young man are qualities capable of exciting " compassion." " Je n'en veux pas davantage," he asserts. He finds the subject of Bérénice " tres-propre pour le théâtre, par la violence des passions qu'elle y pouvoit exciter."[94] Now it is primarily pity and not fear on which Racine is counting in this play, where he demonstrates more or less conclusively[95] that it is not required " qu'il y ait du sang et des morts dans une tragédie."

Saint-Évremond notices that the " crainte " of his day never goes as far as the " superstitieuse terreur " produced by the

---

[87] Bray, *loc. cit.*, refers to *De trag. constitutione* (1611), p. 93. For this distinction expressed in lines of a play, see Albany's speech after the death of Goneril and Regan:

> This judgment of the heavens that makes us tremble
> Touches us not with pity.
>
> (*King Lear*, Act V, scene 3.)

[88] Louis Racine treats this question in his *Traité de la Poésie Dramatique*, chap. IV (*Œuvres*, VI, 379-381).

[89] 1631.   [90] 1636.

[91] *La Poétique* (1640), pp. 18, 21, cited by M. Bray, *op. cit.*, pp. 318-319. Cf. also Wilma Holsboer, *Hist. de la Mise en Scène dans le Théâtre Français de 1600-1657*, p. 164.

[92] " Je sais bien que la compassion est le plus parfait sentiment qui règne au théâtre." (Cited by M. Bray, p. 319.)

[93] *Au Lecteur* and *Examen* to *Nicomède* (1651). (*Œuvres*, V, 501, 505.)

[94] *Préface.*

[95] Louis Racine reiterates an unfavorable judgment on the play: " Une pièce qui n'excite que la pitié sans la crainte, *comme Bérénice*, est une tragédie imparfaite." (*Traité de la Poésie Dramatique*, chap. IV, *Œuvres*, VI, 381.)

Greek plays. It is in truth nothing more than an "agréable inquiétude" or the "cher intérêt" we take in characters that have won our affection. Pity, he remarks, is no longer a weakness. It has been stripped of its enervating character and remains merely a charitable and humane attitude toward the misfortune of others. He is even willing to weep sometimes at the misery of a character, but, as a true partisan of Corneille, he insists that

ces larmes tendres & généreuses regardent ensemble ses malheurs & ses vertus, & qu'avec le triste sentiment de la pitié nous ayons celui d'une admiration animée, qui fasse naître en notre âme comme un amoureux désir de l'imiter.[96]

Saint-Évremond and Rapin point out that the gradual mollification of terror chimes in with the French tendency toward *tendresse* in tragedy. In a letter that the former wrote to the comte de Lionne after a cursory reading of *Andromaque* and *Attila,* he concludes that Corneille's tragedy would have been admirable in the time of Sophocles and Euripides, "où l'on avait plus de goût pour la scène farouche et sanglante que pour la douce et la tendre." In his day, however, the rôle of Attila, especially if played by an actor like Montfleury,[97] would produce too strong an impression " sur les âmes tendres." [98] Although it is susceptible of much abuse, Saint-Évremond notices that love helps to do away with those "noires idées" produced by the ancient plays.[99] It is not without regret that Rapin likewise notes that perhaps

le génie de notre Nation ne pourroit pas aisément soûtenir une action sur le Theatre, par le seul mouvement de la terreur et de la pitié. . . . Peut-être que notre Nation, qui est naturellement galante, a été obligée par la nécessité de son caractère à se faire un Système nouveau de Tragédie, pour s'accommoder à son humeur. . . . Nos Poëtes ont crû ne pouvoir plaire sur le Theatre que par les sentimens doux et tendres: [100]

---

[96] *De la Tragédie Ancienne et Moderne* (1672). (*Œuvres*, I, 179.)

[97] He points out that Montfleury's recent death (attributed to over-exertion in playing the rôle of Oreste) was no subject for regret as far as that rôle was concerned. *Andromaque,* on the other hand, needed to be sustained by actors of Montfleury's caliber.

[98] *Œuvres*, III, 33-34.

[99] *De la Tragédie ancienne et moderne.* (*Œuvres*, I, 179.)

[100] Chappuzeau attests the same tendency: "On veut de l'amour, et en quantité, et de toutes les manières" (*le Théâtre français*, p. 41.)

en quoi ils ont peut-être eu quelque sorte de raison. Car en effet les passions qu'on représente deviennent fades et de nul goût, si elles ne sont fondées sur des sentiments conformes à ceux du Spectateur.[101]

Rapin, then, makes the external *bienséance* of an age of gallantry responsible for the change in the elemental tragic emotions.

Apart from requiring a "douce terreur" and a "pitié charmante," Boileau says nothing in the *Art Poétique* concerning purgation. But the practical nature of his work, its briefness, and its verse form would indeed preclude any technical or detailed treatment of the process. We have, however, Brossette's account of a conversation with Boileau on the subject of katharsis. The critic began by saying that Corneille and "even" Dacier had not fully grasped Aristotle's meaning, namely, that in artificially exciting pity and fear, which are the two saddest of emotions tragedy can make gay a man who was sad, "c'est-à-dire, le purger de la tristesse." He alleges the eagerness of a sad person to hear pitiable things, in which he little by little takes an interest, and

ces passions nouvelles qu'elle (tragedy) excite en luy, chassent les autres passions, les autres mouvemens de son âme qui y causoient la tristesse: ainsi les passions tristes de la tragédie ont le pouvoir de nous purger de semblables passions.[102]

In other words the pity and fear called forth under the excitation of art expel the sadness or "like passions" that we bring with us from real life. Whether or not this simple, yet sensible interpretation of katharsis is the one he held to in the early seventies, when he was composing the *Art Poétique*, it is impossible to say. There is, moreover, the possibility that Brossette in transcribing Despréaux's words made of katharsis a simpler matter than Boileau intended. This commentator, honest though he was, seems to have been extremely literal-minded,[103] and, in his efforts to be clear, he would tend to simplify the explanation he was recording.

Cf. also l'*Art Poétique*, vss. 93 *et sqq.*, where Boileau says that love has taken possession of the theater.

[101] *Réflexions sur la Poétique*, chap. XX. (*Œuvres*, II, 186-187.)

[102] *Mémoires* of Oct. 22, 1702. (Laverdet, p. 537.)

[103] Cf. his letters to Boileau asking about various lines of his poetry. The poet finally wearied of his commentator's scrupulosity. Cf. *supra*, p. 84.

We conclude this part of our study by saying that both Racine and Boileau believed that the main purpose of tragedy was to please. Both were primarily concerned with arousing pity and fear, which they considered the main tragic passions, and both counted much on love because it conduces to these emotions. There is no question of the purgative process as such either in the *Préfaces* or in the *Art Poétique*. Boileau seems to have had a very general and practical idea of its working, while Racine, if we may judge from the explanation he inserted in his translation of Aristotle and which dates probably from his initiation into æsthetic studies, was more inclined to split hairs. But for all his ingenuity in discerning three steps in the purgative process, in the *Préfaces* he seemed willing to ignore the matter of the purifying and allaying of the emotions and was occupied only with the excitation of pity and fear.

The Characters

We come now to the theoretical treatment of character in the *Préfaces*. It will be well to recall at this point in our study Racine's summary of Aristotle's theory of character [1] found in the margin of Heinsius' dissertation: " Quatre choses à observer dans les mœurs. Boni, convenientes, similes, æquales." [2] In his copy of Vettori, the poet translated the same passage, enlarging upon Aristotle's definition of the last two requirements for tragic characters.[3] We have already seen [4] that as he read and annotated the Greek tragedies he was constantly seeking and pointing out the application of the Aristotelian rules in regard to the portrayal of character.

In order to grasp the full significance of Racine's discussion of character, it is necessary to bear in mind not only the four precepts of Aristotle, but also the Horatian idea of decorum [5] with all its modern implications. This principle, under the name

---

[1] *Poetics*, chap. XV.
[2] Mesnard, VI, 290.
[3] *Ibid.*, V, 484-485.
[4] *Supra*, pp. 118 *et sqq.*
[5] Horace develops Aristotle's second requirement, namely, propriety, and adds a description of the various ages of man modeled after that of the *Rhetoric* (Bk. II, chaps. XII-XIV). Cf. *Ars Poetica*, vss. 114-124 and 156-178.

of *bienséances*,[6] took on an almost overwhelming importance during the seventeenth century in France. Chapelain, La Mesnardière, d'Aubignac, the abbé de la Pure, Saint-Évremond, and Rapin—to mention only its most important advocates—all bear testimony to the preponderance of the new precept. The latter calls it the most universal of the rules, the *sine qua non* of verisimilitude.[7]

M. Bray, after pointing out with remarkable clarity the development of this complex rule, concludes that " on pourrait dire de la poétique classique que c'est la poétique des bienséances." [8] The clearest contemporary statement of the new rule is that given by Nicole in 1659: " reason teaches us that an object is beautiful when it harmonizes with its own nature and with ours." [9] In accordance with this precept, a work of art must correspond not only with the thing imitated, but also with the ideas, taste, and beliefs of those to whom the work is designed to give pleasure.[10] The *bienséances* are therefore like verisimilitude in that they require the poet to follow the opinion of the public or, as Racine puts it, " l'idée que nous avons maintenant de cette princesse." [11] The necessity of conforming to contemporary notions of *honnêteté* introduces, moreover, a moral factor into seventeenth-century poetics. This new rule makes the task of the French poet a very delicate one, for while

[6] According to M. Bray (p. 220), La Mesnardière was the first to use the term in the plural.

[7] *Réflexions sur la Poétique*, chap. XXXIX, *Œuvres*, II, 153.

[8] P. 230.

[9] *Traité de la vraie beauté*, p. 171, cited by M. Bray, p. 216.

[10] Without the latter conformity, it would be impossible to arouse fear and pity, as we can not be interested in the destiny of persons utterly unlike ourselves. One of the most exaggerated expressions of the necessity for external *bienséance* is found in the dedication of Pradon's *Hippolyte*. Addressing the duchesse de Bouillon, he says of the hero: " Ne vous étonnez pas, Madame, s'il vous paroît dépouillé de cette fierté farouche et de cette insensibilité qui lui estoit si naturelle, mais en auroit-il pu conserver auprès des charmes de Votre Altesse? Enfin si les Anciens nous l'ont dépeint comme il a esté dans Trézène, du moins *il paroîtra comme il a dû estre à Paris*; et n'en déplaise à toute l'Antiquité, ce jeune Héros auroit mauvaise grâce de venir tout hérissé des épines de Grèce dans une Cour aussi galante que la nostre." (Cited by Bussom, *The Life and Dramatic Works of Pradon*, p. 56).

[11] *Seconde Préface* to *Andromaque*.

internal *bienséance* tends toward historical realism, external *bienséance* militates against it and makes for modernity of treatment. "Adoucir sans changer"[12] and "respecter en accommodant"[13] were ways in which the difficulty was met.

We shall consider first how Racine applied the principle of *bienséance* to Aristotle's four requirements for character. In his *Préfaces*, the poet only grazes the first qualification: "It (the character) must be good."[14] When he does so, it is in connection with the canons of pity and fear, and the matter has been treated under the heading of the katharsis of these emotions.[15]

Aristotle's second requirement is that the character be true to type. From a study of Racine's plays, it is evident that the *bienséances* affect to a considerable extent his application of this rule. For while internal *bienséance* prescribes, in the imitation of characters, fidelity to type, social class, epoch, and country, external *bienséance* requires a certain harmony between the psychology and milieux of the characters imitated and those of the public for which the tragedy is written. Racine's practice shows him to be singularly aware of the necessity of making his characters modern and French types.[16] On examining the *Préfaces*, however, we find no admission that external *bienséance* influenced the poet's procedure with regard to the rule of propriety. On the contrary he stresses several times his close adherence to the truth of history.

Bajazet is a case in point. Corneille's murmurings are well known: there is not one single personage in *Bajazet* who has the sentiments that he should have and that one has at Constantinople; they all have, underneath their Turkish costumes, the sentiments that one has in the heart of France.[17] His criticism was soon repeated with various nuances of irony by de Visé,[18]

---

[12] Le Laboureur in his *Préface* to *Charlemagne* (1666). (Cited by M. Bray, p. 226.)

[13] Mlle de Scudery's *la Manière d'inventer*. (Cited *loc. cit.*)

[14] *Poetics*, chap. XV.

[15] Cf. *supra*, p. 167. For his tendency to notice the goodness of a character as it affects pity, see his notes on the Greek plays, *supra*, p. 118.

[16] Cf. for instance the gallantry that takes from the heroic stature of Alexander or the utter lack of exoticism in the character of Porus.

[17] *Segraisiana*, p. 58, cited by Mesnard, II, 452.

[18] "Le sujet de cette tragédie est turc à ce que rapporte l'auteur dans

Robinet,[19] and Mme de Sévigné.[20] The latter had apparently remained unconvinced by Racine's definite but mild assertations in the *Première Préface:* [21]

La principale chose à quoi je me suis attaché, ç'a été *de ne rien changer, ni aux mœurs ni aux coutumes de la nation.* Et j'ai pris soin de ne rien avancer qui ne fût conforme à l'histoire des Turcs et à la nouvelle Relation de l'empire Ottoman, que l'on a traduite de l'anglois. Surtout je dois beaucoup aux avis de Monsieur de la Haye, qui a eu la bonté de m'éclaircir sur toutes les difficultés que je lui ai proposées.

When Racine wrote the *Seconde Préface* in 1676, he judged it necessary to speak more in detail of his characters and of their trueness to life. We note that he is aware of the limitations that the actual knowledge of Turkish manners places on both the poet and the public.[22] He explains why the women are so experienced

sa préface (it had not yet appeared) . . . Je ne puis être pour ceux qui disent que cette pièce n'a rien d'assez turc: il y a des Turcs qui sont galants; et puis elle plaît, il n'importe comment; et il ne coûte pas plus, quand on a à feindre, d'inventer des caractères d'honnêtes gens et de femmes tendres et galantes, que ceux de barbares qui ne conviennent point au goût des dames de ce siècle, à qui sur toutes choses il importe de plaire." (*Mercure galant,* Jan. 9, 1672, cited by Mesnard, II, 453).

[19]   " Champmeslé, dessus ma parole,
           De Bajazet soutient le rôle
           En Turc aussi doux qu'un Français
           En musulman des plus courtois."
           (*Lettre en vers,* Jan. 30, 1672, cited by Mesnard, II, 448.)

[20] " Les mœurs des Turcs y sont mal observées; ils ne font point tant de façons pour se marier." (Letter of March 16, 1672, *Lettres,* II, 535.)

[21] It appeared in the princeps, which came off the press on Feb. 20, 1672.

[22] Fontenelle in his *Histoire du Théâtre* directed against Racine a remark that contains a grain of truth and deserves to be cited here. *Bajazet* was successful only because the public did not know more about Turkish manners: " Quand nous voyons que l'on donne notre manière de traiter l'amour à des Romains, à des Grecs, et qui pis est, à des Turcs, pourquoi cela ne nous paraît-il pas burlesque? C'est que *nous n'en savons pas assez*; et comme nous ne connaissons guère les véritables mœurs de ces peuples, nous ne trouvons point étrange qu'on les fasse galans à notre manière: il faudrait pour en rire, des gens plus éclairés. La chose est assez risible, mais il manque de rieurs " (Cited by La Harpe, *Cours de Litt. ancienne et moderne,* II, 255). L. Racine (*Mémoires,* Mesnard, I, 256) refutes this remark, observing that those who know these peoples best esteem the tragedies most.

and subtle in their love while the men, even in this passion, retain the "férocité de la nation." The low price his characters set on their own lives seems to require the corroboration that only historical facts can give. The passage is a long one, but since it is Racine's principal pronouncement on propriety we cite it in its entirety:

Je me suis attaché à bien exprimer dans ma tragédie *ce que nous savons des mœurs et des maximes des Turcs*. Quelques gens ont dit que mes héroïnes étoient trop savantes en amour et trop délicates pour des femmes nées parmi des peuples qui passent ici pour barbares. Mais sans parler de tout ce qu'on lit dans les relations des voyageurs, il me semble qu'il suffit de dire que la scène est dans le Serrail. En effet, y a-t-il une cour au monde où la jalousie et l'amour doivent être si bien connues que dans un lieu où tant de rivales sont enfermées ensemble, et où toutes ces femmes n'ont point d'autre étude, dans une éternelle oisi- veté, que d'apprendre à plaire et à se faire aimer? Les hommes vrai- semblablement n'y aiment pas avec la même délicatesse. Aussi ai-je pris soin de mettre une grande différence entre la passion de Bajazet et les tendresses de ses amantes. Il garde au milieu de son amour la férocité de la nation. Et si l'on trouve étrange qu'il consente plutôt de mourir que d'abandonner ce qu'il aime et d'épouser ce qu'il n'aime pas, il ne faut que lire l'histoire des Turcs. On verra partout le mépris qu'ils font de la vie. On verra en plusieurs endroits à quel excès ils portent les passions; et ce que la simple amitié est capable de leur faire faire. Témoin un des fils de Soliman, qui se tua lui-même sur le corps de son frère aîné, qu'il aimoit tendrement, et que l'on avoit fait mourir pour lui assurer l'Empire.[23]

Racine also invokes the principle of propriety in the *Préfaces* to *Esther* and *Athalie*. Seeking indulgence for the length of the final chorus sung by the Jewish maidens in the former play, he claims that it is in perfect accord with the "praiseworthy custom of their nation, whereby, upon receiving a signal favor from God, they thanked Him forthright in long canticles." He adduces the example of Mary, sister of Moses, of Deborah, and of Judith as well as the thanksgiving which the Jews still give each year in commemoration of their delivery from the cruelty of Aman. By the same token, Racine is uneasy lest Joas be con- sidered too precocious for his years. He points out that at an early age this extraordinary child was instructed by the high priest in the duties of his religion and his royal station, that

---

[23] This paragraph was suppressed in editions after that of 1687.

Holy Scripture was taught to Jewish children " dès la mamelle," to use the words of St. Paul, and that the kings copied it in their own handwriting twice during their lives. Finally he cites the eight-year-old duc de Bourgogne as an instance of what can be expected from a gifted nature combined with an excellent education. He adds:

Si j'avois donné au petit Joas la même vivacité et le même discernement qui brillent dans les reparties de ce jeune prince, on m'auroit accusé avec raison d'avoir péché contre les règles de la vraisemblance.

Phèdre's action in accusing Hippolytus seemed to Racine to be wanting in propriety, and he therefore introduced a very important change in his play. In explaining the modification, he uses the word " convenable," which is the French equivalent for " true to type ":

J'ai cru que la calomnie avoit quelque chose de trop bas et de trop noir pour la mettre dans la bouche d'une princesse qui a d'ailleurs des sentiments si nobles et si vertueux. Cette bassesse m'a paru plus convenable à une nourrice, qui pouvoit avoir des intentions plus serviles, et qui néanmoins n'entreprend cette fausse accusation que pour sauver la vie et l'honneur de sa maîtresse.[24]

Racine treats of trueness to type on two other occasions.

In the Première Préface to Britannicus, he flays the partisans of Corneille who apparently enjoy declamation in which the actors say precisely the opposite of what they should say. With a sidelong glance at the older dramatist, he instances such flagrant lapses in propriety as a

héros ivre, qui se voudroit faire haïr de sa maîtresse de gaîté de cœur,[25] un Lacédémonien grand parleur,[26] un conquérant qui ne débiteroit que des maximes d'amour,[27] une femme qui donneroit des leçons de fierté à des conquérants.[28]

[24] Préface.

[25] Attila, in Corneille's tragedy by that name.

[26] Agésilas or Lysandre, in Agésilas.

[27] Professor H. C. Lancaster argues convincingly that Racine here had in mind not César of Corneille's Pompée as Mesnard suggests, but the hero of Quinault's Pausanias (1668). Cf. " A Passage in the First Preface of Britannicus," Modern Language Notes, LI (1936), 8-10.

[28] Professor Lancaster differs again from Mesnard, who thought Racine here referred to Cornélie in Corneille's Pompée. He believes that Racine's slur is aimed at the heroine in la Mort d'Annibal of Thomas Corneille. (Loc. cit.)

In defending the *Alcestis* in the *Préface* to *Iphigénie,* Racine corrects an erroneous reading of the play caused by the omission, in a certain edition of Euripides, of an "Al." to indicate that Alcestis is speaking. Many readers were consequently thrown off the track and thought it was Admetus who urged his wife to hasten her sacrifice. Racine says of the impropriety erroneously inferred:

Ce sentiment leur a paru fort vilain. Et ils ont raison. Il n'y a personne qui n'en fût très-scandalisé.

Aristotle's third requirement for character is that it be true to life. After translating this precept in the margins of Vettori, Racine explains what is meant by making characters "semblables":

C'est-à-dire que les personnages qu'on imite doivent avoir au théâtre les mêmes mœurs que l'on sait qu'ils avoient durant leur vie.[29]

Racine again marks the poet's dependence on what his audience knows of antiquity.

In the *Première Préface* to *Andromaque,* Racine says that inasmuch as the characters are very famous he has rendered them "tels que les anciens nous les ont donnés," allowing himself only one liberty: that of softening a little "la férocité de Pyrrhus," which Seneca and Virgil have pushed farther than he thinks would be proper in his play. Some critics,[30] he tells us, still think Pyrrhus too little resigned to the will of his mistress. Impatient of this complaint inspired by the *bienséances,* the poet falls back on the precept of Aristotle and Horace [31] requiring that a character be true to life:

J'avoue . . . que Céladon a mieux connu que lui le parfait amour. Mais que faire? Pyrrhus n'avoit pas lu nos romans. Il étoit violent de son naturel. Et tous les héros ne sont pas faits pour être des Céladons. . . . Je les (critics) prie de se souvenir que ce n'est pas à moi de changer les règles du théâtre. Horace nous recommande de dépeindre Achille farouche, inexorable, violent, tel qu'il étoit, et tel qu'on dépeint son fils.

---

[29] Mesnard, V, 485.

[30] The prince de Condé among others.

[31] *Ars Poetica,* vss. 120-124, where Horace develops Aristotle's precept by giving examples.

As regards the trueness to life of Pyrrhus' character, we see that although Racine made some concessions to external *bienséance,*[32] it was, in theory at least, internal *bienséance* that prevailed. The poet insists on keeping a certain " férocité " which he evidently considers the proper stuff out of which to fashion this tragic hero.

When we come to the character of Andromaque, however, we see that despite the claims of the earlier *Préface,* it was external *bienséance* that obtained. In the *Seconde Préface,* written nine years after the first, the poet frankly admits altering Euripides' subject. We have already spoken of this change, but since it affects the character of the heroine it must be mentioned again here. Molossus is suppressed in the French version, and it was in order to conform to the " idea that we now have of that princess " that the change was made. Racine, with an eye to pity, is again reckoning with the knowledge and disposition of his audience:

La plupart de ceux qui ont entendu parler d'Andromaque, ne la connoissent guère que pour la veuve d'Hector et pour la mère d'Astyanax. *On ne croit pas qu'elle doive aimer ni un autre mari, ni un autre fils.* Et je doute que les larmes d'Andromaque eussent fait sur l'esprit de mes spectateurs l'impression qu'elles y ont faite, si elles avoient coulé pour un autre fils que celui qu'elle avoit d'Hector.

Racine finds in Ronsard and in Euripides precedents for changing the number of years that Astyanax lived. The child's age, he asserts, is merely an " incident." Since it does not destroy the " principal fondement d'une fable," the poet should not be haggled for the variation.[33] We know, of course, that it was external *bienséance* that obliged the poet to depart from history in this instance, the change in the subject and in the character of the heroine necessarily involving modification in the legendary character of Astyanax.

Racine takes great pains to establish the truth of Nero's character. It is to be that of a " monstre naissant." With a clear statement of the domestic character of his subject, he puts on

---

[32] Later critics found that Racine had " softened " the character of Pyrrhus too much. Monchesnay says that even Boileau considered him a " héros à la Scudéri." Cf. *supra,* p. 69.

[33] *Seconde Préface.*

the right track those who objected to Nero's cruelty on the
grounds that in the early years of his reign he was an " honnête
homme " :

Il ne faut qu'avoir lu Tacite pour savoir que s'il a été quelque temps
un bon empereur, il a toujours été un très-méchant homme. Il ne s'agit
point dans ma tragédie des affaires du dehors. Néron est ici dans son
particulier et dans sa famille. Et ils me dispenseront de leur rapporter
tous les passages qui pourroient bien aisément leur prouver que je n'ai
point de réparation à lui faire.[34]

We recall that at first Racine wanted to make Britannicus two
years older than he was. In the *Seconde Préface,* however, he
tacitly admits the futility of changing anything so well known
as the age of that prince and sets to stressing the precociousness
of his fifteen-year-old hero.[35] The poet's care, in portraying
Mithridate, to include almost all the " striking deeds " recorded
in his life and to " insert everything that could throw light on
the character and sentiments of that prince " [36] has already been
mentioned. The poet felt free, however, to " rectify " Junie's
character because she was little known.[37] He could likewise
paint Ériphile as he pleased since history was silent in regard
to all but her birth.[38]

Racine translated and enlarged upon Aristotle's fourth requirement for character, namely, consistency :

Il faut qu'elles (mœurs) soient uniformes ; car quoique le personnage
qu'on représente paroisse quelquefois changer de volonté et de discours,

[34] *Première Préface* to *Britannicus.*

[35] La Mesnardière said it was permissible to represent a child on the
stage: " Que cet enfant paraisse non pas certes un Caton, puisqu'à bien
juger des choses, cet excès de sévérité serait tout à fait ridicule; mais
comme un esprit avancé qui ait autant de lumières à l'âge de quinze
ou seize ans, que l'ordinaire des hommes en a raisonnablement sur la
fin de l'adolescence." (*Poétique,* p. 125, cited by Delaporte, *op. cit.,*
III, 14-15.)

[36] *Préface.*

[37] *Première Préface* to *Britannicus.* In the *Seconde Préface* this
sentence is suppressed although the rest of the passage remains essentially the same. Racine evidently feels that he no longer needs to
justify the alteration in Junie's character.

[38] *Préface* to *Iphigénie.*

il faut néanmoins [qu'il soit toujours le même dans le fond, que tout parte d'un même principe, et] [39] qu'il soit inégalement égal et uniforme.[40]

As he read the Greek plays, Racine watched very closely the application of this rule.[41]   In his discourse pronounced at the reception of Thomas Corneille to the French Academy, he commended the older Corneille for his characters " toujours uniformes avec eux-mêmes." [42]   Although consistency is a precept that the poet observed rigorously, he invokes it only once in the *Préfaces*.   It is apropos of the change he effects in the legendary Phèdre by subtracting from her character the odious accusation. He feels that there is something too low and too darksome about calumny to put it in the mouth of a princess " qui a d'ailleurs des sentiments si nobles et si vertueux." That he does not mention it more frequently in his *Préfaces* is, however, not surprising if we bear in mind that they were almost always written to justify what had appeared or was likely to appear wrong to critics.[43]   Now no one, to our knowledge, has ever accused Racine of failing in respect to the consistency of his characters. There was, then, of course no need to take the matter up in the *Préfaces*.

Racine's fragmentary translation of the *Poetics* includes the passage in which Aristotle, with a view to arousing pity and fear, recommends a tragic flaw in the hero.[44]   The downfall of an utter villain, he says, would inspire neither of these emotions, and the spectacle of a perfectly good man brought from prosperity to adversity would produce their very opposites.   Since " pity is aroused by unmerited misfortune, fear, by the misfortune of a man like ourselves," [45] the goodness of the hero must be tempered with some frailty, error, or excess that, without entirely vitiating the character, links him with our common humanity and leads ultimately to his downfall.

[39] The part between brackets is Racine's explanatory paraphrase.
[40] Mesnard, V, p. 485.
[41] Cf. *supra*, p. 119.   [42] Mesnard, IV, 367.
[43] " Je prie seulement le lecteur de me pardonner cette petite préface, que j'ai faite pour lui rendre raison de ma tragédie. Il n'y a rien de plus naturel que de se défendre quand on se croit injustement attaqué." (*Première Préface* to *Britannicus*.)
[44] Mesnard, V, 480-482.   [45] *Poetics*, chap. XIII.

Racine sets forth Aristotle's theory succinctly in the *Première Préface* to *Andromaque*. Pyrrhus was considered too violent by those who judged him according to the "perfect" lovers of 1667. The poet, in defense of his hero, not only invokes the Horatian principle of *semblance,* but also has recourse to Aristotle, who " far from requiring perfect heroes "

veut au contraire que les personnages tragiques, c'est-à-dire ceux dont le malheur fait la catastrophe de la tragédie, ne soient ni tout à fait bons, ni tout à fait méchants. Il ne veut pas qu'ils soient extrêmement bons, parce que la punition d'un homme de bien exciteroit plutôt l'indignation que la pitié du spectateur; ni qu'ils soient méchants avec excès, parce qu'on n'a point pitié d'un scélérat. Il faut donc qu'ils aient une bonté médiocre, c'est-à-dire une vertu capable de foiblesse, et qu'ils tombent dans le malheur par quelque faute qui les fasse plaindre sans les faire détester.

The character of Britannicus is from this viewpoint a very interesting one. In the original *Préface* [46] the author recalls, for the benefit of those critics who are "scandalized" at the extreme youth of his hero, that he has previously [47] stated Aristotle's opinion in regard to a tragic character: "bien loin d'être parfait, il faut toujours qu'il ait quelque imperfection." Now he tells them that this is a case in point. A young prince seventeen years old " qui a beaucoup de cœur, beaucoup d'amour, beaucoup de franchise et beaucoup de crédulité" has the highest claim to compassion, which is all the poet is seeking after. His youth, as will be plain when we examine the play, is the flaw that hurries Britannicus forward to his doom; his utter indifference to political power can not atone for his credulity and want of practical insight.[48]

[46] Although in the *Seconde Préface* Racine enlarges upon the idea of the "monstre naissant" of the earlier *Préface,* insisting that the character of Nero lies between the two extremes of vice and virtue, he is there reckoning with fidelity to history and with verisimilitude rather than with *hamartía.* We know from the *Prémière Préface* of *Andromaque* that he considers a tragic flaw necessary only to those characters whose downfall constitutes the catastrophe of the play.

[47] *Première Préface* to *Andromaque.*

[48] In the *Seconde Préface,* Racine seems no longer concerned with refuting the critics and justifying the youthful age of his hero. He now admits that the age of Britannicus is so well known that he can not represent him otherwise than as a fifteen-year-old hero—he had made

Racine's reckoning with *hamartía* in his conception of the tragedy *Iphigénie* caused him to introduce some important changes in the fable. The *deus ex machina* ending of the Greek legend was out of the question, as it would appear " absurd " and " incredible " to a modern audience. A bloody ending with Iphigénie as victim was likewise impossible inasmuch as she lacked a tragic flaw :

Quelle apparence que j'eusse souillé la scène par le meurtre horrible d'une personne aussi vertueuse et aussi aimable qu'il falloit représenter Iphigénie ? [49]

He found the solution of his problem in the sacrifice of another Iphigénie who could be represented as having a character defect that brings her to her ruin. Her fatal jealousy does not, however, make her unworthy of compassion :

Je puis dire donc que j'ai été très-heureux de trouver dans les anciens cette autre Iphigénie, que j'ai pu représenter telle qu'il m'a plu, et qui tombant dans le malheur où cette amante *jalouse* vouloit précipiter sa rivale, *mérite en quelque façon d'être punie, sans être pourtant tout à fait indigne de compassion.*[50]

The *Préface* to *Phèdre* also contains a significant passage on *hamartía*. The poet has changed the traditional character of Hippolytus, transforming the chaste, untamed woman-hater of antiquity into a bashful but ardent lover. In order to parry criticism, the author tells us that he introduced the change in order to avoid the perfect hero precluded by Aristotle. We cite the passage in full :

---

him seventeen years old in the *Première Préface*. He makes no apology for his youth except to say that Britannicus enjoyed the reputation of having " beaucoup d'esprit." There is this time no question of his age's constituting a tragic flaw. Racine, in view of the success of his hero, no longer considered it necessary to lean on Aristotle and his doctrine of *hamartía*. After all, what people objected to most was a *change* in Britannicus' age, and the poet had already submitted on this point of internal *bienséance*. In enumerating the " usual qualities of a young man," moreover, Racine omits " beaucoup de crédulité " which, after his love, is precisely the trait which wrecks his life. We do not believe, however, that this omission was anything more than a stylistic variation to give better balance to the sentence.

[49] *Préface.*   [50] *Ibid.*

13

Pour ce qui est du personnage d'Hippolyte, j'avois remarqué dans les anciens qu'on reprochoit à Euripide de l'avoir représenté comme *un philosophe exempt de toute imperfection*: ce qui faisoit que la mort de ce jeune prince causoit beaucoup plus d'indignation que de pitié. J'ai cru lui devoir donner quelque foiblesse qui le rendroit un peu coupable envers son père, sans pourtant lui rien ôter de cette grandeur d'âme avec laquelle il épargne l'honneur de Phèdre, et se laisse opprimer sans l'accuser. J'appelle foiblesse la passion qu'il ressent malgré lui pour Aricie, qui est la fille et la sœur des ennemis mortels de son père.

According to this, Hippolytus' love, involving as it does disregard for paternal authority, is the tragic flaw that is his undoing.[51]

There are good reasons for believing that Racine was dissembling somewhat in the passage we have just quoted. He seems to be concealing under the pretense of a need for a tragic flaw the real motives of the change wrought in his hero. Although he affirms that the " ancients " found fault with Euripides for making Hippolytus " free of all imperfection," no one has ever succeeded in tracing that criticism farther back than Vettori,[52] and even that commentator suspected that the youth's scorn of Venus might be his tragic defect, for " est vero erratum non parvum graveque crimen committere quicquam contra Deum aliquem." [53] That an over-forward chastity was his *hamartía* is perfectly clear from such lines in Euripides' play as the one in which Artemis tells Hippolytus:

> Thine own heart's nobleness hath ruined thee.[54]

Now Racine was not one to miss textual indications of this kind, and it was consequently a flagrant stretching of his point to say that the Greek hero was a " philosophe exempt de toute imper-

---

[51] It is well to note that Hippolytus' flaw was more of a defect to a seventeenth-century audience than it is today when paternal authority has weakened. Hippolytus is fully aware of the grievousness of his fault in loving the mortal enemy of his father. Cf. *Phèdre*, vss. 101-112.

[52] It is of course possible that Racine might have erroneously, yet in good faith, attributed to the " ancients " a criticism that he had read in Vettori.

[53] Vettori's passage is cited by Mesnard, V, 481, n. 1. Schlegel pointed out the fallacy in Racine's argument in his *Comparaison entre la "Phèdre" de Racine et celle d'Euripide*, pp. 95-96. Cf. Mesnard, III, 301, n. 1.

[54] Vs. 1390 of Way's translation. Cf. also vss. 1400 and 1403.

fection." We have seen once or twice before that he was not averse to bending the facts slightly to fit the immediate needs of his apology.[55]

What was the poet's real intention in making Hippolytus a lover, and why should he wish to conceal it? Scorn of a goddess "jealous for honour, wroth with chastity" [56] is manifestly not a flaw likely to appeal to a French audience. If Racine told us that he had changed the traditional character partly [57] in order to give his hero a defect more in keeping with the taste of his time, he would be far more convincing. He was, however, unwilling to do this in public although he seems to have made such an acknowledgment more or less confidentially to his friends.[58] The alteration was indeed a bold one in that it was made in the direction of the much-criticized tendency toward *tendresse* and thus again laid Racine open to the charge of being a "*doucereux*." [59] It also went counter to two very important precepts: *semblance* and internal *bienséance*. Now it is a notable fact that in his *Préfaces* it is almost always the internal *bienséance* of his characters that Racine is trying to establish. Knowing what critics by and large considered to be his vulnerable spot, the poet strained every point to protect himself against their attacks. It is not, in fact, until the *Seconde Préface* to *Andromaque,* written in 1676, that Racine comes out openly with what had been thus far a kind of professional secret: external

[55] Cf. *supra,* pp. 139 and 140.

[56] *Hippolytus,* vs. 1403 of Way's translation.

[57] The real reason is perhaps to be found in the inherent possibility of intensifying Phèdre's passion under the lash of jealousy.

[58] Brossette (cf. Mesnard, I, 282, n. 2), and L. Racine (*Mémoires, loc. cit.*) say that the poet feared lest fidelity to the chaste and savage beauty of the Greek rôle would incur facetious comment from the fops of that day. "Qu'auroient pensé nos petits-maîtres d'un Hippolyte ennemi de toutes les femmes? Quelles mauvaises plaisanteries n'auroient-ils pas faites?" asks L. Racine. Furetière (*Furetériana,* p. 64) says the same thing without, however, attributing the words to Racine. For the tendency to reduce all subjects to love, as a part of the universalizing process that marks French classic literature, see Lanson, *Esquisse d'une Hist. de la Trag. fr.,* p. 90, Dubos, *op. cit.,* I, 129, and verses 63 and 535 of Racine's *Phèdre.*

[59] Corneille's letter to Saint-Évremond [1666]. (Lanson, *Choix de Lettres du XVIIe Siècle,* p. 129.)

bienséance places certain limitations on the dramatist's fidelity to history. It is evident from a study of his plays that embodying in his character "l'idée que nous avons maintenant de cette princesse," with all the deference to common opinion and contemporary taste that it implies, was always Racine's esoteric purpose. In changing Hippolytus he goes one step farther in harmonizing a character with common opinion or taste. Instead of determining his character according to "l'idée que nous avons maintenant" of that prince, he takes into account the idea that *we should now like to have* of him. Although Subligny,[60] Arnauld,[61] and Fénelon [62] pointed out the violation of history, the success of the play more than vindicates Racine's infringement of the rule of *semblance*. Louis Racine's attitude is a telling one. Although, at heart, averse to seeing at the feet of a mistress the man so famous in antiquity for his hatred of the sex, he prefers the French Hippolytus, whom he finds more modest and more appealing than his Greek prototype.[63]

Under the pretext of giving Hippolytus a tragic flaw, Racine makes a change in his character that is at least comparable to portraying " Caton galant, et Brutus dameret." [64] The result is, however, an immense gain in modernity and consequently in the tragic emotions of pity and fear. Although Racine seems unwilling to declare it too openly and thereby incur the attacks of the advocates of a narrow internal *bienséance,* his art consists in effecting a certain harmony between the subject and his seventeenth-century audience. *Phèdre,* for instance, is a magnificent synthesis in which the murky atmosphere, the strange beauty of Greek character, and a tragic sense of doom are blended with the chivalrous ideal of the *Cortegiano* and the religiosity and elegance of the age of Louis XIV.[65]

[60] *Dissertation sur les tragédies de " Phèdre " et " Hippolyte "* (1677), p. 392, cited by Mesnard, III, 270.

[61] According to the *Mémoires* of L. Racine (Mesnard, I, 282).

[62] *Lettre à M. Dacier sur les occupations de l'Académie* (1714). (*Œuvres Complètes*, VI, 633.)

[63] *Comparaison de l' " Hippolyte " d'Euripide avec la tragédie française sur le même sujet.* (*Œuvres*, VI, 126.)

[64] *Art Poétique, Chant III*, vs. 118.

[65] Lanson explains clearly how the seventeenth century was not cramped by following the ancients: " Il arrivera bien plus communé-

Turning now to Boileau, we find that he, too, sets forth the four requisites for tragic heroes. It is in connection with *hamartía* that he implies vaguely the first qualification, namely, goodness.[66]   Boileau next enjoins trueness to life, and, like Horace,[67] adds examples to the precept:

> Qu'Agamemnon [68] soit fier, superbe, intéressé;
> Que pour ses dieux Enée ait un respect austère;
> Conservez à chacun son propre caractère.[69]

In the portrayal of love, he insists upon nuances in keeping with the temperament of the character. Achilles as a lover should not resemble Tircis.

A very curious couplet giving a rational basis for *semblance* and *convenance* serves as a transition to the latter requirement:

> Des siècles, des pays étudiez les mœurs:
> Les climats font souvent les diverses humeurs.[70]

It is at first baffling to find the critic of the French classical period giving such clear expression to the theory of relativity. It is possible, however, to account for the idea and to fit it into the ensemble of Boileau's doctrine.   Looking to the whole tenor of the precept, we discover that it is a more or less sterile literary tradition springing from Horace's warning not to make a Colchian speak like an Assyrian or a citizen of Thebes like one

---

ment qu'on trouvera dans les œuvres anciennes la nature contemporaine, crue éternelle; et si elle n'y est pas, on l'y trouvera cependant.   En d'autres termes, le xviie siècle fera les anciens à son image, plus encore qu'il se fera à l'image des anciens, et—son absence de sens historique venant en aide à son rationalisme—il *modernisera* l'antiquité! " (*Hist. de la Littérature fr.*, 4e Partie, Livre III, chap. II, 3.)

[66] Toutefois, *aux grands cœurs*, donnez quelques faiblesses."

(*Chant III*, vs. 104.)

[67]   ". . . Honoratum si forte reponis Achillem:
impiger, iracundus, inexorabilis, acer,
jura neget sibi nata, nihil non arroget armis;
sit Medea ferox invictaque, flebilis Ino,
perfidus Ixion, Io vaga, tristis Orestes."

(*Ars Poetica*, vss. 120-124.)

[68] Racine's play, *Iphigénie*, was performed shortly after the publication of the *Art Poétique*.   This is perhaps a discreet allusion to Racine's forthcoming piece.

[69] *Chant III*, vss. 110-112.   [70] *Chant III*, vss. 113-114.

from Argos.[71]   Vauquelin translated it freely, bidding poets
make distinctions in portraying Germans, Swiss, Spaniards, and
Italians.[72]   La Mesnardière went so far as to list the qualities
that poets should attribute to characters of different nationality.[73]
Ogier,[74] d'Aubignac,[75] and Rapin [76] also pointed out that national
tastes vary widely.   Godeau, as early as 1630, seeking the reason
for such differences found it in the theory of climate and laid
the foundation for that discussion of relationships between climate and temperament, temperament and genius, genius and
government [77] that gathered force in the late seventeenth and

[71] *Ars Poetica*, vs. 118.   [72] *L'Art Poétique*, Livre I, vss. 867-870.
[73] Cited by Delaporte, *op. cit.*, II, 274.   We cite as an example his
unflattering appreciation of English traits: " J'ai vu, par la fréquenta-
tion, que les Anglais sont infidèles, paresseux, vaillants, cruels, amateurs
de la propreté, ennemis des étrangers, altiers et intéressés."
[74] *Préface* of *Tyr et Sidon*, p. 17.
[75] *La Pratique du Théâtre*, pp. 87-88.
[76] " Les Grecs qui étoient des États populaires, & qui haïssoient la
Monarchie, prenoient plaisir, dans leurs spectacles, à voir les Rois
humiliez, & les grandes fortunes renversées: parce que l'élévation les
choquoit.   Les Anglois nos voisins aiment le sang, dans leurs jeux, par
la qualité de leur temperament; ce sont des insulaires, separez du
reste des hommes: nous sommes plus humains; la galanterie est
davantage selon nos mœurs, & nos Poëtes ont crû ne pouvoir plaire sur
le Théâtre, que par des sentimens doux & tendres." (*Réflexions sur la
Poétique*, chap. XX, *Œuvres*, II pp. 186-187.)
[77] There is in *Cinna* (Act II, scene 1) an interesting statement of the
influence of geography on the " *génie* " and the institutions of a nation
which has not, to our knowledge, been pointed out in this connection:
   Maxime:

> J'ose dire, Seigneur, que par tous les climats
> Ne sont pas bien reçus toutes sortes d'États;
> Chaque peuple a le sien conforme à sa nature,
> Qu'on ne sauroit changer sans lui faire une injure:
> Telle est la loi du ciel, dont la sage équité
> Sème dans l'univers cette diversité.
> Les Macédoniens aiment le monarchique,
> Et le reste des Grecs la liberté publique;
> Les Parthes, les Persans, veulent des souverains,
> Et le seul consulat est bon pour les Romains.

   Cinna:

> Il est vrai que du ciel la prudence infinie
> Départ à chaque peuple un différent génie;
> Mais il n'est pas moins vrai que cet ordre des cieux
> Change selon les temps comme selon les lieux.

early eighteenth centuries [78] and culminated in the idea of progress. Godeau explains that climate affects one's physical being and that, since "l'âme se sert des organes du corps pour exercer ses fonctions," [79] climate would necessarily influence one's temperament and way of thinking. Complaining that Porus was not Indian enough, Saint-Évremond wrote in 1666:

Un autre ciel, pour ainsi parler, un autre soleil, une autre terre y produisent d'autres animaux et d'autres fruits; les hommes y parois-sent tout autres par la différence des visages, et plus encore, si j'ose le dire, par une diversité de raison: une morale, une sagesse singulière à la région y semble régler et conduire d'autres esprits dans un autre monde. [80]

This criticism of Saint-Évremond, coupled with the later develop-ment of the theory, [81] is evidence that discussions concerning the influence of climate on character were being carried on during the time that Boileau was writing his *Art Poétique*. Quick to discern new ideas and eager to give an air of actuality to his work, the poet seized upon the argument that happened to enforce Horace's precepts. If this assumption is correct, it was not with eyes on the dramatic performances of his day that Boileau said what he did about climates and epochs.

[78] M. Mornet (*la Pensée Française au XVIIIᵉ Siècle*, p. 71) finds the theory outlined in Baillet, Fénelon, Chardin, La Motte-Houdard, Huet, Fontenelle, and the abbé Dubos. M. Bray without exhausting the subject traces it back to Godeau (*op. cit.*, p. 174).

[79] *Discours sur la traduction de Giry*, pp. 263-264, cited by M. Bray, *loc. cit.*

[80] *Dissertation sur Alexandre le Grand* (1666). (*Œuvres*, I, 199.)

[81] On Nov. 18, 1701, Boileau put to the Académie Royale des Mé-dailles et des Inscriptions a question on the pronunciation of Latin and another as to whether or not Frenchmen felt the real harmony of Latin verse. The account of the discussion and the conclusions drawn were published by Ch. H. Boudhors in *RHLF*, XXXX (1933), 175. Harmony, having "un rapport nécessaire à nostre ame, à nos organes, et à nos sens" is not an absolute thing. "Or nostre climat, nostre institution et nostre goust se trouvent bien différents du climat, du goust, et de l'institution des anciens Romains" with the result that the French would never enjoy perfectly the harmony of Latin verse. The fullest expressions of the theory of climate from the littérateur's angle of vision are found in Baillet, *Jugement des Savants*, I, 122, cited by Delaporte, II, 277-278 and in Dubos, *Réflexions Critiques sur la Poésie et sur la Peinture*, II, 246 et sqq.

As regards the next requisite for characters, namely, trueness to type,[82] Boileau's principal admonition, provoked this time by Mlle de Scudéry's travesty of antiquity, is to avoid giving

L'air, ni l'esprit français à l'antique Italie.[83]

It is in letting the tendency to *tendresse* run riot that poets are likely to offend.[84] Lapses in *convenance* such as those found in *Clélie* may be overlooked in fiction,[85]

Mais la scène demande une exacte raison:
L'étroite bienséance y veut être gardée.[86]

We should be wary, however, about resting Boileau's opinion of *semblance* and *convenance* entirely upon the rigid rules which are here set forth. We must decide whether Boileau's point of view in this particular passage is mainly one of observation or whether it is a purely literary one. His indebtedness to Horace and his allusion to the theory of climates would lead us to believe that it is the latter. An encomium on Louis XIV found at the end of the *Art Poétique* contains an indication that seems to confirm this opinion. In exhorting poets to celebrate the glory of the king, Boileau says of his friend:

Que Racine, enfantant des miracles nouveaux,
De ses héros sur lui (the king) forme tous les tableaux.[87]

---

[82] Boileau's imitation (*Chant III*, vss. 373-390) of Horace's passage on the different ages of man (*Ars Poetica*, vss. 156-178) is included in the treatment of comedy. It ends with this admonition:

Ne faites point parler vos acteurs au hasard,
Un vieillard en jeune homme, un jeune homme en vieillard.

[83] *Chant III*, vs. 116.

[84] " Et, sous des noms romains faisant notre portrait,
Peindre Caton galant, et Brutus dameret." (*Ibid.*, vss. 117-118).

[85] *Le Dialogue des Héros de Roman* and a letter which he wrote to Brossette on Jan. 7, 1703, show him to be far less indulgent in this respect. He writes in the latter: "C'est effectivement une très grande absurdité à la Demoiselle . . . d'avoir choisi le plus grave siècle de la République Romaine pour y peindre les caractères de nos Français" (Laverdet, p. 122). We have already noticed that it is in works not destined for the public that our critic is most severe in his criticisms of Mlle de Scudéry. Cf. *supra*, p. 27, n. 64.

[86] *Chant III*, vss. 122-123.

[87] *Chant IV*, vss. 197-198.

Boileau's vivid sense of fact made him fully aware of the extent
to which Racine interpreted antiquity in terms of Versailles and
Paris. Contemporaries, moreover, report only one objection that
Boileau is said to have made to a character of Racine on the
grounds that *semblance* or *convenance* is violated. Monchesnay
testifies that Boileau branded Pyrrhus a " héros à la Scudéri."
If he did, there is strong likelihood that it was long after the
publication of the *Art Poétique.*[88] An allusion to the censors
of Pyrrhus found in *Épître VII* [89] seems to exclude Boileau
from their number before 1677. Brossette, moreover, claims
that the critic ranked the tragedy of *Andromaque* second only to
that of *Phèdre.*[90] This does not argue a serious condemnation
of the hero at any time, much less during the years when the
critic was composing the *Art Poétique.* We have no account of
his disapproval of the change made by Racine in the legendary
character of Hippolytus. On the contrary we have seen how
he told Arnauld expressly that *Phèdre* was " according to the
rules." [91] It would seem that this was an instance where Boileau,
satisfied that pleasure had been given, would proscribe " vaines
subtilités " [92] and recognize that genius sometimes goes beyond
the pale of rules.[93] Thus we reach the end of our study on
bienséance as it affects the representation of character. Boileau
staying close to Horace [94] in the *Art Poétique* favors an " étroite
bienséance " for the drama. On the other hand he gives his full

[88] Cf. *supra,* pp. 69-70.
[89]   " Et, peut-être, ta plume, aux censeurs de Pyrrhus
         Doit les plus nobles traits dont tu peignis Burrhus."
                                                     (Vss. 53-54.)
[90] Cf. *supra,* p. 147, n. 83.   [91] Cf. *supra,* p. 172.
[92] " Lorsqu'un endroit d'un discours frappe tout le monde, il ne faut
pas chercher des raisons, ou plutôt de vaines subtilités, pour s'empêcher d'en être frappé, mais faire si bien que nous trouvions nous-
mêmes les raisons pourquoi il nous frappe." (*XIᵉ Réflexion Critique,*
Œuvres, III, 270.)
[93] Boileau admits that
         Quelquefois, dans sa course, un esprit vigoreux,
         Trop resserré par l'art, sort des règles prescrites,
         Et de l'art même apprend à franchir leurs limites.
                                          (*Chant IV,* vss. 78-80.)
[94] It is only the modern implications of Horace's precept of decorum
that constitute what M. Bray calls external *bienséance.*

approval to Racine, whose art consists precisely in blending the beauty of antiquity with modern sentiment.

What Boileau says of the consistency required of characters is an exact translation of the corresponding passage in the *Ars Poetica*: [95]

> D'un nouveau personnage inventez-vous l'idée?
> Qu'en tout avec soi-même il se montre d'accord,
> Et qu'il soit jusqu'au bout tel qu'on l'a vu d'abord.[96]

Boileau, like Racine, enjoins *harmartía,* but with a slight change in emphasis. We have seen that when the dramatist speaks of a tragic flaw it is by way of accounting for the disaster that wrecks a character's life or with a mind to exciting pity and fear by the misery of a man who, like us, has some imperfection. Boileau, on the other hand, not mentioning these effects, stresses the fact that a slight defect in a hero makes us recognize nature and gives pleasure in that way:

> Des héros de roman fuyez les petitesses.[97]
> Toutefois, aux grands cœurs, donnez quelques faiblesses:
> Achille déplairait, moins bouillant et moins prompt;
> J'aime à lui voir verser des pleurs pour un affront.
> *A ces petits défauts marqués dans sa peinture,*
> *L'esprit avec plaisir reconnaît la nature.*[98]

---

[95]   " Si quid inexpertum scenæ committis, et audes
        personam formare novam: servetur ad imum
        qualis ab incepto processerit, et sibi constet." (Vss. 125-127.)
Cf. also Vauquelin's literal rendering of the passage in his *Art Poétique,* Livre I, vss. 887-890.

[96] *Chant III*, vss. 124-126.

[97] The *Dialogue des Héros de Roman* makes it clear what are the " petitesses " that the poet has in mind. There he ridicules heroes like Astrate, " la mollesse peinte sur le visage," always weeping for his queen, and those whose enthrallment causes them to leave off fighting and think only of their love. He cannot brook their pretty verse, enigmas, impromptus, and the like. He excoriates the " faux clinquant " of their words. In fine, the soldiers of antiquity made over into simpering shepherds are not to his liking. He says as much in the *Art Poétique.* While admitting amorous heroes, he warns poets:

        Mais ne m'en formez pas des bergers doucereux. (Vs. 98.)
All this harks back to what we have said regarding his opinion of love as a tragic subject: if it is to be used, it must be a furious and destructive passion, not one that expresses itself in the " petitesses " we have listed.

[98] *Chant III*, vss. 103-108.

Emphasis on " la nature " is, of course a characteristic feature of Boileau's poetics—we might say of his philosophy. What he says in regard to *hamartía* does not have the air of a merely bookish remark. It is something far more deeply ingrained in the poet's system of thought. A passage in his *Épître* to Seignelay, written in 1675, illustrates what we mean. The poet regrets that we hardly ever dare appear to be just what we are. We would, however, be more pleasing if we were more sincere in this respect. A person " né triste et pesant," but wishing to seem " folâtre, évaporé, plaisant " becomes straightway a bore because

> Le faux est toujours fade, ennuyeux, languissant.
> *Mais la nature est vraie, et d'abord on la sent;*
> C'est elle seule en tout qu'on admire et qu'on aime;
> *Un esprit né chagrin plaît par son chagrin même;*
> *Chacun pris dans son air est agréable en soi;*
> Ce n'est que l'air d'autrui qui peut déplaire en moi.[99]

It is quite evident that as far as inspiration goes these two passages of Boileau are very closely related. What is more, the verses in the *Art Poétique* on the defects that tragic heroes should have are not imitated from Horace, who has said nothing regarding this Aristotelian precept.[100]

Looking back over what Boileau and Racine said concerning the portrayal of character, we see that in the main Racine stresses his fidelity to the truth of history as it is commonly known. On the other hand, his admission that he is following in *Andromaque* " l'idée que nous avons maintenant de cette princesse " indicates that he is guided to a very considerable extent by the demands of external *bienséance*. Although in the *Art Poétique* Boileau speaks only of a narrow internal *bienséance,* we find that at the time when he was writing the poem he gave his full approval to Racine who showed in practice a very opposite tendency. The two poets recommend *harmartía* but with a different emphasis. Racine looks upon a tragic flaw as conducive to pity and fear. Boileau sees in this imperfection the earmark of nature.

---

[99] *Épître IX*, vss. 85-90.
[100] When Horace recommended portraying Achilles

    impiger, iracundus, inexorabilis, acer   (vs. 121),

he was speaking not of a tragic flaw but of trueness to life.

The Action

We now turn to our last consideration: the action in tragedy. Racine, in his critical writings, reveals very few secrets of that art of invention which, according to him, consists " à faire quelque chose de rien." [1] Although his processes are more clearly discernible in the tragedies themselves, we can discover a few indications in the *Préfaces*. It is not, he affirms, a bloody catastrophe that makes a tragedy.[2] Twice he deprecates the contemporary taste which runs to those plays representing a " quantité d'incidents qui ne se pourroient passer qu'en un mois." [3] He taboos surprising " jeux de théâtre," especially if they are improbable.[4] On the other hand, he commends action sustained by violent passions, beauty of sentiment, and elegance of expression.[5] There are, in addition to these general hints, more precise indications as to what Racine made tragic action to consist in. We have in the first place his judgment on a play of Seneca. It occurs in the *Préface* to *la Thébaïde* written in 1676. It is, then, as a mature poet that he condemns the *Phœnician Women* [6] as " l'ouvrage d'un déclamateur qui ne savoit ce que c'étoit que tragédie." He refuses for that reason to ascribe it to Seneca. Second, he praises the *Œdipus* which, " quoique tout plein de reconnoissances," is more simple than even the simplest tragedy of his day.[7] Lastly he outlines clearly in the *Préface* to *Iphigénie* the process technically known as peripeteia.[8] He felicitates himself upon having found in history a second Iphigénie, who

---

[1] *Préface* to *Bérénice*.   [2] *Ibid.*

[3] *Première Préface* to *Britannicus*. Cf. also *Préface* to *Bérénice*: " Et quelle vraisemblance y a-t-il qu'il arrive en un jour une multitude de choses qui pourroient à peine arriver en plusieurs semaines? . . . Tout ce grand nombre d'incidents a toujours été le refuge des poëtes qui ne sentoient dans leur génie ni assez d'abondance ni assez de force pour attacher durant cinq actes leurs spectateurs par une action simple. . . ."

[4] " Un grand nombre de jeux de théâtre, d'autant plus surprenants qu'ils seroient moins vraisemblables." (*Première Préface* to *Britannicus*.)

[5] *Préface* to *Bérénice*.   [6] Racine refers to it as *la Thébaïde*.

[7] *Préface* to *Bérénice*.

[8] We cite from Walter Lock's article based on Vahlen's study of peripeteia. When used in a technical sense, it is " any event in which

tombant dans *le malheur où cette amante jalouse vouloit précipiter sa rivale*, mérite en quelque façon d'être punie, sans être tout à fait indigne de compassion.

Not only is her intention thwarted, but it is overruled to produce the very opposite of that intention. Although Racine merely adverts to peripeteia and recognition in his *Préfaces*, it is plain from a study of his plays that these are the great dramatic resources upon which he relies.[9] His setting little by

any agent's intention is overruled to produce an effect which is the direct opposite of that intention. It belongs to the class of actions half-voluntary, half-involuntary, discussed in the *Ethics* (III, i), in which the action is deliberate, but the result is not intended, but is produced contrary to the agent's intention, owing to his ignorance of the exact circumstances of the case. . . . The act may be that of the hero of the drama, or of any subsidiary character: it may or may not produce a change of fortune: it may, with equal probability, produce a change to happiness or unhappiness: it may take place suddenly or gradually: but the change of fortune is not connotated by the word and is always a subsequent result which can be separated in thought and generally in time from it. It is not so much a 'specific kind of change of fortune' (Butcher) as one means by which a change of fortune is brought about" ("The Use of Peripeteia in Aristotle's *Poetics*," *Classical Review*, IX (1895), 251). For Butcher's revised opinion see *op. cit.* (4th ed.), p. 329, n. 2. In the *Rhetoric* Aristotle, listing the things that produce pity, mentions this case: "if some misfortune comes to pass from a quarter whence one might have reasonably expected something good" (Book II, chap. viii).

[9] The late Professor Lanson (*Esquisse*, etc., p. 86) is, to our knowledge, the only scholar who has, in a published work, hinted at these two mainsprings of action in Racine's plays. Professor Nitze, in his course in Racine (Summer, 1932), emphasized their importance in the structure of Racinian tragedy. With their suggestions as a point of departure, we are considering in another study the examples of recognition and peripeteia in Racine's plays. We find one or the other, or both in every tragedy. We cite a few of the most striking examples. Oreste kills Pyrrhus in order to win Hermione's love; he earns instead her implacable hate. In her effort to regain control of Nero and of the state, Agrippine makes use of a threat: if Nero remains indocile, she will supplant him and restore Britannicus, the rightful heir. But by her maneuvers and by the frequent mention of Britannicus' name, she so irritates Nero that he poisons the young prince. "Agrippine perdoit en lui sa dernière espérance" (*Seconde Préface*). By the same token she "recognizes" that she herself will die at his hand. Almost the only action in *Bérénice* is the heroine's gradual recognition of her situation: Titus loves her, but he will not marry her. The opening of Theseus'

Seneca's *Phœnician Women* becomes full of meaning in the light of this consideration. Although this play has a certain kind of action sustained by violent passions, beauty of sentiment, and elegance of expression—things that Racine professedly set a value upon—we find that it has no peripeteia nor recognition scenes. This is doubtless the reason why Racine considered it to be the work of someone who did not know what a tragedy was.

Further evidence tending to show Racine's grasp of peripeteia and recognition, which Aristotle considered the " most powerful elements of emotional interest in Tragedy " [10] and which he made the basis of his classification of plots into Simple or Complex,[11] lies in Racine's translation and paraphrase of Chapter XVI of the *Poetics*. This is the passage in which the different kinds of recognition are described. In treating of the first kind, recognition by means of tokens, Aristotle says that " even these admit of more or less skilful treatment," alleging two such recognitions in the *Odyssey*, one by the nurse in the Bath Scene,[12] the other, a less artistic one, made by the swineherds when Ulysses shows his scar with the express purpose of making himself known. Racine thus enlarges and clarifies Aristotle's thought, bringing out the fact that in one instance Ulysses' intention is frustrated:

Car il y a moins d'art dans cette dernière, où Ulysse découvre exprès sa cicatrice pour se faire reconnoître et pour vérifier son discours; au lieu que dans l'autre, c'est sa nourrice qui le reconnoît d'elle-même en

---

eyes in regard to Hippolyte's innocence and Phèdre's guilt fills the last two acts of *Phèdre*.

[10] *Poetics*, chap. VI.

[11] " An action which is one and continuous. . . . I call Simple, when the change of fortune takes place without Reversal of the Situation (Butcher's rather unsatisfactory rendering of " peripeteia ") and without Recognition. A Complex action is one in which the change is accompanied by such Reversal, or by Recognition, or by both." (Chap. X.)

[12] " Now Odysseus sat aloof from the hearth, and of a sudden he turned his face to the darkness for anon he had a misgiving of heart lest when she handled him she might know the scar again, and all should be revealed. Now she drew near her lord to wash him, and straightway she knew the scar of the wound that the boar had dealt him with his white tusk along ago." (*Odyssey*, chap. XIX, trans. by Butcher and Lang.)

voyant cette cicatrice. Ainsi il n'y a point de dessein dans cette reconnoissance; il y a, au contraire, une surprise *qui fait une péripétie; et
les reconnoissances de cette nature sont bien meilleures que ces autres
qui se font avec dessein.*[13]

Racine seems to have considered that the other kinds of
recognition, namely, those invented by the will of the poet and
those depending on memory or on a process of reasoning, did
not need to detain him, for in his translation he skips to the
concluding paragraph of Aristotle's chapter, which he renders as
follows:

La plus belle des reconnoissances est celle qui, étant tirée du sein même
de la chose, se forme peu à peu d'une suite vraisemblable des affaires,
et excite la terreur et l'admiration: comme celle qui se fait dans l'*Œdipe*
de Sophocle et dans l'*Iphigénie*; car qu'y a-t-il de plus vraisemblable à
Iphigénie, que de vouloir faire tenir une lettre dans son pays? Ces
reconnoissances ont cet avantage par-dessus toutes les autres, qu'elles
n'ont point besoin de marques extérieures et inventées par le poëte, de
colliers et autres sortes de signes. Les meilleures, après celles-ci, sont
celles qui se font par raisonnement.[14]

Now the former is precisely the type of recognition that
Racine is going to make use of. He will not, however, limit its
application to the discovery of persons. In fact he so changed
the seventeenth-century practice in this regard and brought
about his recognitions by such natural means that many critics
believe that he did not use the *procédé.*[15]

We have already seen how Racine invokes Horace's dictum
that whatever a poet does must have a certain simplicity or
oneness about it.[16] He criticizes Rotrou's *Antigone* for the
duplicity of its action; [17] he commends the *Ajax, Philoctetes,*

---

[13] Mesnard, V, 487. [14] *Ibid.*, p. 488.

[15] De la Porte and Chamfort in their *Dictionnaire dramatique* (1776),
p. 404, express surprise that in Racine the catastrophes " ne soient
jamais l'effet d'une reconnoissance." Even M. Bray restricts recognitions almost exclusively to comedy and for that reason considers that
in his chapter " la Tragédie," Aristotle's list of the different kinds of
recognition " ne présente aucun intérêt pour nous." (*Op. cit.*, 323.)

[16] " Que ce que vous ferez, dit Horace, soit toujours simple et ne soit
qu'un " (*Préface* to *Bérénice*). Cf. *Ars Poetica*, vs. 23.

[17] " Mais il faisoit mourir les deux frères dès le commencement de son
troisième acte. Le reste étoit en quelque sorte le commencement d'une
autre tragédie, où l'on entroit dans des intérêts tout nouveaux. Et
il avait réuni en une seule pièce deux actions différentes, dont l'une sert

and *Œdipus* for their simplicity.[18]   From certain remarks in
the *Préface* to *Mithridate,* we infer that he was at one with
d'Aubignac on the manner in which the life of a historical character should be treated.   The author of *la Pratique* counsels
poets to represent not the entire life of a hero but rather one
outstanding action in which the rest can be included

comme en abrégé, & par la représentation d'une seule partie faire tout
repasser adroitement devant les yeux des Spectateurs, sans multiplier
l'action principale, et sans en retrancher aucune des beautez necessaires
à l'accomplissement de son ouvrage."[19]

This is precisely what Racine does in his tragedy.   The subject
is the death of Mithridate.   There are, however, scarcely any
" actions éclatantes " in the life of that hero which do not find
place in the play.   Leaning hard on history, he has " inserted
everything that could throw light on the character and sentiments of that prince "; yet he assures us that, in accordance
with the rule of necessity, everything is closely linked with the
main action.

In the first *Préface* that he wrote, we find Racine, very conscious of his technique, stressing two corollaries to unity of
action: continuity and the necessity of linking scenes.   The
young dramatist wonders what his critics find to complain of

si toutes mes scènes sont bien remplies, si elles sont liées nécessairement
les unes avec les autres, si tous mes acteurs ne viennent point sur le
théâtre que l'on ne sache la raison qui les y fait venir, et si, avec peu
d'incidents et peu de matière j'ai été assez heureux pour faire une pièce
qui les a peut-être attachés malgré eux, depuis le commencement jusqu'à
la fin ? [20]

---

de matière aux *Phéniciennes* d'Euripide, et l'autre à l'*Antigone* de
Sophocle.   Je compris que cette duplicité d'actions avoit pu nuire à sa
pièce, qui d'ailleurs étoit remplie de quantité de beaux endroits. (*Préface* to *la Thébaïde* written for the collective edition of 1676.)   Mesnard
points out that there is a sort of epilogue of some 300 verses in Euripides' play and shows that Rotrou is not so far from Euripides as
Racine would have us believe.   (*Op. cit.,* I, 403, n. 4.)

[18] *Préface* to *Bérénice.*

[19] He then adduces the example of the ancients who " n'ont pas laissé
de remettre devant l'esprit des Spectateurs, soit par des narrations, par
des entretiens, par des plaintes, et par d'autres délicatesses de l'art
toutes les plus signalées circonstances des histoires qu'ils ont traittées."
(*Op. cit.,* pp. 104-105.)

[20] *Première Préface* to *Alexandre* (1666).

The rule of continuity is again alluded to in the *Préface* to *Mithridate*:

On ne peut prendre trop de précaution pour ne rien mettre sur le théâtre qui ne soit très-nécessaire. Et les plus belles scènes sont en danger d'ennuyer, du moment qu'on les peut séparer de l'action, et qu'elles l'interrompent au lieu de la conduire vers sa fin.

His annotations on copies of Euripides show that several times he found fault with that dramatist for violations of the rule of necessity.[21]

Unity of action also implies completeness. Early in his career Racine was much preoccupied with this dramaturgic detail inferred from Aristotle's definition of tragedy.[22] The French poet held that action should " advance by degrees toward its end " [23] and that " cette action n'est point finie que l'on ne sache en quelle situation elle laisse ces mêmes personnes." [24] Hence the reappearance of Junie who has nothing more to say than that she is on her way to the apartments of Octavie.[25] For the benefit of those who maintain that the play should end with the *récit* of Britannicus' death, he recalls the practice of Sophocles in the *Antigone,* where

il emploie autant de vers à représenter la fureur d'Hémon et la punition de Créon après la mort de cette princesse, que j'en ai employé aux imprécations d'Agrippine, à la retraite de Junie, à la punition de Narcisse, et au désespoir de Néron, après la mort de Britannicus.[26]

It will be interesting to note how, as the poet becomes more skilled, his endings are swifter and less obviously " complete." His remarks on the dénouement of *la Thébaïde* are telling. In his first tragedy he carried out Aristotle's counsel to the letter. Twelve years later in publishing the *Préface* to the play, he admitted that

[21] Cf. *supra,* p. 120.
[22] *Poetics*, chap. VI. It is an " imitation of an action that is complete."
[23] *Première Préface* to *Britannicus.*
[24] *Ibid.*
[25] Act V, scene 6, in the princeps. It was later suppressed.
[26] *Première Préface* to *Britannicus.* We have seen that Racine could also argue on the other side of the question. Four years later in criticizing the double action in Rotrou's *Antigone,* he disregards all that happens in the epilogue of Euripides' play. Cf. *supra,* p. 207, n. 17.

14

la catastrophe de ma pièce est peut-être un peu trop sanglante. En effet, il n'y paroît presque pas un acteur qui ne meure à la fin. Mais aussi c'est *la Thébaïde*. C'est-à-dire le sujet le plus tragique de l'antiquité.

This implies that he thought he had applied the precept of completeness too rigorously in his earliest tragedy.[27]

Racine tells under what circumstances it is permissible to replace by a *récit* the actual representation of an action. He claims in the original *Préface* to *Britannicus* that Junie's reappearance is necessary. It would be contrary to the rules merely to relate the definitive situation of the young heroine because "une des règles du théâtre est de ne mettre en récit que les choses qui ne se peuvent passer en action." Racine seems to have in mind a rule of d'Aubignac.[28] Horace is not nearly so categorical; he merely specifies that what is unfit for stage representation [29] should be related in a *récit*.[30] Racine, moreover, changed his mind later on, deleting the scene [31] that had been the subject of criticism and letting Albine tell in a *récit* what becomes of the heroine.

The marginalia in the *Trachiniæ* attest the poet's dissatisfaction with long narrations that are not "sincères." He questions whether such long reports, if false, are "dignes de la tragédie." [32]

We are now in a position to consider what Racine said concerning unity of time. There are in the *Préfaces* only two references to this rule, and both times Racine is defending his choice of a simple subject. Unity of time, he asserts, precludes any other kind of subject.[33] In the *Première Préface* to *Britannicus*,

[27] All the characters die at the end, even those like Hémon, Antigone, and Créon, who live on in other versions of the story. Créon's death, clumsy and unmotivated, is obviously a make-shift finishing off of the character.

[28] The rule is "de ne point faire par récit ce que les principaux acteurs peuvent vray-semblablement faire eux-mêmes sur la Scène." (*La Pratique*, p. 366.)

[29] Acts of excessive cruelty or those which on account of the difficulty of execution would be likely to appear *invraisemblables*.

[30] *Ars Poetica*, vss. 179-188.

[31] Act V, scene 6, in the original edition.

[32] Mesnard, VI, 249.

[33] D'Aubignac had advised against representing "toute une grande histoire" or the entire life of a hero, for the result would be an "ouvrage de confusion" and would shock "la vray-semblance, la bien-

he bans subjects of intrigue on the grounds that many incidents
are not likely to occur "en un jour." "Quelques heures" are
roughly designated in the *Préface* to *Bérénice* as the limit he
would place on action. Hence the obvious necessity for a simple
plot. Whether this argument is an expedient to justify the subjects of his predilection, or whether, at least at the outset of his
career, he was really guided in his choice of a subject by the
generally accepted unity of time,[34] it is extremely difficult to
say. The question will probably never be satisfactorily concluded. We can be concerned here only with what Racine
actually said: his choice of a simple subject is justifiable as that
is the only kind that verisimilarly admits of treatment in accordance with the unity of time.[35]

The poet mentions unity of place only once in his critical
writings. His statement is comprehensive: in his secular tragedies he observed the rule rigorously, and, although he takes some
liberties in *Esther*,[36] even there he may be said to follow the rule
in its freer application. He writes:

On peut dire que l'unité de lieu est observée dans cette pièce, en ce que
toute l'action se passe dans le palais d'Assuérus. Cependant, comme on
vouloit rendre ce divertissement plus agréable à des enfants, en jetant
quelque variété dans les décorations,[37] cela a été cause que je n'ai pas

---

séance, et l'imagination des Spectateurs." The poet would be obliged
either to go beyond the prescribed time limits or else to "précipiter
tous les Incidens, les accumuler les uns sur les autres, sans grâce aussi
bien que sans distinction, étouffer et perdre tous les endroits pathétiques,
et enfin nous donner une figure monstrueuse et extravagante." (*Op.
cit.*, pp. 103-104.)

[34] D'Aubignac holds out for the sunrise to sunset interpretation of the
rule (*la Pratique*, p. 154) and testifies that, although for a long time
it was not observed in France, it is quite generally accepted in his day.

[35] It should be mentioned here that his earlier tragedies mark off the
time more obviously than do the later ones.

[36] Mme de Maintenon had expressly stated that his reputation as a
poet was not to be at stake and that it did not matter if the rules were
not observed in the piece. (*Souvenirs de Mme de Caylus*, p. 164.)

[37] D'Aubignac testifies to the pleasure derived from a change in deco-
ration providing it be a legitimate one. While he maintains that the
"terrain" can not change, he admits that "il n'est pas de même du
fond, et des cotez du Théâtre. . . . Ils peuvent aussi changer en la
representation; et c'est en cela que consistent les changemens de Scènes,
et ces Décorations dont la variété ravit toûjours le peuple, et même

gardé cette unité avec la même rigueur que j'ai fait autrefois dans mes tragédies.[38]

We shall study Boileau's ideas on action under the three headings he has outlined: exposition, complication, and dénouement.

With Horace[39] as a point of departure, Boileau tells how a tragedy should begin. The passage teems with actuality:

> Que, dès les premiers vers, l'action préparée
> Sans peine du sujet aplanisse l'entrée:
> Je me ris d'un acteur, qui, lent à s'exprimer,
> De ce qu'il veut, d'abord, ne sait pas m'informer;
> Et qui, débrouillant mal une pénible intrigue,
> D'un divertissement me fait une fatigue.[40]
> J'aimerais mieux encor qu'il déclinât son nom
> Et dît: "Je suis Oreste, ou bien Agamemnon," [41]

---

les habiles, quand elles sont bien faites." He then authorizes opening up a temple and showing a perspective of columns, etc. (*Op. cit.*, pp. 127-128.)

[38] *Préface* to *Esther.*

[39]   " Semper ad eventum festinat, et in medias res,
    non secus ac notas, auditorem rapit."
                            (*Ars Poetica*, vss. 148-149.)

[40] Corneille, although advising against too much narration of antecedent action, seems to be proud of *Héraclius*, one of those plays which require extraordinary efforts on the part of both the poet and the spectator and often prevent the latter from taking " un plaisir entier aux premières représentations tant ils le fatiguent " (*Discours des Trois Unités, Œuvres*, I, 105). Cf. also the *Examen*, where he makes the same admission. D'Aubignac had, before Boileau, warned dramatists against narrations including " un grand nombre de Noms, une suitte de différentes actions brouillées les unes dans les autres par le temps, ou par les dépendances; d'autant que le spectateur ne veut pas se donner la peine de garder en sa mémoire toutes ces différentes idées, ne venant au théâtre que pour avoir du plaisir, et faute de s'en souvenir il demeure dans une confusion, et une obscurité qui ne luy donne que du dégoust de tout le reste " (*op. cit.*, p. 381).

[41] D'Aubignac insisted that the characters should be named and the place indicated so as to avoid confusion in the minds of the spectators: " Le Poëte ne doit mettre aucun Acteur sur son Théâtre qui ne soit aussitost connû des Spectateurs, non seulement en son nom et sa qualité; mais encore au sentiment qu'il apporte sur la scène; autrement le Spectateur est en peine, et tous les beaux discours qui se font lors au théâtre, sont perdus; parce que ceux qui les écoutent, ne sçavent à qui les appliquer. . . . J'ai veû depuis peu de temps une Pièce, où pas un

> Que d'aller, par un tas de confuses merveilles,
> Sans rien dire à l'esprit étourdir les oreilles.
> Le sujet n'est jamais assez tôt expliqué.
> Que le lieu de la scène y [42] soit fixe [43] et marqué.[44]

Acteur n'estoit nommé, excepté deux, dont les noms ont esté changez par l'Autheur, jusques-là même, qu'après la Catastrophe on ne sçavoit de quel pays estoient les Acteurs, ny si le Sujet estoit tiré de l'histoire d'Angleterre, ou d'Espagne. Or on ne verra point que les Anciens manquent jamais à cette règle, à quoy les Chœurs, qui ne sortoient point du Théâtre, leur estoient fort utiles pour les Personnages qui leur pouvoient estre connûs; . . . s'il estoit étranger et inconnû au Chœur, il faisoit luy-même entendre ce qu'il estoit. . . .

Quant à nous qui n'avons point de Chœurs, il faut, au lieu d'eux, faire parler quelques-uns des Acteurs qui sont déjà sur la scène; . . . ou bien quand ils sont inconnus à ceux qui sont sur la scène, il faut employer les deux autres moyens dont nous venons de parler; c'est à dire, faire entendre ce qu'ils sont, ou *par leur bouche*, ou par celle de quelqu'un de leur suitte. . . ." (*Op. cit.*, pp. 357-358.) Cf. also *ibid.*, p. 68. For Racine's marginal notes commending Sophocles' practice in this regard see *supra*, p. 116.

[42] This " y " we understand to refer to the exposition. The sense of the verse is closely connected with what precedes, and it serves also as a transition to Boileau's treatment of the unities. It is not, however, the formula for unity of place.

[43] This precept, if we interpret it aright, requires that it be clear from the exposition where the action is going to take place. As d'Aubignac (*op. cit.*, p. 122) put it, the action should be "sur un Theatre déterminé." The *Dictionnaire de l'Académie française* gives this meaning of "fixe."

"Marquée" should be taken in the sense of "clearly specified" (*ibid.*). D'Aubignac even takes care to warn poets against being too meticulous in following this rule. They should not describe the columns, the porticoes, ornaments, architecture of a temple, the espaliers and different flowers in a garden, nor the names and number of trees in a forest. These details concern the " Ingenieurs," not the poet (*op. cit.*, p. 72). Boileau's verse was perhaps aimed at plays like *Clitandre* (1630) where, until the edition of 1644, the place of the action was professedly left " au choix du lecteur " (*Préface, Œuvres*, I, 263), and particularly at a shift Corneille recommended in his *Discours*. The latter admitted of an " élargissement pour le lieu comme pour le temps." He would allow action to take place in two or three parts of the same city providing that the changes occur between acts, the decorations remain unchanged, and only the general place name be given (*Discours des Trois Unités, Œuvres*, I, 118-120). La Mesnardière in *la Poétique*, p. 269 (cited by Stewart, "Stage Decorations and the Unity of Place in France in the Seventeenth Century," *MP*, X, 398), has a curious

214 RACINE AND THE 'ART POÉTIQUE' OF BOILEAU

According to Monchesnay,[45] Boileau is here inveighing against
the practice of Corneille, whose expositions contain too much
empty declamation. Whether or not it is the opening verses of
Corneille's plays that he is criticizing in the negative part of the
precept, there can be no doubt that it is Racine's expositions that
he has in mind as models of clarity and economy of words. In
precluding involved narrations of antecedents, and in requiring
that from the very beginning the action be ready to move forward, he is obviously thinking of Racine's practice. " L'action
préparée " [46] fits exactly the latter's tragedies, in the opening
scene of which we invariably see a passion of already long
duration [47] and a situation that straightway precipitates the
crisis. The pregnant reference to Agamemnon should also
be noted. In *Iphigénie,* the play that Racine had under way
while the *Art Poétique* was being completed, we find this opening verse telling whom the actor represents:

> Oui, c'est Agamemnon, c'est ton roi qui t'éveille.

In a pendant to this study, we shall point out how Racine's
expositions, patterned after those of the ancient dramatists,
fulfill to the letter Boileau's requirements; it would doubtless
be more exact to say that they inspired them.

remark that puzzled d'Aubignac quite as much as it does us: " Nous
permettons aux Dramatiques d'étendre en ces occasions les bornes de
leur Théastre et de partager leur Scène en plusieurs cartiers différens,
pourveu qu'ils fassent écrire, *Cet endroit figure le Louvre, et Cy est la
Place Royale.*" There is no evidence that in France signs were used to
" mark " the scene in the seventeenth century. Stewart finds only one
instance in the Middle Ages where such a device was used (Rouen,
1474). Boileau, a partisan of the strict observance of the unities, did
not, of course, recommend a labeling of the unique scene represented.

[44] *Chant III,* vss. 27-38.

[45] " Il n'avoit point de termes assez forts pour exalter *Cinna,* à la
réserve des vers qui ouvrent la Pièce, dont il avouoit s'être moqué dans
son troisième Chant de l'Art Poétique. La raison qu'il en donnoit,
c'est qu'ils ne signifient rien, & sentent trop le Déclamateur." (*Bolœana,*
p. 131).

[46] D'Aubignac counseled poets to " ouvrir le Théâtre le plus près
possible de la catastrophe " (cited by Arnaud, *Étude sur la Vie et les
Œuvres de l'abbé d'Aubignac,* p. 118). Jean de la Taille had considered this one of the principal secrets of art (*loc. cit.*).

[47] Le Bidois calls attention to this very important fact. (*La Vie
dans la Tragédie de Racine,* pp. 41 et sqq.)

We pass now to Boileau's recommendations concerning the middle part of the plot. As we have already seen, he bans the *invraisemblable* in the stage representation and enjoins the use of the *récit* to relate what must not be shown. The passage is patterned on a more extensive treatment of the subject in the *Ars Poetica.*[48] It contains nothing that is not found in Horace. With the "incroyable" as a point of departure, Boileau writes:

> Ce qu'on ne doit point voir, qu'un récit nous l'expose:
> Les yeux, en le voyant, saisiraient mieux la chose;
> Mais il est des objets que l'art judicieux
> Doit offrir à l'oreille et reculer des yeux.[49]

Like Chapelain,[50] d'Aubignac,[51] Corneille,[52] and Racine,[53]

[48] Vss. 179-188.

[49] *Chant III*, vss. 51-54. D'Aubignac's treatment of the subject is more practical. Besides giving precise rules dictated by verisimilitude (*op. cit.*, p. 396), he explains how a *récit* can be made dramatic: the words must be "soûtenuës par le mélange des divers sentimens de celuy qui parle et de celuy qui écoute" (*ibid.*, p. 388). He points out that, when narrations are made "à la personne intéressée" by another party concerned in the affair, or vice versa, "elles sont toûjours lors accompagnées d'espoir et de crainte, de tristesse et de joye, ce qui retient l'esprit du Spectateur attentif, et avec plaisir" (*ibid.*, 396). This will be the consistent practice of Racine. It is the essential difference between his *récits* and those of Corneille which, with the exception of the one in *Horace*, tend to be epic in character. Cf. Le Bidois, *op. cit.*, p. 105. That the same principle holds for comedy is pointed out by Dorante in the *Critique.* He maintains that the *récits* of the *École des Femmes* are actions, inasmuch as they are made innocently "à la personne intéressée, qui, par là, entre à tous coups dans une confusion à réjouir les spectateurs, et prend, à chaque nouvelle, toutes les mesures qu'il peut, pour se parer du malheur qu'il craint." (Sc. VII.)

[50] "Dans le premier acte, les fondemens de l'histoire se jettent. Dans le seconde, les difficultés commencent à naistre. Dans le troisiesme, *le trouble* se renforce. Dans le quatriesme, les choses sont désespérées. Dans le cinquiesme, le désespoir continuant, le nœud se desmesle par des voyes inespérées et produit la merueille" (*IIe Dissertation Inédite* of Chapelain, edited in the Appendix of Arnaud's *Étude sur la Vie et les Œuvres de l'Abbé d'Aubignac*, p. 348).

[51] He recommends that the acts be of nearly equal length and that "les derniers ayent toûjours quelque chose de plus que les premiers, soit par la nécessité des événemens, ou par la grandeur des passions, soit par la rareté des spectacles." (*Op. cit.*, p. 295.)

[52] *Examen* of *Rodogune*. (*Œuvres*, IV, 421.)

[53] *Première Préface* to *Britannicus.*

the author of the *Art Poétique* insists that dramatic interest rise from scene to scene. The plot must finally unravel smoothly.[54] He says:

> Que le trouble,[55] toujours croissant de scène en scène
> A son comble arrivé se débrouille sans peine.[56]

---

[54] He insists likewise for comedy
> Que son nœud bien formé se dénoue aisément.
>
> (*Chant III*, vs. 406.)

[55] The idea of "roiled" is inherent in the French word "trouble." It means an "agitation désordonnée" (*Dict. de l'Acad. fr.*) and, taken figuratively, it designates an emotional disturbance (*ibid.*). It is Racine's stock word for deep anxiety and emotional excitement whatever the cause. It often carries, moreover, a strong suggestion of its original meaning and indicates the confused mental state that will be cleared up by the recognition, e. g., Thésée's supplication:

> Dieux, éclairez mon *trouble, et daignez à mes yeux*
> Montrer la vérité, que je cherche en ces lieux.
>
> (*Phèdre*, vss. 1411-12.)

Chapelain, in two of his *Dissertations Inédites* obviously uses the word in the sense of an "agitation désordonnée." Describing the crescendo movement in a tragedy, he notes that in the third act "le *trouble* se renforce" (cf. *supra*, p. 215, n. 50. D'Aubignac lists it among the "agitations" obviously psychological in character with which the stage should be filled continuously: "quelques desseins, attentes, passions, *troubles*, inquietudes et autres pareilles agitations" (*op. cit.*, p. 111). He also says that, while comedy implies a certain amount of bustling about—"mouvemens du corps"—"les *troubles* de l'esprit" constitute tragic action (*ibid.*, p. 320).

Rapin, on the other hand, uses the word most often in the sense of confusion or disorder in affairs: "L'intrigue brouille les choses, en jettant le *trouble* et la confusion dans les affaires; le dénoüement y remet le calme (*op. cit.*, chap. XXI, *Œuvres*, II, 129). Again he says of tragedy: "Tout y doit être dans le *trouble* et le calme n'y doit paroître, que quand l'action finit, par la catastrophe" (*ibid.*, chap. XXXI, *Œuvres*, II, 189-190). Racine will use it in precisely this sense in the *Préface* to *Athalie*. He claims that Joad's prophecy "sert beaucoup à augmenter le *trouble* dans la pièce, par la consternation et par les différents mouvements où elle jette le chœur et les principaux acteurs."

It would be very interesting to know whether the idea of emotional disturbance or of the commotion inherent in a tragedy of intrigue was uppermost in Boileau's mind when he wrote the couplet. "Se débrouille" would indicate that it was the latter, while "croissant," not "se compliquant" or "s'expliquant" (cf. vs. 159) would fit the former

We come now to a passage that invites very close attention. Boileau says that the surprise element in a plot is conducive to pleasure:

> L'esprit ne se sent point plus vivement frappé
> Que, lorsqu'en un sujet d'intrigue *enveloppé*,
> D'un secret *tout à coup* la vérité connue
> Change tout, donne à tout une face imprévue.[57]

The first verse is obviously written from the spectator's angle of vision, that is, it is his "esprit" that is "vivement frappé" by the sudden and unexpected turn of affairs. At first sight one is inclined to look upon the next three verses as Boileau's statement of recognition as it was practised by Racine: the actor in the dark regarding a certain situation, light finally dawning upon him and producing the change in fortune proper to tragedy.

Five considerations, however, hold us back from this tempting conclusion: (1) Boileau's speaking from the spectator's angle of vision in verse fifty-seven and the implication that he kept that viewpoint in the lines immediately following; (2) the type of subject described as being "d'intrigue *enveloppé*," [58] (3) "*trouble*" in verse fifty-five, which may well indicate imbroglio, complication, and the like; (4) the idea of suddenness that is,

---

better. These distinctions will have to be kept in mind when we are considering to what extent Boileau's tenets summarize Racine's practice.

Saint-Marc (*Œuvres de Boileau*, II, 73), recognizing a difficulty in the word *trouble*, suggests a slightly different interpretation. He believes that it is Boileau's technical term to designate the second part of the action that Vauquelin called "le brouil." Delaporte (*op. cit.*, II, 234, n. 2) and Pellissier, in his edition of the *Art Poétique*, follow Saint-Marc.

⁵⁶ *Chant III*, vss. 55-56.   ⁵⁷ *Ibid.*, vss. 57-60.

⁵⁸ "Caché" (*Dict. de l'Acad. fr.*). The word was used by Vauquelin in exactly the same sense and apropos of the plot complication. In speaking of the part of comedy that follows the exposition, he had said:

> La seconde sera comme un *Env'lopement*,
> Un trouble-feste, un brouil de l'entier argument;
> De sorte qu'on ne sçait qu'elle en sera l'issue,
> Qui tout' autre sera qu'on ne l'avoit conceue.

(*Art Poétique, Livre III*, vss. 117-120.) Molière uses the word in the *Critique*: Climène complains that all the "ordures" of the *École des Femmes* are "à visage découvert" and that they have not "la moindre enveloppe qui les couvre." (Sc. III.) Cf. Chapelain's use of the word in 1670: he insists that the poet, in portraying "sales amours," use delicate words; "cela s'appelle *envelopper* les ordures." (*Lettres*, II, 685.)

in general, foreign to Racine's recognitions; and lastly, the literary antecedents of this passage. This last consideration can not be summarily dismissed. Aristotle held that fear and pity are best produced " when events come upon us by surprise " and that " the effect is heightened when at the same time they follow as cause and effect." [59] Keeping a balance between suspense and the proper preparation of the dénouement becomes the delicate task of the dramatist. Horace does not speak of the surprise element. During the Renascence, dramatists tended to neglect it; woe came upon the hero early in the play and the greater part of the piece was devoted to lyric lamentation. Sixteenth-century theorists, however, adhered to the idea of intrigue and the resultant suspense.[60] French doctrinaires all recommend suspense.[61] In the first quarter of the seventeenth century, perhaps through the influence of the tragicomedy,[62] practice falls in with theory, and the pathetic tragedy of the Renascence is superseded by a new kind in which intrigue—psychological for the most part in Corneille—predominates. This dramatist's tendency to depend on suspense [63] increases. In *Rodogune* he disposes everything in view of the enigma to be resolved in the last act. He claims that this tragedy, " à cause des incidents surprenants " purely of his invention, is more his own than any that preceded it.[64] We have mentioned the satisfaction he took in the obscure intrigue

---

[59] *Poetics*, chap. IX.

[60] Cf. Castelvetro's " ingegno a trovare," *Poetica d'Aristotele vulgarizzata et sposta*, cited by Miss McPike, *Aristotelian and Pseudo-Aristotelian Elements in Corneille's Tragedies*, p. 32.

[61] Cf. M. Bray, *op. cit.*, pp. 322-323. Chapelain two years before the *Cid* wrote: " Le plus digne et plus agréable effet des Pièces de Théâtre est lors que, par leur artificielle conduitte, le Spectateur est *suspendu*, de telle sorte qu'il est en peine de la fin et ne sçaurait juger par où se terminera l'aventure." (*De la poésie représentative, IIIᵉ Dissertation*, Arnaud, *op. cit.*, p. 350.) Cf. also the *IIᵉ Dissertation*: " L'action scénique a deux parties principales: le nœu et le desnouement. *Le plaisir exquis est dans la suspension d'esprit*, quand le poëte dispose de telle sorte son Action, que le spectateur est en peine du moyen par où il en sortira " (edited in the Appendix, p. 348, of Arnaud's work).

[62] Cf. Lanson's *Corneille*, pp. 65-66, and his *Esquisse d'une Histoire de la Trag. fr.* (1920), p. 62.

[63] Cf. the *Examen d'Horace* (*Œuvres*, III, 278).

[64] *Examen* (*Œuvres*, IV, 420-421).

of *Héraclius,* a play that he tells us must be seen more than once
"pour en remporter une entière intelligence." [65] He believes
that the " constitution assez extraordinaire " [66] of *Nicomède* does
honor to his ingeniousness as a poet and boasts that in *Œdipe,*
by obscuring the oracles and Laius' answer, he was able to complicate the plot and to keep secret what Sophocles had disclosed
early in his play.[67]

M. Mornet [68] calls attention to the complicated plots that
were in vogue between 1650 and 1667. Astonishing recognitions
arising from situations in which the hero passed for someone
else, a prince was ignorant of his rank and real identity, or
women were disguised as men, were not infrequent even in the
plays of Thomas Corneille, Quinault, Boyer, and Gilbert, not
to mention a generation of writers already in their decline. The
fact that d'Aubignac [69] and, a decade later, Guéret,[70] while condemning the *romanesque* plots of their day, make a point to
except the older Corneille, also indicates to what extremes other
dramatists had gone. Racine, moreover, is obviously not beating

---

[65] *Examen* (*Œuvres,* V, 154).   [67] *Examen* (*Œuvres,* VI, 130).
[66] *Examen* (*Œuvres,* V, 505).   [68] *Racine: Théâtre,* pp. 11-16.
[69] The beauty of a piece lies not in the intrigue or action but in the
"discours." After affirming that Sophocles surpasses Euripides in this
respect and pointing out that Seneca's tragedies, for all their irregu-
larities, pass for excellent in view of their forceful and beautiful " discours," he says: " Nous en avons une preuve sensible dans les Pièces
de M. Corneille; car ce qui les a si hautement élevées par dessus les
autres de nostre temps, n'a pas esté l'intrigue, mais le discours; leur
beauté ne dépend pas des Actions, *dont elles sont bien moins chargées
que celles des autres Poëtes,* mais de la manière d'exprimer les violentes
passions qu'il y introduit " (*op. cit.,* pp. 372-373). Rapin, in listing
the faults of contemporary tragedies, leans hard on this passage of
d'Aubignac. He complains that " on ne comprend point assez, que ce
ne sont pas les intrigues admirables, les événemens surprenans et merveilleux, les incidens extraordinaires qui font la beauté d'une tragédie:
ce sont les discours quand ils sont naturels et passionnez." Without
making any acknowledgment, he then gives d'Aubignac's comparison
between Sophocles and Euripides (*op. cit.,* *Œuvres,* II, 190).
[70] Making an exception for Corneille, he arraigns the poets of his day
who " ne connoissent pas davantage la Poëtique d'Aristote & de
Scaliger que le Talmud. . . . . Ils s'embarrassent dans des intrigues
qu'on ne sauroit suivre, & qu'ils ne peuvent eux-mêmes dénoüer." (*Le
Parnasse Réformé,* p. 73.)

the air when in his two *Préfaces* [71] written in 1670 and 1671 he impugns the contemporary taste for complicated intrigue. D'Aubignac's more or less shifting position is for us full of interest. He recommends " des surprises extraordinaires." [72] On the other hand, he affirms that " une Pièce qui n'aura presque point d'Incidens, mais qui sera soûtenuë par d'excellens discours, ne manquera jamais de reüssir." [73] After explaining what he means by subjects of intrigue and of passion, he affirms that the " mixtes " are best of all. His passage on subjects of intrigue is so similar in wording and content to Boileau's treatment of suspense that it deserves to be quoted here. Departing from Aristotle's classification,[74] he distinguishes three kinds of subjects :

Les premiers sont d'incidents, intrigues ou evenemens, lors que d'Acte en Acte et presque de Scène en Scène il arrive quelque chose de nouveau qui *change la face* [75] des affaires du Theatre ; quand presque tous les Acteurs ont divers desseins, & que tous les moiens qu'ils inventent pour les faire reüssir, s'embarrassent, se choquent, et produisent des accidens impréveus : ce qui donne une merveilleuse satisfaction aux Spectateurs, une attente agreable, et un divertissement continuel.[76]

The points of similarity between d'Aubignac's discussion of subjects of intrigue and the passage in the *Art Poétique* are immediately obvious : (1) their general import is the same ; (2) the context is identical, Boileau's treatment of suspense following directly his recommendation of " le trouble toujours croissant de scène en scène," which occurs at the beginning of that same sentence ; and (3) the verbal likeness. We know that Boileau and his generation held d'Aubignac's theories in high regard.[77] Now if, as everything would seem to indicate, Boileau

[71] Those of *Britannicus* and *Bérénice*.
[72] *Op. cit.*, p. 158.
[73] *Ibid.*, p. 374.
[74] *Poetics*, chap. X.
[75] In his analysis of the *Ajax*, d'Aubignac shows how " le *Poëte* a bien sceû fournir son théâtre, *en changeant toûjours la face des choses.*" (*Op. cit.*, p. 489.)
[76] *Op. cit.*, p. 85. He admits, however, that these subjects lose their savor once the intrigue is known. After a paragraph in which he urges strong reasons in favor of subjects " de passions," he discusses " les Mixtes," the kind that we know he prefers. (Cf. *op. cit.*, p. 87.)
[77] Cf. *supra*, p. 92.

is merely restating the traditional ideas on suspense and on the recognitions and change of fortune involved, it follows that he is not thinking especially of Racine's practice, and that there can be no question of peripeteia in the close technical sense in which Racine seems to have understood it [78] and which Vahlen has since defined. La Mesnardière [79] and d'Aubignac [80] use the word peripeteia only in the loose sense of "catastrophe" or "change of fortune." This is also the sense in which Molière uses it in the *Critique de l' " École des Femmes."* Dorante begs the pedant to "humanize" his language and instead of talking of "protase," "épitase," and "péripétie," to say simply the exposition, the "nœud," and the "dénouement." The general meaning is apparently all that Boileau had in mind in this particular passage.[81]

Another interesting question might be raised at this point. Does Boileau, like d'Aubignac, show a real leaning toward subjects of intrigue, or is the passage merely one of literary inspiration and consequently one in which his own taste has little part? Judging from the tragedies which he preferred, we are inclined to believe that Boileau liked a fair amount of intrigue. He is said to have considered *Polyeucte* Corneille's masterpiece.[82] According to him, nothing surpasses the first

[78] Brunetière (*Œuvres Poétiques de Boileau*, p. 209, n. 1) is of the opinion that Boileau here had in mind the "péripétie" of *Iphigénie*, Act III, scene 5. This tragedy was performed five weeks after the publication of the *Art Poétique.*

[79] It is "un événement imprévu qui dément les apparences et, par une révolution qui n'était point attendue, vient *changer la face de* choses." (*La Poétique,* cited by M. Bray, p. 323.)

[80] D'Aubignac, in giving the basis for Aristotle's classification of subjects into Simple and Complex, says that in the latter there is "changement dans les avantures du Theatre par Reconnoissance de quelque personne importante, comme l'*Ion* d'Euripide et par Péripétie, c'est-à-dire par conversion et retour d'affaires de la Scène, lors que le Héros passe de la prospérité à l'adversité ou au contraire" (*op. cit.,* p. 119). Vauquelin had made "Péripétie" equivalent to the final change of fortune in either comedy or tragedy (*Art Poétique,* Livre III, vss. 195-222).

[81] For Boileau's use of the terms "péripétie" and "agnition" to confound de Beaumont, see *supra,* pp. 105-106.

[82] *Bolœana,* p. 131.

three acts of *Horace*.[83] He lacked "termes assez forts pour
exalter *Cinna*, à la réserve des vers qui ouvrent la pièce."[84] He
was transported with admiration as he recited the imprecation of
Cléopâtre in the last scene of *Rodogune*.[85] Moreover, even when
he found fault with Corneille, it was not for his complicated
intrigue, but rather for too much declamation,[86] "fautes de
langue,"[87] an occasional want of verisimilitude,[88] cold "raisonnements,"[89] a lack of tragic action, and the like. Taking no
notice of the *romanesque* plots, he flays Thomas Corneille for
certain "galimatias" occurring in his tragedies.[90] In Quinault
he excoriates the "lubrique morale" of the operas.[91] Among
Racine's plays, Boileau preferred *Phèdre* and *Athalie*, which are
by no means those with the scantiest intrigue. It seems, then,
quite probable that Boileau shared the taste of his generation
for an intrigue which provoked suspense.

In a couplet remarkable for its laconism, Boileau epitomizes
the pseudo-Aristotelian doctrine. It is in the name of reason
and art that he enjoins the rule of the three unities:

> Nous voulons qu'avec art l'action se ménage;
> Qu'en un lieu,[92] qu'en un jour,[93] un seul fait accompli
> Tienne jusqu'à la fin le théâtre rempli.[94]

---

[83] *Loc. cit.* Cf. also the *Préface* to *le Traité du Sublime*.

[84] *Bolœana*, p. 131.

[85] *Loc. cit.*

[86] *Loc. cit.* Cf. also *VIIᵉ Réflexion*. (*Œuvres*, III, 209.) Addison's
letter to Bishop Hough (Lyons, December, 1700), written after a visit
at Auteuil, records the same criticism coming from Boileau.

[87] *VIIᵉ Réflexion*, (*Œuvres*, III, 209.)

[88] Cornélie, in *Pompée*, is thus criticized (*Bolœana*, p. 112). Cf. also
his criticism of Phocas in *Héraclius* (*Bolœana*, p. 110).

[89] He criticized *Othon* and had this play in mind when he wrote vss.
20 *et sqq.* of *Chant III* of the *Art Poétique* (*Bolœana*, pp. 132-133).

[90] *Bolœana*, pp. 129-130.

[91] Cf. *supra*, p. 157.

[92] Unity of place was the last unity to be constructed and formulated.
It was inferred, in the name of false verisimilitude, from Aristotle's
observation that "tragedy endeavors, as far as possible, to confine itself
to a single revolution of the sun, or but slightly to exceed this limit"
(*Poetics*, chap. V). Castelvetro (*Poetics*, 1570), following Scaliger,
narrowed Aristotle's observation, going so far as to identify the time
of action with that of the representation. He then formed, by analogy
with the unity of time, a third unity, that of place. Absolute unity of

Completeness,[95] continuity,[96] and the linking of scenes [97]—all aspects of unity of action—are requisites easily inferred from these terse lines. They are later on prescribed for comedy in the place gained recognition gradually in France. At first the rule allowed a space equivalent to that of a city. Later it limited the locality represented to a single building or to a single outdoor space of similar dimensions. At length the palace or room *à volonté* prevailed. Professor Lancaster calls attention, however, to several exceptions to this rule and concludes in his study of the *Mémoire de Mahelot* (p. 43) that absolute unity of place "ne fut jamais acceptée comme règle invariable pendant la période des grandes pièces classiques." Racine observes the rule rigorously except in *Esther* (cf. *supra*, pp. 211-212), and even there the action is confined to a single palace.

[93] Theorists of the classic period held that the ideal was a perfect correspondence between the time represented in the action and the actual duration of the performance. They admitted that this was impossible under some conditions and then allowed twelve hours for the action. (D'Aubignac, *op. cit.*, pp. 156-157; Corneille, *Discours des Trois Unités, Œuvres*, I, 113; and Dacier, *op. cit.*, pp. 67, 113, and 115.)

[94] *Chant III*, vss. 44-46. The rime words are identical with those of Vauquelin's couplet:

> Le Théâtre jamais ne doit estre *rempli*
> D'un argument plus long que d'un jour *accompli*.
>
> (*Art Poétique*, Livre II, vss. 257-258.)

[95] Cf. d'Aubignac, *op. cit.*, p. 178: " Il faut aussi prendre garde que la Catastrophe achève pleinement le Poëme Dramatique, c'est à dire, qu'il ne reste rien après, ou de ce que les Spectateurs doivent sçavoir, ou qu'ils veuillent entendre: car s'ils ont raison de demander, *Qu'est devenu quelque Personnage intéressé dans les grandes intrigues du Theatre*, ou s'ils ont juste sujet de sçavoir, *Quels sont les sentimens de quelqu'un des principaux Acteurs après le dernier evenement qui fait cette Catastrophe*, la Pièce n'est pas finie, il y manque encore un dernier trait."

[96] Cf. d'Aubignac, *op. cit.*, p. 133: " Le Théâtre ne devroit jamais estre vuide." Cf. also *ibid.*, pp. 111, 113, *et passim*.

[97] Chapelain, while endorsing the linking of scenes, permits poets occasionally to dispense with the rule (*IIe Dissertation inédite*, Arnaud, *op. cit.*, p. 348). D'Aubignac attaches much importance to the rule and describes minutely *liaisons de Présence, de Recherche, de Bruit, et de Temps* (*op. cit.*, pp. 316-320). Corneille affirms that what was with the ancients an " ornement et non pas une règle " has become one in his day " par l'assiduité de la pratique " (*Discours des Trois Unités, Œuvres*, I, 101-102). Chappuzeau testifies that a troupe examining a play with a view to performing it looks to see if " les Scènes sont bien liées " (*le Théâtre français*, p. 65).

usual technical terms.[98]   It is also worthy of notice that in *Satire III*, at Quinault's expense, Boileau had made a point of unity of action.   The stupid country fellow bestows this more than dubious praise on the *Astrate*:

> Et chaque acte, en sa pièce, est une pièce entière.[99]

Thus we reach the end of our investigation of tragic action as it is set forth in the *Préfaces* and in the *Art Poétique*. Boileau, while he says nothing that has not been said in the critical works of his predecessors and contemporaries, is for once more complete and explicit than Racine.   It must be noted, however, that he failed to mention an overruled intention as one of the special forms which peripeteia may assume.   Except for a possible leaning of Boileau toward subjects of intrigue, on the matter of action they see eye to eye.

---

[98] It is required that the action
> Ne se perde jamais dans une scène vide   (vs. 408)
and that the scenes be " toujours l'une à l'autre liées " (vs. 412).

[99] Vs. 198.

CONCLUSION

Racine's early verse and his correspondence concerning it reveal the qualities of an artist. He polished his poems and sometimes rewrote them entirely. He eagerly sought the criticism of others and profited by it. On at least two occasions, however, he flatly rejected the suggestions made. He brought to his task altogether unusual poetic endowments: a keen intelligence; a temperament that was sensitive, restive, and passionate; a thorough knowledge of Greek; and a veneration for Euripides and Sophocles that dates from his sojourn at Port-Royal. Before Boileau cautiously published his first collection of *Satires* in 1666, Racine had given, besides minor poems, two tragedies remarkable for their technical skill, their fashionable gallantry, and excellent prosody, and had thereby won the notice and favor of the king. His technique in *la Thébaïde*, however, as we shall show more fully in another study, is that of a yet too rigid Aristotelian. Although he departed from the Stagirite's precepts in the *Alexandre*, he was brought back, perhaps by the chastening criticism this play evoked. His translation of the passages on tragedy in Aristotle's *Poetics*, and the annotations made in copies of the ancient dramatists attest his serious preparation for a career of letters.

Boileau's reputation, at first unsavory and confined to the habitués of Paris taverns, through his intercourse with persons like the premier président de Lamoignon gradually takes on an air of respectability. But even as late as the spring of 1671, Mme de Sévigné looks askance upon him and his *entourage*. His fame as a man of letters is, however, taking shape; in 1672 after condemning *Bajazet*, Mme de Sévigné triumphantly invokes, in the interests of her beloved Corneille, the authority of none other than Despréaux. The *Art Poétique* and his translation of Longinus finally establish his title to literary pre-eminence and social standing.

The long-credited anecdotes showing that the intimacy between Racine and Boileau dates from the very outset of their careers do not stand scrutiny. It is highly probable, however, that the two poets were acquainted during the sixties, for Paris was not large, and Molière was a common friend to both of them. Their relations appear to have been entirely casual, however, until the end of 1670 or the beginning of 1671. There is no doubt that, from this time on, they exercised a mutual influence upon each other. There are even indications that, of the two, Racine proved himself the more meticulous critic.

Boileau's reminiscences at Auteuil tend to magnify his part in the literary friendship. Having outlived all his other contemporaries, and Racine by twelve years, he seems, looking backward, to have deluded himself into thinking that he had been teacher and guide during the years when Racine's star was rising.

The theory underlying the structure of Racine's plays and Boileau's more dogmatic pronouncements evolves from the general seventeenth-century concern for Aristotle and from the stage practices which had grown out of it. Both poets profited from the growing tendency to pass over Italian commentators and go directly to Aristotle. All around them scholars were occupied in collating works of antiquity with the Stagirite's observations. The records preserved show that Boileau's interest ran to the critical works of antiquity, while Racine seems to have been equally well versed in both the critical writings and the literary masterpieces of the ancients. His love for the latter was, in fact, one of the dominant passions of his life.

Boileau begins his treatment of tragedy with a bookish discussion of the doctrine of imitation; Racine, bent on more practical things, does not advert to it. They both understand the need of verisimilitude if a truly tragic effect is to be secured. They see eye to eye on the question of love as a tragic subject, maintaining that, if it is to be represented, it must be an unbridled and destructive passion. It must be expressed convincingly and must vary with the character of the personages. Boileau insists that it is the surest way of touching the heart of the spectators. Racine upholds a simple subject; Boileau apparently leans to one of intrigue. The possibility of treating a modern subject such as *Bajazet* is not mentioned in the *Art Poétique*.

As regards the function of tragedy, Racine seems to have had in mind only the pleasure of the spectators, if we except the remarks made in the concluding paragraph of his *Préface* to

Phèdre, which should not be considered an integral part of his poetics. As Professor Lancaster puts it, Racine, like Molière, looked upon life and portrayed it as an artist, not as a reformer. In translating Aristotle's definition of tragedy, he explains katharsis as a medical figure and discerns three steps in the process. In his *Préfaces* he is concerned, however, only with the practical aspects of purgation, namely, the excitation of the tragic passions. Indeed he makes everything converge therein; subject, characters, and action are all designed to produce the greatest amount of compassion and a somewhat less degree of fear. Boileau crystallizes this general tendency to soften the tragic emotion of terror and stresses the resultant pleasure when he recommends a " douce terreur " and a " pitié charmante." In his general recommendations to poets, he chimes in with the advocates of a Horatian utility in art by advising them to blend the useful and the beautiful. He implies, however, that he can conceive of a work of art without the adjunct of utility.

The two poets conceive or judge characters according to the Aristotelian requirements which, if we may believe Saint-Évremond, are known to dramatists and spectators alike: goodness, propriety, *semblance*, and consistency. In the application of these rules, Boileau holds out for a narrow internal *bienséance*; Racine in practice plays fast and loose with this last precept, but does not admit it openly until his fame is solidly established. In the 1676 *Préface* to *Andromaque*, he reveals his secret: the portrayal of the heroine " according to the idea we now have of her." To do this he had to keep historical truth in abeyance. Thus external *bienséance* takes precedence over internal *bienséance*. Boileau seems not to have objected to Racine's practice in this regard until long after the publication of the *Art Poétique*; he is reported to have then considered Pyrrhus a " héros à la Scudéry." Both poets recommend a tragic flaw in the hero, Racine in order to heighten pity and fear, Boileau in order to give to the character a " natural " trait.

In theory Racine opposes complicated action because it is not verisimilar that many events should occur in one day. He also bans surprising " jeux de théâtre," especially if they are improbable. Boileau, on the other hand, in a passage that harks back to d'Aubignac, professes a fondness for intrigue and the suspense it entails. Does he prefer the intrigue in Corneille's plays to

Racine's more simple treatment of a subject? He is admittedly unwilling to pronounce judgment on the relative greatness of the two dramatists. Although he mentions a change in fortune, evidence is lacking in the *Art Poétique* to show that he understood Racine's use of recognition and peripeteia as the mainsprings of action. He is reported, however, to have engaged in certain skirmishes in which he worsted his adversaries by introducing a discussion of peripeteia and recognition, on which they were ill prepared to meet him.

They agree that the exposition must be rapid and clear and that the scenes must be linked according to the French rule. Completeness of action is likewise required by both poets. The unities are defended with equal rigor in the *Art Poétique* and in the *Préfaces*.

Are there any procedures that Racine must have got from Aristotle rather than from other French dramatists or theorists? Since he seems to have grasped more fully than his contemporaries the importance that Aristotle attached to tragic pity, and to peripeteia and recognition as means of exciting it, we are inclined to think that this essential part of his dramatic system comes directly from Aristotle. In his extreme care to arouse compassion as well as in his use of the "doucereux," Racine was an *isolé*.

Boileau's poem shows him to be highly eclectic. We know for certain that he drew freely upon Aristotle, Horace, and the common fund of post-Renascence criticism summed up in works like d'Aubignac's *Pratique*. He said nothing that had not been said before him or around him. He mingled with counsels that were purely traditional, certain remarks destined to give an air of actuality to his work. But these observations are banal and superficial. Most of them go no farther than to note that love is the subject most apt to stir a French audience or that the spectators are annoyed by long and muddled expositions. It is probable, however, that the poet here had in mind Racine's clear and direct expositions as the ideal to be attained. Although in his whole treatment of tragedy there is nothing that must necessarily come from Racine, it is reasonable to suppose that while writing this part of the *Art Poétique* Boileau discussed traditional rules and practices with his friend. The latter with his fine critical powers and his practical experience of the theater was admirably fitted to give counsel.

On the other hand, in the *Préfaces* which Racine wrote after their friendship became intimate, there is nothing, with the possible exception of the paragraph on the utility of the theater, that must needs be ascribed to Boileau's influence. On the contrary almost all the precepts that Racine defended after 1670 are opposed either to the letter or to the spirit of Boileau's counsels as stated in the *Art Poétique*. Racine for instance recommends with new emphasis utter simplicity of action. He allows for the use of modern and religious subjects. He openly advocates portraying a character " according to the idea we now have of her." He experiments with choruses and with a broader interpretation of the unity of place. Although these tendencies find no authorization in the *Art Poétique*, Boileau apparently approved each one according as Racine gave it artistic form. His rôle would thus have been to encourage a friend who was too easily dejected by every adverse criticism his plays evoked. It is reasonable to believe that the heartening *Épître* which Boileau addressed to him on the occasion of the momentary failure of *Phèdre* epitomizes both their literary and personal relationships.

BIBLIOGRAPHY

L'Académie française. Dictionnaire. Paris: Veuve de J. B. Coignard, 1694; Lille: L. Danel, 1901. 2 vols.

Aristotle. *Art of Rhetoric,* translation by John Henry Freese. London: William Heinemann, 1926.

Arnaud, Charles. *Les Théories Dramatiques au XVIIᵉ siècle. Étude sur la Vie et les Œuvres de l'abbé d'Aubignac.* Paris: Alphonse Picard, 1888.

Aubignac, Abbé François d'. *La Pratique du Théâtre.* Paris: Denys Thierry, 1669.

————. *La Pratique du Théâtre* éd. par P. Martino. Paris: E. Champion, 1927.

Bédier, J., et Hazard, P. *Histoire de la Littérature française illustrée.* Paris: Larousse, 1923.

Boileau-Despréaux, Nicolas. *Art Poétique,* éd. par Georges Pellissier. Paris: Ch. Delagrave, 1897.

————. *Correspondance entre Boileau Despréaux et Brossette publiée sur les manuscrits originaux par Auguste Laverdet.* Paris: J. Techener, 1858.

————. *Œuvres Complètes,* nouvelle éd. par Berriat-Saint-Prix. Paris: Philippe, 1837. 4 vols. (1ère éd., 1830-34.)

————. *Œuvres Complètes, accompagnées de notes historiques et littéraires et précédées d'une Étude sur sa vie et ses ouvrages par A. Ch. Gidel.* Paris: Garnier Frères, 1870.

————. *Œuvres,* éd. par M. Amar. Paris: Lefèbvre, 1821. 4 vols.

————. *Œuvres de Boileau Despréaux avec des Éclaircissements historiques donnés par lui-même et rédigés par M. Brossette; augmentées de plusieurs pièces, tant de l'Auteur, qu'ayant rapport à ses Ouvrages; avec des Remarques et des Dissertations Critiques par M. de Saint-Marc. Nouvelle édition, augmentée de plusieurs Remarques et de Pièces relatives aux Ouvrages de l'Auteur. Enrichie de figures gravées d'après les desseins du fameux Picart le Romain.* Amsterdam: D. J. Changuoin, 1775. (1ère éd., 1716.)

————. *Œuvres Poétiques,* éd. par Brunetière. Paris: Hachette et Cie, 1918.

————. *Satires,* éd. critique avec introduction et commentaire par Albert Cahen. Paris: E. Droz, 1932.

Bonnefon, Paul. "La Bibliothèque de Racine," in *RHLF,* V (1898), 169-219.

————. *Correspondance de Jean-Baptiste Rousseau et de Brossette publiée d'après les originaux, avec une introduction, des notes et un index par Paul Bonnefon.* Paris: Hachette et Cie, 1910-1911. 2 vols.

Boudhors, Ch. H. "Boileau Inédit," in *RHLF,* XL (1933), 161-185.

Boursault, E. *Théâtre*. Paris: Compagnie des Libraires, 1746. 3 vols.

———. *Lettres Nouvelles*. Paris: la Veuve de Théodore Girard, 1698.

Bray, René. "Boileau et Maucroix en 1666," in *RHLF*, XXXVIII (1931), 99-103.

———. "La Dissertation sur *Joconde*. Est-elle de Boileau?" in *RHLF*, XXXVIII (1931), 337-354 and 497-517.

———. *La Formation de la Doctrine Classique en France*. Paris: Hachette et Cie, 1927.

Brémond, Henri. *Racine et Valéry*. Paris: Bernard Grasset [c1930].

Brienne, Louis Henri de Loménie, comte de. *Mémoires* pub. par Paul Bonnefon. Paris: Renouard, H. Laurens, successeur, 1916-19. 3 vols.

Brossette, C. *See* Boileau-Despréaux, entries 2 and 6, and Bonnefon, entry 2.

Brunetière, F. "Les Ennemis de Racine au XVIIe Siècle," in *Revue des Deux Mondes*, XXXII (1879), 206-217.

———. "L'Esthétique de Boileau," in *Revue des Deux Mondes*, XCIII (1889), 662-685.

Bussom, Thomas W. *The Life and Dramatic Works of Pradon*. Dissertation, University of Minnesota. Paris: Champion, 1922.

Bussy-Rabutin, Roger de. *Correspondance avec sa famille et ses amis*, éd. par Lalanne. Paris: Charpentier, 1858-1859. 6 vols.

Butcher, S. H. *Aristotle's Theory of Poetry and Fine Art with a critical text and translation of the "Poetics."* 11th ed. London: Macmillan & Co., 1927.

Cahen, M. Albert. Compte Rendu of *la Formation de la Doctrine Classique en France*, in *RHLF*, XXXV (1928), 268.

———. *See* Boileau-Despréaux, entry 8.

Cambridge History of English Literature, Vol. VIII. New York: Putnam and Sons, 1912.

Caylus, Mme de. *Souvenirs de la marquise de Caylus*, éd. par M. de Lescure. Paris: Alphonse Lemerre, 1873.

Chapelain, J. *Les Sentimens de l'Académie sur le "Cid."* *See* Gasté, Armand, *La Querelle du "Cid."*

———. *Lettres* pub. par Ph. Tamizey de Larroque. Paris: Imprimerie Nationale, 1880-1883. 2 vols.

Chappuzeau, Samuel. *Le Théâtre français*. Paris: J. Bonnassies, 1875. (1ère éd., 1674.)

Clairon, Mlle. *Mémoires de Mlle Clairon, de LeKain, de Préville, de Dazincourt, de Molé, de Garrick, de Goldoni, avec avant-propos et notices; par M. Fs. Barrière*. Vol. VI. Paris: Firmin Didot Frères, Fils et Cie, 1857.

Clément, P. *Lettres, Instructions et Mémoires de Colbert*. Tome V. Paris: Imprimerie Impériale, 1868.

Corneille, Pierre. *Œuvres Complètes*, éd. par Marty-Laveaux. Collection des Grands Écrivains de la France. Paris: Hachette et Cie, 1862-1868. 12 vols.

Cousin, Jean. "Phèdre n'est pas Janséniste," in *RHLF*, XXXIX (1932), 391-396.

Curtius, Quintus. *De Rebus Gestis Alexandri Magni*, ed. by G. Delbès. Paris: Delalain Frères, 1884.

Dacier, André. *La Poétique d'Aristote traduite en français avec des remarques*. Paris: Barbin, 1692.

Dargan, E. Preston. *See* Nitze, William, joint author.

Delaporte, Victor. *L'Art Poétique de Boileau Commenté par Boileau et par ses Contemporains*. Lille: Desclée, de Brouwer et Cie, 1888. 3 vols.

Deltour, F. *Les Ennemis de Racine au XVIIe Siècle*. 7e éd. Paris: Hachette et Cie, 1912.

Demeure, Jean. "L'introuvable société des 'Quatre Amis' (1664-1665)," in *RHLF*, XXXVI (1929), 161-180; 321-336.

⸺. "Mauroy," in *RHLF*, XLI (1934), 54-71; 215-230.

⸺. "Racine et son Ennemi Boileau," in *Mercure de France*, CCV (1928), 34-61.

Deschanel, Émile. *Le Romantisme des classiques. Racine*. Paris: Calmann Lévy, 1891. 2 vols.

Despois, E. *Le Théâtre en France sous Louis XIV*. 3e éd. Paris: Hachette et Cie, 1886.

Despréaux. *See* Boileau.

Dubos, Abbé Jean-Baptiste. *Réflexions Critiques sur la Poésie et sur la Peinture*. 4e éd. Paris: Pierre-Jean Mariette, 1740. 3 vols.

Egger, Émile. *Essai sur l'histoire de la Critique chez les Grecs*. 3e éd. Paris: Pedone-Lauriel, 1887.

Euripides. *English Translation*, by Arthur S. Way. London: William Heinemann, 1916; New York: G. P. Putnam's Sons, 1916. 4 vols.

Fairchild, A. H. R. "Aristotle's Doctrine of Katharsis and the Positive or Constructive Activity involved," in *Classical Journal*, XII (1916), 45-56.

Fénelon, François de Salignac de la Mothe. *Œuvres Complètes*. Paris: Leroux et Jouby & Gaume frères, 1850. 9 vols.

Furetériana. *Ana ou Collection de Bons Mots, Contes, etc. des Hommes Célébres*. Tome I. Amsterdam: Visse, 1789.

Gasté, Armand. *La Querelle du "Cid." Pièces et Pamphlets pub. d'après les originaux*. Paris: H. Welter, 1898.

Granet, François. *Recueil de Dissertations sur plusieurs Tragédies de Corneille et de Racine*. Paris: Gissey & Bordelet, 1740. 2 vols.

Gudeman, Alfred. *Aristoteles Poetik*. Berlin and Leipsig: Walter de Gruyter & Co., 1934.

Guéret, Gabriel. *Le Parnasse Réformé*. 2e éd. (1ère éd., 1668.) Paris: Th. Jolly, 1669.

Guiffrey, Jules M. *Comptes des Bâtiments du roi sous le règne de Louis XIV*. Paris: Imprimerie Nationale, 1881-1901. 5 vols.

Holsboer, S. Wilma. *L'Histoire de la Mise en Scène dans le Théâtre Français de 1600 à 1657*. Paris: E. Droz, 1933.

Homer. *Odyssey*, translation by S. H. Butcher and A. Lang. New York: P. F. Collier & Sons [c1909].

Horace. *Ars Poetica*, éd. par Taillefert. Paris: Hachette et Cie, 1894.

Jacoubet, H. "A Propos d'un Passage de la Première Préface de *Britannicus*," in *RHLF*, XXXII (1925), 416-420.

———. "Le Problème d'Andromaque: Si Racine l'a voulue coquette," in *RHLF*, XXXVI (1929), 409-415.

Janet, Paul. *Les Passions et les Caractères dans la Littérature du XVIIᵉ Siècle.* 3ᵉ éd. Paris: Calmann Lévy, 1898.

Lachèvre, Frédéric. *See* Le Verrier.

La Fontaine, Jean de. *Œuvres*, éd. par Henri Régnier. Collection des Grands Écrivains de la France. Hachette et Cie, 1883-1927. 11 vols.

La Grange, Charles Varlet de. *Registre* pub. par les soins de la Comédie Française. Paris: J. Claye, 1876.

La Harpe, Jean-François de. *Lycée ou Cours de Littérature ancienne et moderne.* Tome II. Paris: Verdière, 1817.

Lancaster, H. C. *French Dramatic Literature in the Seventeenth Century.* Parts I, II, and III. Baltimore: Johns Hopkins Press, 1929-1936.

———. *Le Mémoire de Mahelot, Laurent et d'autres décorateurs du XVIIᵉ Siècle,* éd. par H. C. Lancaster. Paris: Champion, 1920.

——— and Méras, E. A. *Racine: "Andromaque" – "Britannicus" – "Phèdre."* New York: Charles Scribner's Sons [ᶜ1934].

Lanson, Gustave. *Boileau.* Grands Écrivains Français. Paris: Hachette et Cie, 1900.

———. *Choix de Lettres du XVIIᵉ Siècle.* Paris: Hachette et Cie, 1922.

———. *Choix de Lettres du XVIIIᵉ Siècle.* Paris: Hachette et Cie, 1921.

———. *Corneille.* Paris: Hachette et Cie, 1913.

———. *Esquisse d'une Histoire de la Tragédie Française.* New York: Columbia University Press, 1920.

———. *Histoire de la Littérature Française.* 11ᵉ éd. Paris: Hachette et Cie, 1909.

———. *Méthodes de l'Histoire Littéraire.* Paris: Société d'édition "les Belles Lettres." 1925.

La Porte, Joseph de, and Chamfort, S. R. *Dictionnaire dramatique contenant l'histoire des théâtres, les règles du genre dramatique, les observations des maîtres les plus célèbres.* Paris: Lacombe, 1776.

La Rochefoucauld, François. *Œuvres*, éd. par M. D. L. Gilbert. Collection des Grands Écrivains de la France. Paris: Hachette et Cie, 1868.

Laverdet, Auguste. *See* Boileau-Despréaux, entry 2.

Le Bidois, Georges. *La Vie dans la Tragédie de Racine.* 6ᵉ éd. Paris: Gigord, 1929.

Lemaître, J. *Corneille et la Poétique d'Aristote.* Paris: Lecène, Oudin et Cie, 1888.

———. *Impressions de Théâtre.* Paris: Lecène, Oudin et Cie, 1890.

———. *Jean Racine.* Paris: Calmann Lévy [n. d.].

Lemoine, Jean. " Boileau contre Racine," in *Revue de Paris*, VI (Nov.-
Déc., 1902), 861-870.

Le Verrier, Pierre. *Les Satires de Boileau commentées par lui-même et
publiées avec des notes par Frédéric Lachèvre. Reproduction du
Commentaire inédit de Pierre Le Verrier avec les corrections autographes de Despréaux*. Le Vesinet (Seine-et-Oise) : Courménil
(Orne), 1906.

Lock, Walter. " The Use of περπέτεια in Aristotle's *Poetics*," in *Classical
Review*, IX (1895), 251-253.

Lucas, F. L. " The Reverse of Aristotle," in *Classical Review*, XXXVII
(1923), 98-104.

McKeon, Richard. " Literary Criticism and the Concept of Imitation
in Antiquity," in *MP*, XXXIV (1936), 1-35.

McPike, Elizabeth. *Aristotelian and Pseudo-Aristotelian Elements in
Corneille's Tragedies*. Unpublished doctor's dissertation, The
University of Chicago, 1923.

Magne, E. *Bibliographie Générale des Œuvres de Nicolas Boileau-
Despréaux et de Gilles et Jacques Boileau suivie des luttes de
Boileau, Essai bibliographique et littéraire, Documents inédits*.
Paris: L. Giraud-Badin, 1929. 2 vols.

Mahelot, Laurent. *Le Mémoire de Mahelot, Laurent et d'autres décorateurs du XVIIe Siècle*, éd. par H. C. Lancaster. Paris: Champion,
1920.

Michaut, G. *La Bérénice de Racine*. Paris: Lecène, Oudin et Cie, 1907.

———. *Les Luttes de Molière*. Paris: Hachette et Cie, 1925.

Monchesnay, Jacques de Losme de. *Bolœana ou Bons Mots de M.
Boileau*. Amsterdam: L'HONORÉ, 1742.

Monglond, André. " Dernières Années d'un Ami de Racine. Valincour
et ses Lettres au Président Bouhier," in *RHLF*, XXXI (1924),
365-403.

Morel, Jean-Émile. "La Vivante Andromaque," in *RHLF*, XXXI
(1924), 604-619.

Morillot, P. *Boileau*. Paris: Lecène, Oudin et Cie, 1897.

Mornet, Daniel. *La Pensée Française au XVIIIe Siècle*. 2e éd. Paris:
Armand Colin, 1929. (Dernière éd., 1937.)

———. *Racine: Théâtre*. Paris: Mellottée [n. d.].

———. Compte Rendu of Albert Cahen's edition of the *Satires*, in
RHLF, XXXIX (1932), 465-468.

Nadal, Augustin. *Œuvres Mêlées*. Paris: Briasson, 1738. 3 vols.

Nisard, Désiré. *Histoire de la Littérature*. 18e éd. Paris: Firmin-
Didot [1881?]. 4 vols.

Nitze, William A., and Dargan, E. Preston. *A History of French Literature*. New York: Henry Holt and Co., 1928.

Olivet, Pierre Joseph d'. *See* Pellisson, Paul, joint author.

Parfaict, Frères. *Histoire du Théâtre Français depuis son origine jusqu'à
présent*. Paris: André Morin et Flahault, vol. I; le Mercier et
Saillant, vols. II-XV, 1734-1749. 15 vols.

Patin, Gui. *Lettres*, éd. par J.-H. Reveillé-Parise. Paris: J. B. Baillière, 1846. 3 vols.

Pellet, Eleanor J. *A Forgotten French Dramatist: Gabriel Gilbert.* Baltimore: Johns Hopkins Press, 1931.

Pellisson, Paul, et Olivet, Pierre Joseph d'. *Histoire de l'Académie Française*, éd. par Livet. Paris: Didier, 1858.

Racine, Jean. *Œuvres*, éd. par M. Paul Mesnard. Collection des Grands Écrivains de la France. Paris: Hachette et Cie, 1865-1929.

Racine, Louis. *Œuvres*. Paris: Le Normant, 1808. 6 vols.

Rapin, Père René. *Œuvres*. Vol. I. Amsterdam: Pierre Mortier, 1709; vols. II and III, La Haye: Pierre Gosse, 1725.

Reese, Helen Reese. *La Mesnardière's "Poëtique" (1639): Sources and Dramatic Theories.* Baltimore: Johns Hopkins Press, 1937.

Revillout, C. "La Légende de Boileau," in *Revue des Langues Romanes*, XXXIV-XXXVIII (1890-1895).

Robert, Pierre. *La Poétique de Racine. Étude sur le système dramatique de Racine et la constitution de la tragédie française.* 2e éd. Paris: Hachette et Cie, 1891.

Rostagni, Augusto. *Arte Poetica di Orazio. Introduzione e Commento.* Torino: Chiantore, 1930.

———. *La Poetica di Aristotele con introduzione, commento e appendice critica.* Torino: Giovanni Chiantore, 1928.

Rousseau, J.-B. *See* Bonnefon, entry 2.

Rousseau, J.-J. *Lettre à D'Alembert sur les Spectacles*, éd. par L. Flandrin. Paris: Hatier [n. d.].

Sainte-Beuve, Ch. Augustin de. *Causeries du Lundi.* Paris: Garnier Frères [n. d.].

———. *Nouveaux Lundis.* Paris: Michel Lévy, 1864-1870.

———. *Portraits Littéraires.* Paris: Garnier Frères [n. d.].

———. *Port-Royal.* 7e éd. Paris: Hachette et Cie, 1908. 7 vols.

Saint-Évremond, Charles de. *Œuvres*, pub. par René de Planhol. Paris: la Cité des Livres, 1927. 3 vols.

Saint-Simon. *Mémoires.* Collection des Grands Écrivains de la France. Paris: Hachette et Cie, 1879-1919.

Sand, Hedwig Crawford. *The Three Unities in Racine.* Unpublished Master's dissertation. The University of Chicago, 1928.

Seneca. *Tragedies*, translation by Ella Isabel Harris. London: Henry Frowde, 1904.

Sévigné, Mme de. *Lettres.* Nouv. éd. Collection des Grands Écrivains de la France. Paris: Hachette et Cie, 1862-1868. 14 vols.

Sophocles. *Tragedies* translated into English Prose by Sir Richard C. Jebb. Cambridge: University Press, 1928.

Spingarn, J. E. *A History of Literary Criticism in the Renaissance.* 2d ed. New York: Columbia University Press, 1920.

Stewart, D. C. "Stage Decorations and the Unity of Place in France in the 17th Century," in *Modern Philology*, X (1913), 393-406.

Taine, H. *Nouveaux Essais de critique et d'histoire.* Paris: Hachette et Cie, 1901.

Truc, Gonzague. "Le Cas Racine." I. "A Uzès," in *RHLF*, XVII (1910), 531-544; II. "La Conversion et la Vieillesse de Racine," in *ibid.*, XVIII, 566-585; III. "La Solution," in *ibid.*, XIX, 570-587. The same study was published in book form by Garnier Frères in 1921.

Vahlen, J. "Beiträge zu Aristotles Poetik," in *Sitzungsberichte der phil.-hist.* Vienna, 1865-1867.

Van Roosbroeck, G. L. *Boileau, Racine, Furetière, etc. Chapelain Décoiffé: A Battle of Parodies.* New York: Institute of French Studies, 1932.

Vauquelin de la Fresnaye. *L'Art Poétique,* éd. par Georges Pellissier. Paris: Garnier Frères, 1885.

Vossler, Karl. *Jean Racine.* München: Max Hueber, 1926.

[1] This is an index of authors, of books, the titles of which are placed, as far as possible, under the names of their authors, and of persons who lived in the sixteenth and seventeenth centuries.